D0955498

Chrétien de Troyes Revisited

Twayne's World Authors Series Revisited
French literature

David O'Connell, Editor
Georgia State University

TWAS 855

YVAIN WITH HIS LION, MS GARRET 125.

Reproduced by permission of the Garrett Collection of Medieval and Renaissance Manuscripts, Department of Rare Books and Special Collections, Princeton University Libraries.

Chrétien de Troyes Revisited

Karl D. Uitti with Michelle A. Freeman

Princeton University

L.C.C.C. LIBRARY
DISCARD

Twayne Publishers • New York
Maxwell Macmillan Canada • Toronto
Maxwell Macmillan International • New York Oxford Singapore Sydney

Twayne's World Authors Series No. 855

Chrétien de Troyes Revisited
Karl D. Uitti

Copyright © 1995 by Twayne Publishers
All rights reserved. No part of this book may be reproduced or transmitted in any form
or by any means, electronic or mechanical, including photocopying, recording, or by any
information storage and retrieval system, without permission in writing from the
Publisher.

Twayne Publishers   Maxwell Macmillan Canada, Inc.
Macmillan Publishing Company   1200 Eglinton Avenue East
866 Third Avenue   Suite 200
New York, New York 10022   Don Mills, Ontario M3C 3N1

Library of Congress Cataloging-in-Publication Data

Uitti, Karl D.
   Chrétien de Troyes Revisited / Karl D. Uitti with Michelle A. Freeman.
      p.   cm.—(Twayne's world authors series; TWAS 855. French literature)
   Includes bibliographical references and index.
   ISBN 0-8057-4307-3 (alk. paper)
      1. Chrétien, de Troyes, 12th cent.—Criticism and interpretation. 2. Arthurian
romances—History and criticism. I. Freeman, Michelle A. II. Title. III. Series:
Twayne's world authors series; TWAS 855. IV. Series: Twayne's world author series
French literature.
PQ1448.U38   1994   94–33948
841'.1—dc20   CIP

The paper used in this publication meets the minimum requirements of American
National Standard for Information Sciences—Permanence of Paper for Printed Library
Materials. ANSI Z3948-1984. ∞™

10 9 8 7 6 5 4 3 2 1

Printed in the United States of America

Alfred Foulet,
In memoriam

Contents

Acknowledgments

My thanks go to Princeton University for granting me a sabbatical and to the University Committee on Research in the Humanities and Social Sciences for financial support, which enabled me to consult various manuscripts in European libraries containing works by Chrétien de Troyes. I also express here gratitude to my students, whose questions and interests, articulated in seminars and classes over the past quarter century, I have endeavored to address in this monograph. My debt to Dr. Michelle A. Freeman, with whom I have had the pleasure of discussing aspects of the work of Chrétien de Troyes for, quite literally, hours on end over a period of some 20 years, is incalculable. Thanks are due to my research assistant, Miss Bronwyn Low (Princeton '96) for help with references, and to Ms. Nancy Danch who helped with the index. Finally, let me declare my indebtedness to the late Edward Billings Ham and to my dear friend, the late Alfred Foulet, for having taught me whatever I know concerning Old French textuality.

Note on Sources

Texts by Chrétien de Troyes quoted in this study are taken from the following editions: *Erec und Enide*, vol. 3 of Christian von Troyes, *Sämtlichen erhaltene Werke*, ed. Wendelin Foerster (Halle, Germany: Max Niemeyer, 1890; Amsterdam: Éditions RODOPI, 1965); *Cliges*, vol. 1 of Christian von Troyes, *Sämtlichen erhaltene Werke*, ed. Wendelin Foerster (Halle, Germany: Max Niemeyer, 1884; Amsterdam: Éditions RODOPI, 1965); *Le Chevalier au Lion (Yvain)*, ed. Karl D. Uitti (with Modern French translation by Philippe Walter), in Daniel Poirion, ed., *Œuvres complètes de Chrétien de Troyes*, Bibliothèque de la Pléiade (Paris: Gallimard, 1994); *Le Chevalier de la Charrette (Lancelot)*, ed. Alfred Foulet and Karl D. Uitti (with facing page Modern French translation), Classiques Garnier (Paris: Bordas, 1989); *"The Story of the Grail," or "Perceval"*, ed. Rupert T. Pickens (with facing page English translation by William W. Kibler), Series A: Garland Library of Medieval Literature (New York and London: Garland, 1990). Unless otherwise noted, English translations are mine. Other editions and translations are listed in the Bibliography. For the most part, I shall refer to these works by their Modern French titles:*Érec et Énide, Cligés, Le Chevalier au Lion (Yvain), Le Chevalier de la Charrette (Lancelot)*, and *Le Conte du Graal (Perceval)*, or by the name of the eponymous hero. The standard edition of *Philomena* is that of Cornelis De Boer (Paris: Geuthner, 1909); his lyric poems are to be found in *Les Chansons courtoises de Chrétien de Troyes: Édition critique, avec introduction, notes et commentaire*, ed. Marie-Claire Zai (Bern: Herbert Lang, 1974; Frankfurt: Peter Lang, 1974).

Chronology

1155   Frederick Barbarossa named Roman emperor.

1160–1165   Rome taken by Frederick Barbarossa. Marie de France, *Lais*.

1165   Notre-Dame of Paris erected; Chrétien de Troyes, *Érec et Énide*.

1170   Assassination of Thomas Becket at Canterbury cathdral.

1174   Canonization of Saint Bernard of Clairvaux. Guernes de Pont-Sainte-Maxence, *Life of Thomas Becket* (Old French vernacular). Béroul and Thomas, *Tristan and Iseut* romances. Canterbury cathedral completed.

1176–1178   Chrétien de Troyes, *Cligés*. Earliest branches of the *Roman de Renard*. Gautier d'Arras, *Éracle*; *Ille et Galeron*. Raimbaud d'Orange and Bertrand de Born (troubadours).

1179–1180   Philip-Augustus, king of France (1180). Chrétien de Troyes composes *Le Chevalier de la Charrette (Lancelot)* and *Le Chevalier au Lion (Yvain)* simultaneously. The former was written at the command of Marie, countess of Champagne.

1185   Andreas Capellanus, *De arte honesti amandi*.

1187   French lose Jerusalem to Saladin.

1189   Richard Lion-Heart, king of England.

ca. 1190   Chrétien de Troyes dedicates *Le Conte du Graal (Perceval)* to Philip of Alsace, count of Flanders; the poem remains unfinished, due, it is presumed, to Chrétien's death.

1191   The Third Crusade. Saint-John of Acre and Cyprus taken. The Old French lyric poems of Conon de Béthune and Gace Brulé. Joachim of Flore, *Expositio in Apocalypsim*. Gautier Map, *De nugis curialium*.

1190s   Verse continuations of Chrétien's *Le Conte du Graal*. Chartres cathedral completed.

1200   Royal privileges granted to the University of Paris. Renaut de Bâgé, *Le Bel Inconnu*. Jean Bodel, *The Song of the Saxons* and *Play of Saint Nicholas* (Old French vernacular). Sharp criticism of the mendacity of verse narrative arises, "truthful prose" favored. Beginning of the triumph of "dialectic" (logic) over "grammar" (literary study) in schools.

1204   Taking of Constantinople by Western Crusaders during the Fourth Crusade; establishment of the Latin Empire of Constantinople.

1208   Geoffrey of Villehardouin, *Chronicle of the Taking of Constantinople* (Old French vernacular).

1209   Start of the Crusade against the Albigensians.

1214–1215   Victory of Philip-Augustus at Bouvines. Fourth Lateran Council. Magna Charta.

1220–1225   *Quest of the Holy Grail*; *Prose Lancelot*; *Prose Tristan*. Saint Francis of Assisi, "The Canticle of Brother Sun."

1226   Louis IX ("Saint Louis"), king of France; death of Saint Francis of Assisi.

Chapter 1
Biography and General Background

As is typical of our knowledge of many twelfth-century vernacular French writers, we possess very few facts concerning the life of Chrétien de Troyes.[1] Archival records mentioning him are nonexistent. What we know has had to be inferred from various sources: (1) writings attributed to him in manuscripts copied from 30 to over 100 years after his death—statements he himself made, presumably, alongside references to him made by the scribes who copied his works; (2) remarks about him contained in the works of other writers; (3) reworkings of and responses to his compositions (as well as "continuations" of his unfinished poems), which proliferated in the closing years of the twelfth century and well beyond; and (4) our knowledge—still very imperfect—of medieval literary practices and vernacular authorship.

Uncertainty prevails, then, concerning Chrétien de Troyes as a person.[2] Numerous hypotheses have been advanced. Almost everything we shall say in this chapter is open to at least some doubt. The critical and scholarly commentary to which, of course, we are deeply indebted[3] abounds in gratuitous assertion and controversy, some of which has been acerbic.[4] Consequently, to attempt to present a fair and plausible picture of who (and what) Chrétien de Troyes was, and what he came to represent in Western literature, is not an easy task. It is clear, however, that he existed and that he was a truly major figure—one of the handful of writers to whom the adjective "seminal" properly applies. His accomplishment is such that it certainly merits our best efforts to understand and appreciate it.

Let us constantly bear in mind, though, that being a writer, especially a vernacular writer, in a twelfth-century French court was socially, artistically, and intellectually quite different from being the writer as individual to whom we have become accustomed in more recent centuries. It is true that Chrétien de Troyes represented for his coevals writing and learning—something of which he and certain fellow writers of his time were rightly quite proud. However, he was not primarily of the

First Estate, that is, of the church hierarchy that in his day was univer-
sally recognized as the repository and guardian of both intellectual and
spiritual matters. He spent his life in the employ of aristocratic patrons
whom he was obliged constantly to please and entertain; in this role he
resembled other clerics employed by kings and counts in their varied
ministerial bureaucracies. To an important degree Chrétien was a man of
the Third Estate, a worker-craftsman, a producer of stories that he
"made"—he used the verb *faire*, "to make, to do"—according to the
principles of his craft out of material that was either given to him by his
patron or that he "found" (or "invented") in the books and stories that
were available to him. He saw himself as a participant in an ongoing cultural tradition of bookishness—as the renewer of, or successor to, Ovid
and other bookish men of the past. It surely would be no exaggeration to
say that this participation in bookishness—what Chrétien and others
called *clergie*—constituted a significant source and one of the very purposes of his identity, as he saw it. His works prove this aspect of his self-
belief; they are replete with references to the writer's participation in
clergie.

For that matter, Chrétien may well have been the senior member of a
team—or "workshop"—of court functionary-poets attached to the court
of Champagne during the late 1170s and beyond. Two romances, written conjointly at about the same time (around 1180), seem to testify to
this possibility. Thus a clerkly figure who identifies himself as Godefroi
de Leigni claims that Chrétien did not bring to completion the romance
undertaken at the behest of Countess Marie de Champagne, *Le Chevalier
de la Charrette (Lancelot)*. Godefroi declares that he himself, with
Chrétien's full approval, completed this romance according to the master's initial plans; he furthermore states his unwillingness to tamper with
the romance for fear of damaging the story.

A similar theme pervades the final verses of *Le Chevalier au Lion
(Yvain)*. Here the narrator figure, who specifically does not identify himself with the romance's author, explains that "Chrétien . . . has finished
. . . his romance thus," and that he who would be so bold as to add to it
would be "adding lies."[5] We shall return to this (and the *Lancelot*) passage later; for now it suffices to note that in this instance Chrétien cre-
ates (or "invents") another person in the figure of the narrator, a
journeyman responsible to him, the master of this particular workshop.
This creation depends entirely on his audience's willingness to accord
him magisterial authority and status.

Chrétien's dates of birth and death are unknown. His literary activity spanned a number of decades in the second half of the twelfth century; he must have commenced work on *Le Conte du Graal (Perceval)*, his last, unfinished romance, no later than 1 June 1191, the date on which Philip of Alsace, count of Flanders and the patron to whom Chrétien dedicated this poem, died. (It is generally—and plausibly—assumed that Chrétien, even if he did live as long as the count, must not have survived Philip by a lengthy period of time.) Since Chrétien's verse narratives—his romances—bear traces of the influence of other Old French (OF) texts composed during the 1150s and early 1160s (such as romances by the Anglo-Norman Wace; the *Le Roman d'Énéas*; possibly even the *Le Roman d'Alexandre* and the *Lais* of Marie de France), it is thought that his own production must have started no earlier than the late 1150s or early 1160s. His career began in earnest in the late 1160s or around 1170.

Much depends on what is meant by Chrétien's literary production. Five lengthy romance-type narratives may securely be attributed to him, and two (or more) surviving courtly lyric songs are also thought to be his; in addition, a curious non-Arthurian, semihagiographic narrative entitled *Guillaume d'Angleterre* (William of England), signed by an otherwise undescribed "Crestïens," has been ascribed to him at times. Most present-day scholars deny this attribution, however, and we shall not deal with this text in the present study. Finally, in the listing of his works provided by Chrétien in the prologue to the second romance of certain attribution, *Cligés*, several titles of texts no longer extant are given. One of these, however, has survived in a reworked version included in the late-thirteenth-century—or early-fourteenth-century—compilation known as the *Ovide moralisé*. These lost narrative poems, whose OF titles are given by Chrétien as the *Comandemanz Ovide* (Ovid's commands; the *Remedia Amoris?*), the *Art d'Amors* (Art of love; that is, Ovid's *Ars amandi*), the *Muance de la Hupe, de l'Aronde et du Rossignol* (The transformation of the hoopoe, the swallow and the nightingale; which is the story of Philomela and Procne, from Ovid's *Metamorphoses*, VI), the *Mors de l'espaule* (The bitten shoulder; the tale of Pelops, *Metamorphoses*, VI), and *Del roi Marc et d'Iseut la Blonde* (King Mark and the blond Iseut; an episode from the Celtic legend of *Tristan and Iseut*).

With the exception of *Del roi Marc*, all these works consist of short narratives adapted from the classical author Ovid.[6] In this they resemble two surviving short OF narratives, also imitated from Ovid (*Metamorphoses*, III and VII, respectively), entitled *Narcisus* and *Piramus et*

Tisbé, which were composed around 1160 and which, like the *Lais* of Marie de France, must have appealed to the courtly audiences of that period, especially, perhaps, to audiences predominantly made up of aristocratic women, like that surrounding the new queen of England, Eleanor of Aquitaine. The works' not being a part of the more masculine, lineage-centered Arthurian stories or the "histories" of the Bretons and the Normans (such as Wace's *Roman de Brut* and *Rou*), and their classical antecedents (such as Virgil's *Æneid*, the *Thebaid* of Statius, or the story of Troy)—all of which were "translated" into the OF vernacular during the 1150s and early 1160s—might help explain why they were not copied in the immense thirteenth-century codices to which we owe the survival of Chrétien's lengthy romances.

Chrétien's poetic corpus, then, undoubtedly consists of five surviving major romance narratives, all composed in octosyllabic rhyming couplets (called *rimes plates* in French).[7] With the exception of the second, these works are known by the titles given to them by Chrétien himself: *Érec et Énide*, v. 19: "D'Erec, le fil Lac est li contes" (The story is about Érec, son of Lac); but compare *Cligés*, v. 1: "Cil qui fist d'Erec et d'Enide" (He who wrote about Érec and Énide)[8]; *Le Chevalier au Lion (Yvain)*, vv. 6814–15: "Del *Chevalier au Lyeon* fine / Crestïens son romans ensi" (Concerning *The Lion Knight*, Chrétien finishes his romance thus); *Le Chevalier de la Charrette*, vv. 24–25: "Del *Chevalier de la Charrete* / Comance Crestïens son livre" (Concerning the *Knight of the Cart* / Chrétien begins his book); and *Le Conte du Graal (Perceval)*, vv. 66–67: "Ce est li *Contes del Graal*, / Don li cuens li bailla le livre" (It is the *Story of the Grail* / About which the count gave him the source-book).[9]

Chrétien refers to himself only once by the full name we now ascribe to him, Chrétien de Troyes (or, Crestiiens de Troyes), in *Érec et Énide*, v. 9. The name *Crestiiens*[10] is repeated in v. 26 of that same romance, and also in *Cligés* (v. 23, where it is associated with the author of the aforementioned list of works; also in v. 45, "Crestiiens comance son conte," and in v. 6784); in *Yvain* (v. 6817); in *Lancelot* (v. 25, where the name is identified as the person to whom Countess Marie has assigned the task of composing a book recounting a story, the subject matter and "orientation" of which she has furnished him; also in vv. 7127 and 7129, where his continuator, Godefroi de Leigni, identifies himself as having completed the work according to Chrétien's specifications and with his approval); and in *Le Conte du Graal (Perceval)* (vv. 7 and 62, where, once again in the third-person, Chrétien describes himself as toiling at the assignment given to him by his patron, Count Philip of Flanders).

In addition to Godefroi's mentioning him, Chrétien is also singled out by Huon de Méry as a master stylist in French (*Torneimenz Antecrit*, v. 1339);[11] and, as already stated, in copying his works certain scribes also give his name. Other writers refer to him indirectly. We will later discuss aspects of his influence in greater detail. Suffice it at present to state that Chrétien's name was well remembered during at least the first half of the thirteenth century, and that this name was linked both to a specific narrative œuvre and to the person of an admired literary craftsman by subsequent craftsmen who willingly acknowledged their admiration and, in some cases, indebtedness to him.[12]

Chrétien's connection with the city of Troyes in Champagne seems to be confirmed by his aforementioned relationship with Countess Marie, wife of Count Henry II of Champagne (who died in 1181) and daughter of Eleanor of Aquitaine by her first husband, King Louis VII of France.[13] Troyes, with Provins, was the capital of the counts of Champagne, and the site of very important trade fairs held twice a year. These fairs were attended by merchants, entertainers, and others from all over Europe. Given that he called himself "Crestïens *de Troyes*," it is plausible that our author was native to that city—a notion reinforced by numerous Champagne dialect traits present in his language (which is, in other respects, the standard OF, or *francien*, the courtly written language of his time). These assumptions and facts, then, make of Chrétien a person identifiable with the culture and civilization of Champagne, a culture heavily dependent upon France, of course, and closely linked to the values of the French monarchy, yet not totally coterminous with them, and very much open to cosmopolitan currents and culture—especially, one suspects, vernacular cultures and literature—from abroad (England, the Empire, Italy, the Midi). Chrétien probably was also imbued with the aristocratic and Lady-centered behavior one associates with chivalry and courtliness. In fact, Chrétien's œuvre constitutes one of the prime sourcebooks for the medieval notions of *courtoisie* and *chevalerie*. Interestingly, the Kingdom of France, though having inspired many epic *chansons de geste*, was not, with its royal court linked especially to Paris, a significant twelfth-century foyer of vernacular literary creation. Like Normandy and, somewhat later, Picardy and Flanders, Champagne and the court of its counts were the genuine centers of poetic innovation in French during the second half of the twelfth century. Paris, of course, was in the process of becoming a great center of learning because of its schools and their Latin curricula.

It is not known whether Chrétien de Troyes traveled widely or, for that matter, at all. As far as his work is concerned, there was really no need for him to do so. Even the patronage bestowed upon him by Philip of Flanders could have taken place at Troyes, since Philip was a frequent visitor there. Basing their theories on evidence taken from *Érec et Énide*, *Yvain*, and *Cligés*, some scholars have claimed that Chrétien must have known Brittany and parts of England firsthand, but this evidence is skimpy at best.

Of much greater significance is Chrétien's status as *clerc* (cleric). One of his German imitators, Wolfram von Eschenbach, refers to him as *meister Cristján von Troys*; *meister* is equivalent to Latin *magister* (master) and the OF *maistre*. This title designated an individual who had studied formally in the schools, but who was not necessarily a cleric in the sense of having taken holy orders. *Maistre* is also the self-given title of one of Chrétien's best-known predecessors, the Anglo-Norman romancer Wace, who identified himself as *Maistre Guace*, a *clers lisant* (literally, a reading cleric, or clerk).

The twelfth-century view of clerkliness was as an honorable state; ecclesiastical prestige adhered to the term, even when it was applied to nonchurchmen. Interestingly, part of the cleric's effectiveness as a "workman," or "master," at court derived from his having shared in the kind of educational training received by many of the most highly regarded members of the First Estate; this training and its locus surely contributed greatly also to the *clerc*'s moral authority, and, just as surely, lies at the root of his spiritual concerns, even as these are voiced in romance-type narratives of ancient heroes and of the knights of the Round Table. This prestige was denied to many of those whom we would today classify as participants in the processes of vernacular literature during the twelfth century, the jongleurs and minstrels who entertained nobles and laypersons alike with their *chansons de geste* and various other compositions. In the front matter to *Érec et Énide*, Chrétien himself speaks deprecatingly of "loutish story-tellers" who purvey their ill-conceived wares in the courts of kings and counts.

Clerkly prestige also derived from the cleric's constant reiteration of his cultural role and function: the *clerc* is no more and no less than the active memory of his society. Without the cleric we should know nothing of Nineva or of Troy, we should live like beasts (Benoît de Sainte-Maure); thanks to books, and the cleric's rendering of them to us, we "know the deeds of the ancients" (Wace, Chrétien).[14] Without *clercs*, it is suggested, chivalry itself would not exist. In an argument that calls to mind the old conundrum as to whether a tree falling in the forest makes any noise if there is nobody there to hear it crash, the cleric defines himself as he who hears the tree: it is he who registers the crash of chivalric deeds, recording them for his own time and for future generations. The truth of these deeds is his to determine according to the authority vested in him by his learning and moral competence. *Clergie* is thus the indispensable counterpart to *chevalerie*. Together they form an indissoluble couple, for the benefit of everyone concerned. The cleric is deeply involved in the world. In a very profound sense, his task is to restore the relevance—the meaning—of the world.[15]

Several terms deserve our closer attention at this juncture. All of those to be discussed below are used by Chrétien de Troyes.[16]

The first is *conjointure* (conjoining, putting together), a word appearing at v. 14 of *Érec et Énide*. Chrétien speaks here of having "extracted" (*tret*) a *bele* (beautiful) *conjointure* from a (presumably ill-constructed) "adventure story." He is in the process of contrasting his own fine handiwork with those of the despised minstrels. Because of its importance, we shall return to the idea of *conjointure* at the close of this chapter.

The second and third terms are *chevalerie* and *clergie*. In Cligés, after quoting Wace (*Roman de Rou*) to the effect that without books we would not know of the deeds of the ancients or of the world as it once was, Chrétien introduces a well-known topic—that of the *translatio imperii et studii*, or, transferal of *chevalerie* and *clergie* from antiquity to modern times:

> Ce nos ont nostre livre apris,
> Que Grece ot de chevalerie
> Le premier los et de clergie.
> Puis vint chevalerie a Rome
> Et de la clergie la some,
> Qui or est an France venue.
> Deus doint qu'ele i soit retenue,
> Et que li leus li abelisse
> Tant que ja meis de France n'isse
> L'enors qui s'i est arestee.
> Deus l'avoit as autres prestee:
> Car des Grejois ne des Romains

Ne dit an meis ne plus ne mains;
D'aus est la parole remese
Et estainte la vive brese.

(vv. 30–44)

(Our books have taught us that Greece once held of chivalry the first prize, and of learning. Then chivalry came to Rome, as did the sum of learning, which now has come to France. May God grant that she be retained there and the place so please her that the honor never depart from France which has now stopped off there. God had merely loaned it [this honor] to others: for of the Greeks and Romans no more is anything said; silence has enveloped them and their burning embers have died out.)

Translatio is temporal (ancient > modern) and geographic (Greece > Rome > France). The France to which he refers is obviously the Capetian Kingdom of France, but also the area—Champagne, Normandy, England, Flanders—of French cultural and scriptural predominance. One might venture the opinion that for Chrétien de Troyes, the France of these quoted lines is a stand-in for the culture of Latin Christendom, much as it had been in such works as the *Song of Roland* (ca. 1100) and, perhaps, the *Life of Saint Alexis* (ca. 1080–1100), the story of a Roman saint who is described as one "of our ancestors" by the OF poet telling the story.

Translatio imperii has to do with governance—with matters pertaining to the Second Estate—with political power and, as the very term demonstrates, with empire. Thus, at the time of the ancient Theban conflicts and the Trojan War (and during the brief age of Alexander the Great), Greece was at the center of things. Power and imperial governance subsequently passed to Rome, the Rome of the Cæsars, an empire whose prehistory had been explored in Virgil's *Æneid*. Chrétien's France had its origin in both these one-time centers. It was post-Constantine Rome, however, the Christian Rome of *Alexis*, with its pope and its emperors, that may be said to have fathered Chrétien's France most directly. This legendary France knew its greatest moment under the Frankish, or "French," king-emperor Charlemagne, whose "chivalry" was fostered anew, indeed undergoing renewal, at the behest of France's new royal dynasty, the Capetians.[17]

The passage from *Cligés* appears, however, to underscore *studium* even more emphatically than it does *imperium*. France is above all the land of *clergie*, of literary learning and thought. After all, in 1175 French culture and learning, including the French language, were more solidly anchored in such places as England, Normandy, Flanders, and Champagne than French political rule was. To be sure, as duke of Normandy, the king of England was nominally the vassal of the king of France, but, more importantly, he was also his rival as king. Besides, thanks to the Continental dowry of his consort Eleanor, King Henry II possessed a kingdom much larger than his French counterpart. Furthermore, it was virtually impossible to deny the genuine legitimacy of the Italo-German–based Empire. Indeed, for some political thinkers of Chrétien's time, Capetian France had usurped, within France, the political obeisance properly owed to the emperor of the Romans, the imperial, or temporal, leader of Latin Christendom, the real heir to Charles the Great. (It would be some time before the pope would see fit to grant the king of France "imperial" status within his kingdom.) However, the cultural supremacy of France—its being the locus of *studium*—was disputed by no one. Since at least the time of Saint Anselm (later eleventh century) the schools and learning of France were primary in Latin Europe. Besides, although he served the count and countess of Champagne, Chrétien, clearly, was culturally a "Frenchman," as were, for that matter, Wace the Norman and Marie *de France*. Being the natural home of modern *clergie*, "France" was also by definition the home of Chrétien the *clerc*. In Chrétien, then, we find one of the earliest expositions of what we now understand to be the peculiarly universalist character Frenchmen ascribe almost automatically to their culture.

Several other terms to be found in Chrétien's work also reveal his strong intellectual and literary self-consciousness. Three of these appear in the prologue to *Lancelot*, a romance that Chrétien claims to have written at the request of Countess Marie de Champagne. The first two are *matiere* (Modern French *matière*) and *san* (or *sen*).

> Matiere et san li done et livre
> La Contesse . . .
>
> (vv. 26–27)

(The Countess vouchsafed to him the subject matter and the "orientation" he was to give to it . . .)

The story was, in short, the Countess's "invention"; it was she who "found" it for him, who played the role played for Chrétien in other romances by books.

San is harder to grasp. It must be distinguished (at least for writers of Chrétien's generation) from *sans* (or *sens*, which in Latin is *sensu*).[18] The *san* belongs to the literary work; it is embedded in it. And it has to do with how the *matiere* is to be handled by the poet. It is perhaps not entirely unrelated to what we sometimes call nowadays the "moral" of the story. Thus, to take a well-known example, the story, or *matiere*, of Billy the Kid may be made to demonstrate via the young outlaw's early demise that crime does not pay. Or, conversely, that the social outcast, however much he might try, can never hope to beat society at its own game. Or both. Specific *matieres*, in fact, may be almost automatically associated with certain moral outcomes. The *chanson de geste* subgenre known as songs of the Rebellious Vassal recounts stories of noble knights who revolt against, and even at times betray, their liege-lord, not always without strong justification. Yet, almost invariably, no matter how just his cause, the Rebellious Vassal meets defeat and, frequently, death at the hands of the sovereign. Although it is rare, it is not inconceivable that a new *san* be grafted upon a popular *matiere*. For example, it might be suggested that the writer make Billy the Kid fall in love and earn redemption through the love of a Good Woman. Such a twist was in fact introduced into the subject matter pertaining to the biography of Saint Alexis. The saint's return to Rome, at least in the earliest OF versions, was prompted by his affection for his spouse with whom he hoped to taste the incomparable joys of salvation in paradise. In the earliest, Syriac versions of the story, Alexis had been shown as leaving Rome before his marriage takes place: his departure constituted a fleeing from the temptations of conjugal life. The new *san* of the OF (and its immediate Latin antecedent) version required a substantial change in the story's plot.

Chrétien sometimes exhibits a certain playfulness in regard to the *san* of his romances. Thus, the story of Cligés and Fénice is asserted to have caused subsequent emperors of Constantinople to lock up their empresses in order to avoid being cuckolded by them, as was the case with Cligés's uncle Alis, Fénice's first husband, who left his wife a virgin because he was made to believe he had enjoyed her favors on their wedding night, whereas he had only dreamt that he had done so. It was Cligés who possessed, unlike Tristan with Iseut, both the love and the body of his adored Fénice.

The ostensible, and essential, corpus of Chrétien's *matiere* is Arthurian, that is, it is of the vast repository of Celtic tales involving that famous

British king, his queen, and the knights of the Round Table that our poet "found" in books like the *Roman de Brut* by Wace, and the *Historia regum Britanniæ* of Geoffrey of Monmouth, as well as, perhaps, in certain orally transmitted traditions. All five of his romances take place in the time and geographic space of the Arthurian world, although, as we shall see, King Arthur himself and many of its other denizens, including Queen Guenevere, are hardly the model characters one might at first glance be tempted to associate with the inhabitants of that world. Arthur is a bumbling fool in *Lancelot*; in *Perceval* his court is a place of decay and perhaps even of impending ruin. Arthur's seneschal, Kay, is a viper-tongued braggart; his nephew, Gauvain, often plays the fop: he is clearly no match for either Lancelot or Perceval, heroes whose ties to Arthur's court are much looser than Gauvain's. Whereas for Wace, King Arthur and his court are by and large worthy of virtually unrestricted praise, for Chrétien matters are far more problematic. Indeed, there are serious grounds for postulating that in Chrétien's œuvre the very idea of historicity—of historical truth—is to be dissociated from the Arthurian story; this dissociation, in fact, constitutes the basic datum of Chrétien's attitude towards his *matiere*. Chrétien's *matiere* always turns out to be a pretext.

His *san* is also often problematic, even ambiguous, especially in regard to moral questions. Thus, it is true that Lancelot loves Guenevere; his love is, consequently, adulterous, as is her (though somewhat qualified) love for him. Does this fact suffice to make of Chrétien, as certain scholars have averred, the epic poet of courtly, or adulterous, love? No, because although this love is part of the romance's *san* (as imparted to Chrétien by Countess Marie de Champagne), it does not constitute the entirety of this *san*. It is after all Lancelot's passion for Guenevere that impels him to rescue the queen from captivity and to return her, along with many other captives, to their rightful homes in Arthur's kingdom of Logres. In this fashion a great good is accomplished (almost incidentally) precisely because of the existence and overriding power of an ostensibly sinful passion. Meanwhile, it is Lancelot's single-minded concentration on his love for Guenevere that causes the many other maidens and ladies who populate the romance to respect him affectionately and, on many occasions, to help him in his task. Other ladies may pine away with love for him, but none displays an iota of jealousy. At its most profound, Chrétien's *san* is invariably open-ended, never reductive or oversimplified.

The last of the three terms to be found in the *Charrette* prologue is
antancïon. After receiving the *matiere* and the *san* from Marie, Chrétien

> . . .s'antremet
> De panser, si que rien n'i met
> Fors sa painne et s'antancïon.
>
> (vv. 27–29)

([He] puts his mind to it so that nothing be added [to the countess's
command] besides his hard work and his intellectual understanding.)

Elements of both understanding and intent are conjoined in *antancïon*—
clerkly competence and good will. Chrétien will unstintingly do the best
job he can, in service to his patroness, with all the learning and literary
talent he has at his disposal. In fact, the literary, or clerkly, service he
renders to the countess seems to parallel the chivalric service rendered by
Lancelot to Guenevere in the main body of the romance!

Antancïon may perhaps best be understood as the application of *clergie*
to developing most perfectly the *matiere* with which the *clerc* is working,
in terms of the *san* that this *matiere* contains. The cleric's *antancïon* reveals
san in such a way as to serve faithfully the truth of the *matiere* and to proclaim the divine mission of *clergie*.[19] In medieval scholastic thought,
intentio(em), "intention(ality)," from which *antancïon* etymologically
derives, signified the mind as it might be essentially directed toward
some thing or concept. Like *san*, *intentio/antancïon* implies direction and
the necessary presence of will.

A term that has been less analyzed by historians of literature and yet
that had, I believe, important repercussions upon the evolution of OF
narrative is *(par)fenir*, "to finish, to bring to a proper close." The word is
given virtuoso development in the last lines of *Le Chevalier au Lion
(Yvain)*, where it constitutes the basis for an elaborate *adnominatio*[20]:

> Et Lunete rest mout a eise;
> Ne li faut chose qui li pleise,
> Des qu'ele a feite la pes sanz *fin*
> De monseignor Yvain le *fin*,
> Et de s'amie chiere et *fine*.
>   Del *Chevalier au Lyeon fine*
> Crestïens son romans ensi;
> N'onques plus conter n'an oï
> Ne ja plus n'an orroiz conter
> S'an n'i viaut mançonge ajoster.
>
> (vv. 6811–20; emphasis mine)

(And Lunette dwells in contentment; nothing she desires is lacking to her since she arranged the enduring peace between my lord Yvain the well-bred and his dear and courteous beloved. Concerning the Lion Knight Chrétien finishes his romance thus; I have never heard anything more said concerning this subject, nor will you ever hear anything further about it either unless someone is adding lies to the story.)

Closure and completion are obviously at issue here, but *fenir*, as in "fine Crestïens son roman," does not appear to be restricted merely to bringing the plot to a satisfactory conclusion. The idea of completion contained in *fenir* seems, rather, to comprise as well the notion of polishing, of finishing, at every stage of the narrative's and its characters' development; each scene is "finished" so as to integrate itself perfectly into the sequence of scenes making up the whole of the romance (its *conjointure*). Plot is consequently but one of the various elements being "finished"; it is perhaps not even the most important of these elements.

Fenir represents the successful translation of the author's *antancïon*, or complete system of intentions, with regard to the *matiere* he has either chosen or been asked to treat. Although the author himself is usually the agent of this translation, that is not necessarily a requirement. When, as we remember, Godefroi de Leigni declares that he has completed (*parfinee*) Chrétien's *Lancelot*, he says that he has done so according to the precise instructions given him by the master. The section of *Lancelot* composed by Godefroi adheres to Chrétien's *antancïon*; Godefroi is here the agent of this *antancïon*. He shares in Chrétien's *painne*.

To a greater or lesser degree all medieval continuators—that is, the various *clercs* who undertook to continue Chrétien's *Graal*—and, indeed, even many OF scribes, see themselves as agents of an original, authoritative, and justifying *antancïon*. However different from Guillaume de Lorris's "incomplete" poem Jean de Meung's continuation of the *Romance of the Rose* might appear to us today—and, in fact, the two parts of the *Rose* are radically dissimilar—Jean firmly associated himself with the poetic nature of Guillaume's enterprise, as the midpoint of the conjoined two poems clearly demonstrates. The œuvre of Chrétien de Troyes stands exemplarily at the beginning of what might be termed the tradition of a certain "poetics of completion" in medieval vernacular literature. The notion of *fenir* includes *translatio, conjointure, antancïon*, and *san*; it is perhaps that which best characterizes the dynamics of OF poetic creativity. To "complete" a poetic work is to participate in literature, to be a part of *clergie*; this completion constitutes each generation's response to what its predecessor—as it understands this predecessor—summons, and authorizes, it to do.

The notions of "conjoining" and of "putting together" included in Chrétien's term *conjointure* have more far-reaching implications than we have suggested so far. *Conjointure* refers also to "coupling," that is, to the harmony created by the joining of man and woman, in love and, especially in Chrétien's œuvre, in marriage. As we shall see later in more detail, both *Érec et Énide* and *Yvain* deal specifically with marriage and its construction by the couple involved. Marriage is also central to the comic narrative of *Cligés*—the marriage, first of all, of Cligés's parents, Alixandre and Soredamor, and then that of Cligés himself and his beloved Fénice, whose union is contrasted to the false—that is, purely "contractual" and loveless—marriage of Fénice and Cligés's usurping uncle, Alis.[21] In the *Chevalier de la Charrette* the couple formed by Lancelot and Queen Guenevere transcends marriage—it is a perfect love story—and, at the same time, the fact of this couplehood contains foreshadowings of tragic events that will occur precisely because a marriage of the two lovers, as in the case of Tristan and Iseut, is out of the question.[22]

Chrétien's "putting together" of *Érec et Énide* is consequently analogous to what transpires in the plot of that romance. As the two principal characters learn authentically to be "conjoined," so the narrative itself is celebrated as a poetic achievement; the story culminates in an episode called the "Joy of the Court"—an episode of redress that leads to the reestablishment of harmony—and ends with the coronation of the two spouses: together they are ready to rule the kingdom left to Érec by his father. Chrétien's book *is* the triumphant union of husband and wife; their alliance, meanwhile, imparts value and meaning to Chrétien's book as poetic artifact. The couple's *chevalerie* is conjoined with Chrétien's *clergie*. The romance displays analogy as a powerful poetic mode of thought, of both narrative and lyric logic.

Like ripples on the surface of water, the analogy constantly broadens its scope, suggesting ever greater possibilities of significance. Man and woman as a literary topic brings to mind the manner in which those of Chrétien's time expressed their understanding of the relationship of God and His Church (the feminine *Ecclesia*, Bride of Christ), as in the tradition of commentary devoted to the biblical Song of Songs—a commentary most eloquently (and beautifully) articulated in Saint Bernard's *Sermons on the Song of Songs* (1135–38, 1148–53) with which it is impossible to believe Chrétien was not familiar.[23] Poems like the aforementioned *Life of Saint Alexis*, in which the saint, as he lives out his "imitation of Christ," devotes himself in love to the salvation of his bride and to their eventual reunion in God's eternal heaven, where their love will be free of the inevitable corruption and unhappiness found in this world.

For the twelfth-century *chevalier*, two occupations were deemed suitably noble and chivalric: war (or combat) and love. Indeed, chivalric prowess not only increased the esteem in which the knight was held by his fellow knights, but also, and often more importantly, proved him to be worthy of a lady's love. A frequent theme in romance (derived perhaps from Virgil's story of Æneas and Dido) is the problem of disjunction between these two chivalric occupations. Chrétien's romances go further than those of his predecessors in exploiting these disjunctions: the recently wed Érec neglects the practice of arms because of his uxoriousness; Yvain vaingloriously seeks the praise of his fellow knights and abandons the woman he has just married. Over and over again Chrétien insists upon the reconciliation of the affairs that pertain to what we shall call the City of Men—military prowess, concern for lineage, the business of *imperium*—with those that fall within the purview of the City of Ladies: love, the couple, the idea of service. Both Yvain and Érec achieve this reconciliation. Significantly, they succeed thanks to the intervention of women.

The lady is the custodian of the couple; it is she who possesses, in Dante's terminology, the "intellect of love" (*l'intelletto d'amore*). The quality of "lady" corresponds to an individual woman's worth, not necessarily exclusively to her rank at birth or her title. Thus, many a *dame* is a lady in name only, and there are women who aspire to "ladyship" without meriting the designation. A very amusing, and quite scatalogical, poem by the troubadour William IX of Aquitaine describes the poet's encounter with two pretentious would-be ladies whose voracious and indiscriminate sexual appetites serve merely to underscore their vulgarity. Meanwhile, Chrétien's Énide, daughter of a humble and impoverished vavasor, is every bit a lady, and a loves her husband with an ardor that admits no shred of prudishness.

The expertise of ladies in matters of love was recognized in fashionable court circles in Chrétien's lifetime. During the final quarter of the twelfth century, in his *De arte honesti amandi* (On the art of honest love), the cleric Andreas Capellanus described just such a circle of refined women surrounding Chrétien's patroness, Marie de Champagne, who assumed the power and the duty of judging the fitness of various types of love-service. These feminine love tribunals (the existence of which would be periodically renewed well into the fifteenth century) corresponded, in all likelihood, to the practice of separating the men's court from that of the women. When, in his *Roman de Brut* (ca. 1150), Wace portrays the Arthurian court, he mentions a procession made up of knights and ladies repairing together to a church where Arthur and Guenevere are to be crowned king and queen. The knights come out, however, from Arthur's court, while the ladies, conversely, emerge from that of Guenevere. It is in the procession itself that the City of Men is conjoined with the City of Ladies. Similar constructs also prevail in several of Chrétien's romances. Serving Blancheflor in her castle and defending her against a malicious and lubricious enemy, the youthful Perceval is for the first time in his life integrated into the City of Ladies. And when Yvain takes Laudine as a wife he too becomes a part of her world (something Æneas refused to do when invited to stay with Dido in Carthage), only to forsake her in order to play out the empty role of tournament champion at the male court of King Arthur. The consequences of this abandonment are severe for Yvain; he must learn the meaning of charity in order to be worthy of his spouse's love once again.

Formal, poetic *conjointure* thus replicates and reinforces the ardent defense of human coupling we find in all of Chrétien's narratives. "Joining"—coupling man and woman—is invested by Chrétien with the deepest possible meaning and with undisputably spiritual dimensions. To a significant degree, then, his romance œuvre may therefore be said to be a series of meditations on *conjointure*: this meditative quality constitutes both a pretext and an end. His œuvre is highly evocative of the shame-free state of mankind as it once existed, before sin, in prelapsarian Eden; this fact also may be viewed as inspiring Chrétien's definition of *courtoisie* (courtliness, courtesy), the human value to which he accords his greatest esteem. Repeatedly, then, Chrétien's knightly protagonists learn not only to recognize the lady's power but also willingly, even adoringly, to concede its genuineness. This recognition, as it takes place, places the knight on what appears to be the horns of a dilemma. On the one hand, he must sally forth, fully armed, in order to defend by force, and quite aggressively, what he has been charged with defending. On the other hand, he is obliged to shed all armor and confess his defenselessness before he can accede to the grace that only his lady may bestow upon him.[24]

Chapter 2

Schools, the Vernacular, and the Court

Although at the time of Charlemagne (742–814) the royal and imperial court constituted an important center of learning, during the disturbed centuries following Charles's death the study of letters reverted mainly to various monastic centers in France and elsewhere in Europe. The second half of the eleventh century, however, witnessed the rise of the cathedral school, especially in France. These establishments were ostensibly dedicated to the intellectual formation of priests and other types of cleric within the ecclesiastical framework. But as the century progressed, the schools tended to become more and more independent of the cathedral administration, and increased numbers of their former pupils began to hold secular positions, particularly in the areas of government and education. Many *clercs* joined the retinues of royal and great noble houses. Chartres, Tours, Orléans, Laon, and Paris were among the most famous of the cathedral schools. It was in such places that the intellectual renewal now recognized as the Renaissance of the twelfth century largely took place, especially at its beginnings. (The medieval university would not truly come into its own until the thirteenth century.) Monasteries also remained influential; indeed, some monastic establishments attained extraordinary intellectual prestige and power. The Abbey of Saint-Denis in Paris, for example, remained the most active— indeed, the official—center for historiography pertaining to France and its new Capetian dynasty. And it was from Cistercian Clairvaux that its abbot, Saint Bernard (1091–1153), forcefully helped map out the course of events in Western Christendom, often in opposition to what he deemed to be the dangerous unorthodoxies fostered by the schools.

Teaching, reading, and writing were conducted in Latin, the official language of record and of learning throughout the Middle Ages in those areas of Europe identified with Roman Catholicism. The curriculum was based on the arts, or *artes*, and, in the initial section of the curriculum called the *trivium*, or "three-part way," it led young scholars in steps from grammar to rhetoric, and from rhetoric to dialectic (or logic). The language-centered *trivium* was followed by the four mathematical arts—the *quadrivium*—made up of arithmetic, geometry, astronomy and music (or harmony).

Studies in the *trivium* were grounded in a traditional canon of Latin "authors" (the *auctores*), with a component of Greek writers whose works had survived in variously faithful Latin translations. Thus, for dialectic, Boethius's version of Aristotle served as the authoritative sourcebook for that philosopher's thought until the late twelfth century, when Arabic translations from the Greek could be made available in Latin versions to West European readers. Included among the *auctores* we find not only such standard Latin literary classics as Virgil, Ovid, Statius, Cicero, Horace, Suetonius, and many others, but also an immensely important cohort of late-Latin writers and commentarists, including of course such church fathers as Saint Ambrose, Saint Jerome, and Saint Augustine, alongside such other Christian writers as Origen the Scriptural commentator and Eusebius the providentialist historiographer.[1] Among the writers of later Latinity studied in the schools were, in particular, Priscian (the late-Latin grammarian), Macrobius (*Commentary on Cicero's "Dream of Scipio"*), Martianus Capella (*De Nuptiis Mercurii et Philologiæ*), Servius (his commentaries on Virgil), the aforementioned Boethius (*De Consolatione Philosophiæ* [ca. 525]), and Saint Isidore of Seville (ca. 570–636), a personage often referred to as "the last man of Antiquity," among whose copious works the encyclopedic *Etymologiæ* enjoyed a special status. Homer's *Iliad* was known, thanks to stories of the Trojan War attributed to the now-forgotten Dares and Dictys. The influence of Plato, which was pervasive during the twelfth century, was based on a fragmentary Latin version of his dialogue, *Timæus*, and, of course, on certain neo-Platonists whose writings survived into the Middle Ages. (Greek was virtually unknown in Western Christendom.)

These were some of the texts, accompanied by myriad commentaries and glosses, which, with numerous others, made up the canon we associate with Chrétien's practice of *clergie*. And it was with these works, along with Sacred Writ, theological writings, and older hagio-historiographical traditions, against the somewhat obscure backdrop of the vernacular heritage—Celtic, Germanic—of the European populations, that the *clercs* of the time forged new understandings and interpretations of God and nature as they understood them.

A passage from John of Salisbury's *Metalogicon* (ca. 1160) describes the life of pupils at the cathedral school at Chartres, under the direction of its great master, Bernard—the teacher who first compared the ancients to giants and the moderns to dwarfs perched on the shoulders of the ancients. John of Salisbury's text provides a charming—and accurate—picture of early twelfth-century literary learning presented as a discipline; it deserves extensive quotation here:

> In his daily reading of the authors, Bernard pointed out what was simple and in conformity to the rule; he would indicate the grammatical figures, the rhetorical colors, the fine points of reasoning, and the spots at which his text touched upon neighboring disciplines, without, however, saying all there was to say about everything. . . . And since exercise imparts strength to memory and vitality to the spirit, he forced his pupils to reproduce what they had heard, sometimes giving advice, at other times having recourse to the whip and to punishments. . . . The evening exercise, which was called *declinatio*, contained such a dose of grammar that, provided one worked assiduously for a whole year and provided one wasn't too stupid, one would attain mastery of the art of speaking and writing, and one would no longer be ignorant of proper usage. . . . He prized very highly, and taught his pupils to prize, the virtues of *œconomia*, the qualities of thought and of expression, showing what was truly thinness of discourse, acceptable abundance, excess or just proportion. He would recommend to his pupils that they read stories and poems attentively, without hurrying; and he required each one to memorize something new every day. (translation mine)[2]

Bernard the grammarian was not merely initiating young men into the mysteries of the Latin language, he was training them to take part in a literary, or cultural, process based on reading and writing. The process included the fine points of Latin grammar and usage, to be sure; it comprised as well the assimilation of a body of living texts—the *auctores*—which were to be learned and to be imitated, in order that the pupil one day might himself deserve to be imitated by future generations. In a most genuine sense each apprentice cleric is invited here to contribute to an ongoing Book, the significance of which is far greater than what any single individual might compose by himself. Bernard of Chartres—in tune with his century—thus championed a clearly mapped out program, or discipline, of *clergie*. The program is at once permanent and dynamic. To anticipate somewhat the arguments we shall present below, it may be said that the *clerc*, in remaining faithful to Virgil and Ovid as distinguished participants in this ongoing program (or process), rendered himself eventually capable of creating so startlingly new a literary form as courtly romance and of couching it in a highly sophisticated vernacular diction. Chrétien de Troyes's own authorial identity is tied into the process rendered illustrious by forebears like Virgil and Ovid. His "creativity" stemmed from his fidelity to that process.

Bernard's classes were of course conducted orally: the *lectio*, the *explicatio*, and what followed these were spoken and responded to out loud. Pupils also presumably presented their own work orally and were corrected in the same fashion. Great feats of memory were required, with the novice cleric assimilating vast amounts of literary material and precept. Naturally, apart from some written records of scholastic disputations, all this dynamic and spoken give-and-take is lost to us today. However, it may be reconstituted to some degree by our having recourse to certain types of manuscript that record bits and pieces of the process. Surely, too, this school emphasis on orality, strengthened by the oral dissemination of many early saints' lives and epic *chansons de geste*, must have entered into the oral reading of vernacular romances at courts like those of Champagne and of the Plantagenets.

Compendia of the sort of technical knowledge also stressed by Bernard were numerous in twelfth-century France. Ancient authorities on rhetoric—Priscian, Cicero (as well as the pseudo-Cicero of the rhetorical treatise *Ad Herennium*), Quintilian, Saint Augustine, and their followers—and poetics (Horace) were studied, imitated, and cited, even in vernacular works.[3] Chrétien's narrator refers to Macrobius in his *Érec et Énide* as "[he who] teaches me the art of description" (v. 6741) and Marie de France, in the prologue to her *Lais*, paraphrases Priscian's remark concerning the greater literary perspicacity of modern writers over their ancient predecessors. Indeed, the old grammarians and rhetoricians also played an important role in the early development of scholastic thought, with its well-known concern for words, their organization, and their referential power. By the end of the twelfth century, scholastic philosophers had rejected "literary" grammar as too imprecise to permit rigorous logical formulations, and philosophy continued on its way, in opposition to poetry, with the development of a new "speculative" grammar.

Important as this acquisition of grammatic-literary learning was, it was no more important than the twelfth-century "imitations" of certain classical works. Imitation possesses a long and distinguished history in medieval European culture, reaching far back into the early Christian era and continuing more or less uninterruptedly, although waxing and waning in various areas at different times,[4] down to the twelfth century and beyond. Poems recounting the deeds of Germanic heroes and rulers were composed in a Latin grounded in the diction and prosody of Virgil's *æneid*; histories and biographies (Einhard's *Life of Charlemagne* [ca. 820] comes to mind) imitated Cicero and Suetonius. The monastic culture of Carolingian Europe favored the copying, and therefore the preservation, of the authorial canon and its commentarists. And, after the Council of Tours (813), convoked by the Emperor, decreed that henceforth certain portions of the mass would be said or sung in the vernacular (especially the homily and the Alleluia), this same monastic culture presided over the assembling and diffusion of pious vernacular works in both Romance and Germanic.

A veritable explosion of Latin literary composition took place, however, in the twelfth century.[5] Prose history took on new importance. Philosophical—largely neo-Platonic—poems, like the *De mundi universitate* (ca. 1150), written by Bernard Silvestris in imitation of Martianus Capella, and the somewhat later *Anticlaudianus* and *De planctu Naturæ* by Alain de l'Isle (ca. 1128–1202), straddled the intellectual and spiritual terrain of myth, literature, and speculative thought.[6] Early Scholastic treatises, like the *Decretales* of Gratian (ca. 1140), who sought to codify canon law in imitation of the great law codes of Roman antiquity, began to appear and to set a new intellectual tone. The vitally important tradition of what has been called "thinking about thinking"—works on language and on logic (as well as on the limitations of these when applied to the contemplation of God)—was born with Saint Anselm (1033–1109), and continued throughout the twelfth century and beyond, with Peter Abelard (1079–1142) among its most distinguished twelfth-century representatives.[7] Latin songs—sacred and profane—were also composed (the older Abelard regretted having written a few in his younger days), and these laid the foundation for the highly ribald, but sometimes deeply pious, Goliard poetry of the later twelfth and thirteenth century. Dramatic works appeared, many of which were put on stage in monasteries and nunneries. Intense theological debates were also carried on in writing, along with other kinds of polemic. Scholars have unearthed written correspondences—letters exchanged by individuals, sometimes by individuals deeply involved with one another, as was the case with Abelard and his wife, Heloise, to whose correspondence might be added letters of consolation written to Heloise, now a widow, by Peter the Venerable, Abbot of Cluny. Saint Bernard of Clairvaux was also an inveterate correspondent.

Historiographical writings often served political ends. The English cleric Geoffrey of Monmouth, for example, in about 1136 completed his very belleletristic, and "clerkly," *Historia regum Britanniæ*—a history of the kings of ancient Britain based largely on Celtic legends and certain old myths (such as the Trojan origin of Britain via Æneas's descendant Brutus). Geoffrey's *Historia* celebrates in great detail King Arthur and what the author presents as the golden age of pre-Saxon England, thus providing the Norman-Angevin dynasty in England with an anti-Saxon precursor as well as with a worthy rival to the heroic Charlemagne, who was claimed as its forebear by the Capetian house of France. This work would be rendered in OF romance form by the Norman *clerc* Wace less than two decades later; it was Wace, moreover, who first wrote of King Arthur's Round Table.

It is worth mentioning once again that Andreas Capellanus's *De arte honesti amandi* (ca. 1185), a treatise on love ostensibly composed in order to instruct a young man in the etiquette and ways of refined, courtly sentiment, includes among its characters Countess Marie de Champagne, the patroness of Chrétien de Troyes, and her ladies, who considered themselves arbiters of the rules of *fin'amors* (refined, noble love—referred to frequently since the later nineteenth century as *amour courtois*, or "courtly love").[8] The setting for the frame fiction of this treatise is Arthur's court.

Perhaps of greatest interest to us as we try to approach the œuvre of Chrétien de Troyes are certain eleventh- and twelfth-century Latin writers who deal specifically with their own times, indeed with their own thoughts and sentiments. For the most part these are school- or monastery-trained clerics of truly exceptional intellect and insight who express what might well be called a present, "vernacular" consciousness in formal Latin garb. The contributions of Saint Anselm, Abelard, and Saint Bernard of Clairvaux to the new sense of human individuality that was forged in the twelfth century can hardly be overestimated; they were among those who helped bring about and record the transformation of sensibility without which later twelfth-century vernacular romance (and the works of Chrétien) would have been inconceivable.

A sense of humanity pervades this new sensibility, and this aspect led to a revitalization of concern for the Incarnation—God as man—as well as renewed interest both in the personhood of the individual human being and in human society as the object of God's love. The title of one of Saint Anselm's major works is *Cur Deus homo* (Why God became man), composed between 1094 and 1098—a work, as R. W. Southern has observed, which did away once and for all with the notion of man principally as an impotent tragic witness to the mighty combat fought over him between the devil (to whom, in sinning, man had bounded himself over) and God, who, by the strategem of assuming human form and by fooling the devil who claimed Him in death, triumphantly deprived the devil of his power over Man:

> Once this view had been discarded, the story of man's Redemption could be set on another plane. Man had sinned, and Man must redeem. But what the existing race of man was powerless to perform could only be accomplished by a new Man—either by a new creation, or by an Angel become Man, or by God become Man. Anselm attempted to prove that the third of these courses was the one which was logically necessary. . . . The way was now open for a fresh appreciation of the human sufferings of the Redeemer. The figure on the Cross was seen with a new clarity to be that of a Man. The Devil slipped out of the drama and left God and Man face to face. (Southern, 236)

Man's and, in Christ, God's personhood entailed for men and women of the twelfth century the obligation to study themselves, to analyze their deeds and their feelings. Emphasis began to be placed on the examination of one's conscience—on confession and repentance. It is no coincidence that the sacrament of confession was instituted by the Second Lateran Council in 1215. Meanwhile, romancers like Chrétien de Troyes (along with certain predecessors and successors) demonstrate in their works their—and their audiences'—predilection for lengthy confessional monologues of self-analysis in which their heroes and heroines indulge, as well as for shrewd appreciations of what their characters do, think, and feel. Saint Anselm himself, a logician and a systematic philosopher, composed stunningly beautiful and moving prayers in verse; see, for example, the poem he addressed to Saint Mary Magdalene, whose total love for Jesus, he suggests, he can only hope to understand and strive to emulate. Anselm's Mary Magdalene is a woman in love; her exemplary love constitutes for him the key to what divine love might be. Throughout the twelfth century, the vocabulary and syntax of human love provided the verbal means for Man to stand face to face with God. Thus, Anselm's soul—the feminine *anima* in Latin—empathizes with the essentially feminine Magdalene; it is thanks to his *anima* that Anselm was able to articulate his desire for God "truthfully" and passionately.

The son of a minor Breton nobleman, Abelard inherited from his warrior ancestors his taste for combat and public victory; his weapons, however, were verbal arguments, not conventional arms.[9] Quick-tempered, hot-blooded, and never one to mince words, he was a pupil feared by his masters and, later, a master greatly admired—loved even—by his students. His cold-blooded seduction of the intellectually very gifted young Heloise, his falling in love with her and his "secret" marriage to her—all of these events culminating in his brutal emasculation at the hands of thugs hired by Heloise's uncle—provide the stuff of a "real life" romance prototype. This story is told in Abelard's autobiographical account entitled *Historia calamitatum* (1133–36), and it is rehearsed in the extraordinary exchange of letters initiated by Heloise between him and her during the years she remained at the convent of the Paraclete (to which Abelard had sent her) in Champagne, very near Troyes. Abelard continued his theological work, despite the unforgiving opposition of important theologians, above all Saint Bernard of Clairvaux. Finally condemned at the Synod of Sens (1141), his writings burned, Abelard embarked on a trip to Rome in order to plead his case with the pope. Tired and ill, he was received by Peter the Venerable, abbot of Cluny, and nursed until his death in 1142. Peter shipped Abelard's remains to the Paraclete, where Heloise had them interred; she stipulated that upon her death she be buried in the same tomb, alongside her one-time lover and husband, so that they could be joined once again, but eternally, in death as they had only briefly been united in life.[10]

Most of Abelard's earlier work dealt with problems of logic and philosophical language—commentaries and glosses on the Boethian Aristotle, for example. Throughout the late 1120s and 1130s, Abelard's concerns focused increasingly on purely theological matters, especially on the nature of the Trinity (an issue to which he was repeatedly drawn), and, continuing in the path traced by Saint Anselm, on the mystery of the Incarnation—Christ's humanity.

As his correspondence with Heloise and other surviving letters demonstrate, Abelard was very much of his time: he was literate in the sense which a Bernard of Chartres would have attributed to the term, well versed in the *auctores* and attentive to refined Latin style. Running as a constant thread throughout his thought and personal works, however, a never-ceasing tension may be observed between Abelard's frequent professions of orthodox belief and what can only be called the idiosyncrasy of his faith. Although it is not incorrect to see in him an honest and God-fearing thinker, unjustly persecuted by his powerful contemporaries (some of whom were inspired by base motives of jealousy at Abelard's renown), one can nevertheless comprehend the rationale behind this persecution. Abelard seems to slip away from one's grasp; he appears often to want to have his cake and eat it too. Whereas Saint Anselm had clearly drawn the line of demarcation between what could be said truthfully in words and what had to be relegated to silent contemplation, no such borderline appears evident in Abelard. His frequent, almost obsessive, returning to the issue of the Trinity offers a case in point. It is not so much a matter of revising his thought, but, rather, of his successive attempts to contain within it the whole of the meaning of the Trinity, despite the obscurities and contradictions that might emerge when one endeavors to consider the various treatises and monographs as parts or versions of a single totality.

This is the manner of romance, of course. Romance narrative thrives on containing apparent contradictions. The romance itself constitutes a whole context, and within this context it both mirrors the sort of context provided by an individual's life (his "story"), or the entwined lives of two inseparable lovers ("their" story), and legitimizes the genuineness of these individuals' lives. Like Abelard, however, romance narrative also came under severe attack by churchmen and others who accused it of mendacity and subversion.

In the *Historia calamitatum* as well as in his letters to Heloise, Abelard unabashedly presents his seduction of Heloise as sinful lust, because he had planned in advance to seduce her: he had willed this sin. It is in this way that their romance commences, and unfolds with their marriage and the pathetic consequences that follow. The romance ends happily, so to speak, with their afterlife.[11] What are we to make of Abelard's sin? The story, or "romance," appears to argue that it is a kind of *felix culpa*—a sinful human act to which God responds with His charity. Abelard's sinfulness turns out to be an indispensable prerequisite to this—his own— happy ending, as does Heloise's suffering as she lives out her life as prioress of the Paraclete, far from her beloved Abelard. As "read" by Peter the Venerable, the romance of Heloise and Abelard becomes a *bele conjointure*, exactly of the type to the composition of which Chrétien de Troyes will dedicate his life-long *antancïon*.[12] Although the logic of the story (in Peter's reading) is narrative, it is not of a dialectic sort. By placing it, as a number of scholars have done, in the context of a dialectic, one transforms the work that into something either hopelessly muddled or so contradictory as to deserve the double charge of fraud and blasphemy. But when it is read as a "true" narrative (as Peter the Venerable demonstrated), the story becomes that of the redemptive power of God's love on behalf of "real" sinners who "learn" to desire Him; and it is all the more human—or humanly truthful—in Heloise's personal recalcitrance and deep sadness at having to accept the ending of the story. Her

angry grief at having been separated from Abelard and her inconsolable
sorrow at his death serve, for the many twelfth-century readers of the
story who found it fascinating, to prove the ardor of her capacity for
nonselfish love and, therefore, her suitability to receive God's grace.

Dante placed Saint Bernard of Clairvaux in the highest realm of his
Paradise, qualifying him in the *Paradiso* as the "Doctor of Love." In doing
so, Dante simply confirmed what, in the memory of his own time,
Bernard stood for. However, in Bernard's time—he was abbot of
Clairvaux from 1115 to 1153, and leader of a Cistercian network comprising some 350 abbeys (of which he caused to be founded no less than
165)—he acted with forcefulness and energy in the world. He championed the papacy, mediated between kings and emperors, preached on
behalf of the Second Crusade (1146), spoke eloquently at church coun-
cils, and kept up a voluminous correspondence. He acted as reformer in
church matters and pronounced judgment on public morals; he inter-
vened often in the theological debates of the period. He was rightly considered one of the great men of all time by his contemporaries and
successors. He united in himself a public man, very much *en vue*, and an
intensely private, contemplative one. In this dual role-playing, but even
to a much greater degree, he resembled his adversary, Abelard.
Although, so far as we have been able to determine, Bernard does not
give voice to the presence within his soul of a tension between himself as
a man-in-the-world and the contemplative man of God, his life can
arguably be understood as having reflected such a tension. He did not
withdraw from the world of human affairs as Saint Alexis and many
other holy men had done; conversely, he did not totally give himself over
to the world either. A profound thinker and a master of both oral and
written expression, Saint Bernard looked askance at the schools, with
their—to him—dangerous overemphasis on reason and the purely
human capacity for understanding. He was very much a monk, but a
monk of a new, far more public kind; he and his Cistercians, the most
perfectly representative (and energetic) twelfth-century monastic order,
prepared the way for the new wave of religious-in-the-world, which
found its purest articulation a century later in the mendicant orders
founded by Saint Francis and Saint Dominick.

Like the story of Abelard and Heloise and like the lyric expression of
inner longings we find in Saint Anselm, the biography of Saint Bernard
possesses significant romancelike overtones. As he depicts it at its pro-
foundest level, Bernard's life consisted of a disciplined *quest* for union
with God—a kind of journey, composed of steps and of adventures (that

is, unforeseen events or happenings). As Bernard saw it, the soul embarks upon this journey at God's loving invitation at the time of one's birth, for it is already as an infant that one feels an imperious, though selfish, need for the love and the care that can be provided only by others. This need never disappears. Frequently, it is the cause of certain purely human—and consequently sinful—contractual arrangements: in exchange for services rendered, I will be of service to you. Much of what passes for human "love" consists of just such egotistical exchanges, even when God is involved. However, such pseudolove, whether based on the flesh or on reason, is never truly satisfying; it is constantly in need of further proof. When, by rigorous self-discipline, one learns at last to despise this pseudolove, one's desire can be properly and systematically centered on God, spiritually; and in one's love for him, an authentic love for other human beings must also be grounded. This is the Christian's principal quest, as Bernard explained it in his quintessentially important sermons on the Song of Songs, sermons he composed on behalf of young novices attached to his monastery over a period covering two decades, from about 1135 to the time of his death in 1153.

Saint Bernard's commentary on the Song of Songs gives a fairly well-defined shape to the kind of meditation—lyric and narrative—on love that his century found so fascinating. It also invites with fervor its audience to shape their lives—their "biographies"—according to the transcendence permeating his teaching on love. The situation is not without resemblance to that in which Chrétien de Troyes's hero, Perceval, finds himself when he willingly—even passionately—accepts the "calling" to become a knight; this acceptance requires his departure on the quest that will bring him face to face with the mystery of the Grail, the "so *spiritual* a thing" (as Chrétien describes it, in very Bernardian terms), whose mystery he must then go on to try to unravel by initially divesting himself of the selfishness that first prompted him to wish to become a knight. Bernard "calls" his reader to recognize himself, and as he does so, to learn to love God unrestrictedly (in the way that the Shulamite Bride of the Song of Songs loved her Bridegroom), and, concomitantly, to learn to penetrate the mystery of his love for us. This is surely the ultimate "romance," and we can detect echoes of it in virtually all the romance narratives of Chrétien; Bernard's invitation is even more explicitly present in such post-Chrétien romances as the *Perceval Continuations* and the *Prose Lancelot*, and especially, the *Queste del saint Graal*.

In conclusion, then, it is clear that the new intellectual and literary traditions of the late eleventh century and early twelfth century sent down deep roots in the societies that fostered them. To what extent these traditions created the new modes of thought and feeling that came to prevail as the twelfth century progressed is difficult to judge; perhaps they simply mirrored the realities of their time. It seems likely, however, that Saint Anselm, Abelard (and Heloise), as well as Saint Bernard were at once creations of their age and the persons who provided it with its most profound articulation. Historians tell us that after the terrible moment of the first millennium had passed—and let us not forget that for more than a century and a half before the year 1000 Western Christendom endured invasion, pillage, inefficacy of governance, and even starvation—things began to look better for the population at large. Europe experienced a significant demographic and economic growth; the fierce Norsemen had been domesticated and other marauding barbarians had been checked. By the end of the eleventh century, Western Christendom could—and did—envisage taking the offensive against its Muslim adversaries; the Crusade of 1098 witnessed the taking of Jerusalem by a Western army under the command of Geoffrey of Bouillon. Optimism was finally no longer out of the question. People, certainly, were less afraid, more confident in their ability to seek out what they believed—hoped—was true. The kind of trust in God and in His love that we find in Saint Bernard could not help but stimulate human activity and even a certain pride in human works. The discipline and order that could be found in the great works of the *auctores* merited study and emulation. Each "restoration" of the classics invariably puts heavy emphasis on discipline and order; the twelfth century was no exception.

It would be too simplistic to state that during the 1150s a number of clerics made up their minds to transfer into the vernacular, and thereby render accessible to a nonscholarly public, the narrative treasures that had until then belonged exclusively to those familiar with Latin and the Latin literary tradition. It is certainly true, however, that at the mid-century point a new literary consciousness began to make itself felt in the language spoken by the aristocracy on both sides of the English Channel. It is around that time that vernacular romance comes into its own, and that a style we associate with "courtliness" or "courtesy" (*courtoisie*), hitherto pretty much restricted to lyric love poetry, begins to dominate verse narrative.

As has already been mentioned, at the close of Charlemagne's reign over Western Christendom, the Council of Tours, at the emperor's instigation, imposed the use of the *rusticam romanam linguam et theotiscam* (rustic Romance and Germanic languages) in the homily of the mass and allowed its employ in certain other parts of the liturgy. It is consequently from about 815 on that we can date the beginning of the Romance literatures—literatures almost entirely confined to a sacred context. Several ninth- and tenth-century texts in a variety of Gallo-Romance vernacular languages have been preserved: *The Strasbourg Oaths*; a short (and very beautiful) little song recounting the martyrdom of the Spanish Saint Eulalia; fragments of a sermon on the Jonah story; a verse rendition of Christ's trial and Passion; a life of Saint Leodegar. Elements of both what would be distinguished as *langue d'oïl* (Northern Gallo-Romance, including the dialect of Paris, *francien*, or Old French) and *langue d'oc* (the dialects of the Midi, the language of the future Old Provençal troubadours) have been detected in this very adaptable post–Council of Tours Gallo-Romance written vernacular.

By the end of the tenth century, however, the political situation in what is now known as France changed quite radically. Centered in Paris and the Île-de-France, a new dynasty—the Capetians—had come to rule in *langue d'oïl* territory. Although in the beginning the effective rule of the Capetians suffered from severe limitations, due mostly to competition from the great feudal barons, the new royal house was enthusiastically backed by certain ecclesiastical institutions, especially the great Abbey of Saint-Denis outside Paris. Carolingian rule (or what survived of it) was forever broken in the Kingdom of France. Token connections between the empire and the various dukedoms and counties of the Midi were, however, maintained until the thirteenth century, and great swatches of Romance-speaking territory to the north and east of Paris retained more or less strong links to the empire. Slowly but inexorably, these too would be integrated into the French kingdom.

Consequently, the *francien* dialect, centrally located and invested with the prestige of the new French monarchy, slowly began to take precedence over the other spoken dialects of *oïl*. During the second half of the eleventh century, this dialect provided the basis for a new written vernacular (or *scripta*), the language we now call Old French. By the year 1100, two OF literary masterpieces had seen the light of day: the *Life of Saint Alexis* (variously dated, from ca. 1040 to the early twelfth century) and the *Song of Roland* (ca. 1085–1100). Each of these works survives in several twelfth-century manuscripts: MS *L* (Lamspringen, now

Hildesheim) and MS Oxford Digby 23 (ca. 1140?) are generally considered the best representatives of the respective *Alexis* and *Roland* traditions.[13]

Both *Alexis* and *Roland* are specifically oriented to France and are historic-religious in nature. The former text refers to "our ancestors," the Romans, who "received Christianity"; the latter alludes constantly to *douce France* and to *Franceis* as the land (and people) identified with Christendom.[14] Or, to put things another way, France, for the *Alexis*, is the kingdom (represented by the audience to which the poem is addressed) whose subjects are the present-day heirs of the Christianized Romans, although they are depicted as not so pure in their "faith, justice and love" as their ancestors were. Meanwhile, geographically speaking, the France of *Roland* very creatively appears to "confuse" the late-eleventh-century Capetian kingdom with the entirety of Western Christendom identified with Charles the emperor. The French of the *Roland* are both the inhabitants of the aforementioned Capetian kingdom and the "Frankish," or pan-Christian, subjects of the Carolingian empire.

The French as descendants, or heirs, of the Romans—the identification that pervades both *Alexis* and *Roland*—furnishes the ideological backbone to Chrétien de Troyes's rehearsal of the *translatio* topic in the prologue to *Cligés*. The France in which both *chevalerie* and *clergie* have come to reside is therein defined, precisely, in terms of the locus of this residence. France is where *chevalerie* and *clergie*, born in Greece and at one time resident in Rome, now are. This France is opposed by Chrétien to the Britain (identified by him as the former name given to what is now called England) where many of the events of his romances take place; Britain is a *pays de roman*, the place of fiction—a kind of storybook land.

During the twelfth century, France and its capital, the Capetian royal court, was of little literary importance, at least in the vernacular; Paris, of course, was home to the schools. Yet, the idea of "France" exerted a strong magnetic pull upon vernacular literature. That it did so was largely thanks to the *francien* literary *scripta* to which this idea also contributed a great deal.[15] Curiously enough, written *francien* owed its greatest prestige to writers based in lands bordering on France proper—Normandy, Norman-Angevin England, Champagne, Flanders, and Picardy. Already in the 1170s we find in Guernes de Pont-Sainte-Maxence's *Life of Thomas Becket* the claim that because the author was born in France his "language is good," that is, presumably true.[16] However, few twelfth-century texts have come down to us in spotless *francien* redactions; most are, to one degree or another, colored by the presence of dialect traits proper either to the author or to the scribe.

During the course of the twelfth century, literary French acquired a universalist character, especially when viewed in its relationship to other spoken *oïl* dialects, and it was soon to be identified with courtliness and properly aristocratic behavior.[17] At the start of *Le Chevalier de la Charrette (Lancelot)*, Chrétien describes the ladies surrounding Queen Guenevere at Arthur's court in terms that articulate this connection between language and comportment: "Si ot avoec li, ce me sanble, / Mainte bele dame cortoise, / Bien parlant an lengue françoise" (vv. 40–42; There were present next to her, so I believe, many a lovely and courtly lady, well-spoken in the French language").[18]

Chrétien de Troyes stresses the excellence of French and of the *clergie* that has taken up residence in France. With the possible exception of his first surviving romance, *Érec et Énide*, he tends to deny historical value to the Arthurian world that he ostensibly celebrates. The *Le Chevalier au Lion (Yvain)* opens upon a scene in which King Arthur behaves most boorishly to his invited dinner guests;[19] in *Lancelot*, he rashly gives Guenevere, his queen, away, thereby precipitating the events of her rescue by her lover, Lancelot. In *Perceval*, Arthur and his court are but shadows of their former selves; they no longer constitute the center of the world in which the action of that romance takes place. The new center has become the Grail Castle and its mystery, which the protagonist, after having undergone an indispensable spiritual preparation, is called upon to resolve. In Chrétien's view, Arthur and the Round Table are no match for the authentic and truthfully French history of *Alexis* and *Roland*.

If Arthur's court is not the place where true history is made, what does transpire there that makes it a central device in Chrétien's romances? Or is it merely a matter of fashion? Does Chrétien compose Arthurian romances because this is what his patrons require?

Arthur's court—the place of courtliness—is both one and three things. It is where, at certain appointed times during the year, the king summons his barons for advice and aid—a masculine place. A woman-centered court—Guenevere and her retinue of ladies—complements this masculine place. The two courts are separate. However, from time to time, especially on important occasions, the two courts are held together, or jointly. In *Brut*, as was noted earlier, Wace describes Arthur's coronation day—the procession of barons emanating from Arthur's court meeting the procession of ladies coming from that of Guenevere, and their joining together in the church as the king and his queen are crowned. It is necessary to speak here of a "City of Men" conjoined to a "City of Ladies."

Chrétien's romances offer examples of all three sorts of court. Thus, at the beginning of *Érec et Énide*, we learn of Arthur's summoning his court:

> . . . mout i ot buens chevaliers,
> Hardiz et corageus et fiers,
> Et riches dames et puceles,
> Filles a rois, jantes et beles.
>
> (vv. 31–34)

(. . . there were present many fine knights—strong and brave and proud—and powerful ladies and maidens, kings' daughters, noble and beautiful.)

This court is mixed. However, "before this court was dismissed, the king said to the knights present that he wished to hunt the white stag and thereby to revive the old Custom" (vv. 35–38).

Here Arthur is operating within the "City of Men"; the ladies, who might well have objected to Arthur's idea, have left the court: Arthur speaks to the knights. (Nor were they present at Arthur's dinner party in *Yvain*, where his misbehavior so shocked his guests.) Conversely, In *Le Chevalier de la Charrette (Lancelot)*, it is the ladies' court—the City of Ladies—or at least the sector of it comprised by marriageable maidens that proposes the tournament to which all the best knights (including Lancelot) will be invited; this proposal meets with the approval of several *dames*. The king, meanwhile, who "was not in the habit of refusing requests" (v. 5415), subscribes to the idea of Guenevere's attending the tournament. Finally, Guenevere herself approves the venture.

The conjoining of the two courts in Chrétien's romances is usually accompanied by great joy and the depiction of exemplary courtly behavior. Dancing and singing, telling and listening to stories, pleasant flirtation—these are the activities that properly characterize such reunions. As the narrator puts it in the front matter to *Yvain*, "after dining, the knights would come together in these halls where the ladies and the maidens had summoned them. There some would tell stories [*noveles*], others would speak of Love, of its anguishes and pains and of the great pleasures often enjoyed by the disciples of its covenant. . . . But nowadays Love has very few faithful followers, for almost everyone has abandoned Love" (vv. 8–19). Courtliness, therefore, is what is displayed by noblemen and women in mixed company, and the actions of courtliness are expressed in a special, noble vernacular diction.[20]

Chrétien de Troyes's France, it might be said, in giving a home to ancient *chevalerie* and *clergie*, becomes the place in which the values associated with *courtoisie* are most perfectly honored, and where behavior can best be judged. Meanwhile the Arthurian world is fictional—it is not the historically true France of the *chansons de geste* of Charlemagne—and therefore lends itself to the romancer as, essentially, a means for the depiction of behavior and the articulation of values. Thus, Arthur and his court provide the space, the time frame, and the characters for the romancer's dissection of, for example, the discrepancy between what appears to be so and what actually is.

Chrétien's handling of that apparent paragon of courtliness, Gauvain, offers a case in point. In his language and in his actions Gauvain (Arthur's nephew) is the perfect knight. Never is a word of his ugly or base. He betrays no one. He embodies, however, a rule-book brand of *courtoisie*—the standard against which aspiring knights are measured, as in the case of the young Cligés, who fights him in a tourney that ends in a draw. However, in *Yvain, Lancelot,* and *Perceval,* Gauvain is seriously flawed. It is he who convinces his friend Yvain that a fine reputation is to be earned in tournaments rather than in the service of his spouse, and this drives Yvain mad while nearly breaking up his marriage. In the *Chevalier de la Charrette,* unlike Lancelot (who loves Guenevere), Gauvain indignantly refuses to climb into the infamous cart for fear of debasing himself. Therefore, he will not succeed in restoring the queen to Arthur's court. In the *Conte du Graal,* Gauvain's unremitting worldliness bodes ill for his solving the mysteries of the Grail Castle; he becomes the victim of his own foppish superficiality. Nevertheless, throughout Chrétien's œuvre, Gauvain remains entirely likable and eminently charming. His courtesy stands in direct contrast to Kay's nasty tongue, and his willingness to recognize the achievements of others is quite honorable. Chrétien seems to be utilizing the character of Gauvain in order to portray the undeniable merit of *courtoisie* at the same time that he analyzes the limitations of that value system when it is applied merely automatically. A clerkly, or, perhaps, French truth other than the purely Breton truth of Arthurianism appears to be at issue here. Gauvain has the single-minded passion neither of Roland nor of Alexis, and that passion constitutes an integral part of the transcendence that is so indissolubly enmeshed in their stories. Meanwhile, each in his own way, Yvain, Lancelot, and Perceval all evince elements of this same transcendence; they are authen-

tic heroes. Having been "called," they perform works that are suffused
with their faith and their intrepid capacity for chivalric self-sacrifice; in
this performance they also construct, of course, the deeper truth, or
honor, of themselves, building this truth in the case of Yvain, revealing
it in the case of Lancelot. With Perceval both building and revealing take
place. The courtly French language that Chrétien and the other
romancers "invented" in order to tell the stories of these heroes and their
truths was an illustrious vernacular—it partook of *clergie*—that was
understood as renewing the French language of earlier, and highly
prized, saints' lives and *chansons de geste*. Fit to be heard and understood
by ladies, this language purposefully addressed a mixed courtly audience
of gentlemen and gentlewomen.

Chapter 3

Érec et Énide and Cligés: Conjointure, Clergie and Translatio

Érec et Énide

The Story: Having declined to participate, with King Arthur's court, in the traditional Hunt for the White Stag, the young prince Érec, son of King Lac, seeks out Yder, a count whose dwarf had behaved rudely to him and Queen Guenevere. He is given hospitality by an impoverished vavasor and learns that a tourney will take place on the morrow: first prize will be a sparrow hawk, awarded to the knight whose lady is judged to be the fairest. Érec defeats Yder, and the vavasor's daughter, Énide, wins the beauty prize. Érec presents Énide, now his fiancée, at Arthur's court, where the queen welcomes her warmly. Following the completion of the Hunt, or "Custom" of the White Stag, the king bestows a kiss upon Énide, proclaiming her the most lovely lady present. The wedding takes place, to the general joy of all; the couple is rapturously happy. But, given over to the pleasures of wedded bliss, Érec neglects his chivalric duties; people begin to murmur. Distressed, Énide cannot hide her sorrow. Wounded by what he construes to be her accusations, Érec decides to leave the court in order to win back his knightly prestige and prove his worth to her. Although she accompanies him, he has forbidden her to talk to him. A series of combats ensues (against bandits, giants, and noblemen, including the Count of Limors who, as Érec lies as though dead, wants to marry Énide by force), and, despite Érec's having forbade her to speak, Énide warns him at each juncture of the danger facing him. Her utter fidelity prompts him, finally, to "forgive" her. Together, they undertake the most dangerous adventure of all, that of the Joy of the Court (*Joie de la Cour*): Érec triumphs over the giant knight Mabonagrain, who had promised his lady—Énide's cousin—that he would remain with her in a magic orchard until the day he was vanquished by a better knight. Érec and Énide return to King Arthur's court. Upon the death of his father, Érec and his loyal wife are crowned king and queen at a marvelous ceremony held in the city of Nantes.

With *Érec et Énide* (ca. 1170), a new era opens in the history of European storytelling—an era whose effects are still very much with us today. This poem reinvents the genre we call narrative romance; in some important respects it also initiates the vernacular novel. (The term *roman*, used during the Middle Ages to refer to what we in English call "romance," is used indifferently in Modern French to mean "romance" or "novel.") To be sure, romances had been composed in Old French before *Érec et Énide*—during the 1150s, in fact, but mainly in French-speaking Norman-Angevin England by *clercs* attached to the Anglo-Norman royal house. But poems of this type that have survived are translations/adaptations of Latin works: the *Roman de Brut* by Wace renders Geoffrey of Monmouth's *Historia regum Britanniæ*,[1] the anonymous *Roman d'Énéas* offers a version of Virgil's *Æneid*, and so forth. It is quite likely that some OF treatment of the story of Tristan and Iseut was circulating during the 1160s;[2] however, assigning a precise date to an early *Tristan* text is notoriously difficult. *Érec et Énide* constitutes the earliest-known Arthurian romance, as opposed to the "historical" renditions of the Arthurian story to be found in Geoffrey of Monmouth and Wace.[3] It is also the earliest romance to have been composed on soil clearly within the confines of French royal and cultural predominance.[4]

How may this last statement be reconciled with the fact that the prologue to *Érec et Énide* mentions that the story about to be recounted is one that is told by "those who make their livelihood by habitually presenting in corrupt form [such tales] to their aristocratic patrons" (vv. 19–22)? This statement admits the existence of previous versions of the *Érec* subject matter—one, or perhaps several, "conte(s) d'avanture" (v. 13)—from which our author has extracted a "molt bele conjointure."[5] As was suggested in chapter 1, the key word here is *conjointure*, "putting together." Chrétien is creating something qualitatively different from what had been done before, and he is proud of his handiwork: his *estoire* will remain in the memory of man "as long as Christendom" (vv. 23–25). As Jean Frappier puts it, *Érec et Énide* "brings forth a new tonality unknown before him" (Frappier 1968, 103) and that new tonality is due, largely, to Chrétien's pride in his idiosyncratic exercise of *clergie*.

Rather than focusing, as Wace had done, on the "history" of the Arthurian world, Chrétien appears to be adapting to his own ends a Celtic story in which a young prince meets and marries a beautiful maiden whom he later jealously comes to suspect of infidelity. The Arthurian world is but a setting for the acting out, and the resolution, of this tale of a youthful marriage. The emphasis in *Érec et Énide* is placed on the growth of the two protagonists as a couple and on the re-creation of their marriage prior to their being triumphantly crowned king and queen of the kingdom inherited by Érec from his deceased father. In this, Chrétien's romance may be said to respond to the story of Tristan and Iseut, whose adulterous relationship led them inexorably to a kind of tragic transfiguration in death.

Perhaps also the sad, though extraordinarily beautiful and fascinating, tale of the love, marriage, and subsequent separation of Abelard and Heloise was on Chrétien's mind and on that of his courtly public. Abelard was a Breton (born near Nantes, the city of Érec's coronation), and was of noble origin. Possessed, like Érec, of a hot temper, he renounced a life dedicated to feats of arms, and, as Érec experiences conflict between his "career" as a knight and his uxorious sensuality, Abelard was subject to calumny because of his love for Heloise and his marriage to her. There are also parallels between Énide and Heloise. In *Érec et Énide*, when Énide responds to the Count of Limors's query as to whether she is the spouse or the *amie* (mistress) of Érec, that she is *both* spouse and *amie,* one senses the presence of Heloise, whose pride at preferring to be "Abelard's concubine" is matched only by her fierce disdain of the crassness she associated with the conjugal state. As Heloise reproached herself both to Abelard and in public for having been the cause of Abelard's disgrace, so does Énide (v. 2507: "Amis, con mar fus!" [Beloved, how badly it has gone for you!]).[6]

As a number of scholars have pointed out, *Érec et Énide* possesses a tripartite structure, at least on the level of plot. Following immediately upon the prologue, at v. 27, part I of the narrative (designated at its end at v. 1844 as "li premerains vers" [the first verse, or section; prelude]) recounts the story of the Custom of the White Stag; Érec's departure with Guenevere on a promenade; the insult inflicted by a mean dwarf, which Érec determines to avenge by combatting the dwarf's master, Yder; his success in so doing; his meeting the beautiful daughter of an impoverished vavasor—Énide—to whom he becomes engaged; his bringing Énide to Arthur's court, where Énide is declared the most beautiful of all the various knights' *amies.* Part II (vv. 1845–6410) describes the marriage feast, the presentation by Érec of Énide to his father, King Lac, who welcomes both bride and groom equally, Érec's subsequent neglect of his chivalric reputation in order to enjoy to the fullest the charms of his bride, his angry and impetuous departure with Énide in order to prove his chivalric worth, the adventures that befall the couple, and the Joy of the Court episode. Part III (vv. 6411–6958), the shortest of the three, tells of the couple's return to Arthur's court, the death of Érec's father, and the splendorous coronation of the new king and queen at Nantes.

As has been said, this poem is replete with allusions to Wace's *Brut*, to *romans antiques* (like *Énéas*), to the OF *Piramus et Tisbé*, to *Tristan et Iseut*, and to the "real life" narrative of Abelard and Heloise. The story line owes much, of course, to what might be termed the *Proto-Gereint*, that is, the Celtic tale, or *conte d'aventure*, that Chrétien will propagate in worthy form. Underlying these sources and allusions, then, is a set of formal considerations that will effect the transformation Chrétien intends and that will, in his own words, cause his poem to live as long as Christendom. These formal considerations, which also contain profound cultural meanings and values, derive from Martianus Capella's *De Nuptiis Mercurii et Philologiæ (On the Marriage of Mercury and Philology)*, an early-fifth-century Latin work in both verse and prose, from which the European Middle Ages borrowed the notion of the seven liberal arts.

The *De Nuptiis* was enormously popular throughout the Middle Ages, particularly in the schools. Numerous manuscripts of it survive today— some complete, others limited to a section or more. Its decline coincided with the advent of the Renaissance and continued as centuries passed down to our own time. It has been characterized as crazy, vapid, and decadent by modern editors and scholars. However, we should not allow its present-day bad reputation to blind us to its former importance, particularly for twelfth-century intellectual and literary life, nor should we neglect the *De Nuptiis's* carefully wrought structural coherence.[7]

Martianus's work is divided into nine books, yet, like *Érec et Énide,* it also lends itself to a tripartite structuring. Books I and II set up the *fabula* (or myth): Mercury decides to marry, but eligible candidates among the immortals of Olympus are all spoken for; he chooses Philology, a young and beautiful earth maiden, who, poverty-stricken (like Énide), has given over her life to the study of books (Heloise, we recall, was not of noble birth). After some hesitation Jupiter, urged on by Juno, agrees to this match, and Mercury brings Philology up to Olympus after she has drunk from the cup of immortality. Juno outfits her in fine new clothes. The wedding is prepared, guests arrive from all the points in the zodiac,[8] and the ceremonies begin.

Martianus's Books I and II correspond quite closely to the *premerains vers* of *Érec et Énide,* which concludes with Érec proclaiming his love for his bride-to-be before all at Arthur's court. The difference in what we might call the social standing of the god Mercury and the humble earth-maiden Philology is replicated in the similar distance affecting the couple formed by Érec and Énide (as well as, arguably, Abelard and Heloise). This equivalence would underscore the particular, and *natural,* wisdom, as well as the beauty, of Énide: her beauty and wisdom *(sagesse), like* those of Heloise, are simply *there,* and their presence is stunning.

When one compares the prologue to *Érec et Énide* to the 20 lines of verse with which Martianus opens his *De Nuptiis,* Chrétien's purpose is much clarified.[9] Verse 2 mentions the "copula sacra deum," given as "sacred principle of unity amongst the gods" by translator Stahl, whose translation misses the notion of "joining"—the "joining of two," or "coupling"—present in *copula.* Verse 19 suggests that this "coupling," or "principle of unity," is epitomized in what Martianus calls a *connubium diuum* (the wedding of a god, or, perhaps more precisely, a divine wedding, marriage). "Joining," "putting-together," "marrying," "uniting," and "harmony" are all more than merely hinted at here. Martianus specifies further that the "copula sacra deum" (in Stahl's translation) "bind[s] the warring seeds of the world with secret bonds and encourage[s] the union of opposites by your sacred embrace." Stahl's note to these lines is richly informative: "This opening hymn is based on the concept of the universe as composed of varying elements or "seeds" brought into fruitful harmony and coherence by mutual attraction—here personified as Hymen, a god of love and marriage. The concept owes something to Empedocles, but is elaborated by Plato (e.g., *Timæus* 32c; *Gorgias* 508a) and especially by Neoplatonic cosmology (e.g., Macrobius's *Commentary on the Dream of Scipio* II. 2. 18)" (Martianus, 3n2).

Does not the prologue to *Érec et Énide* very pointedly contrast the values we see associated with *copula*—including "coherence"—with the "corrupt and incoherent" adventure tales hawked by minstrels before their audiences of kings and counts? The term *conjointure,* as used by Chrétien, possesses connotations of connubiality as well as of (poetic) "joining," or "putting together," "harmonizing." The adjective *bele* (beautiful), applied to *conjointure,* would appear to indicate the special character of Chrétien's enterprise, and perhaps its great importance, just like Martianus's *copula sacra* and *connubium diuum.* Finally, Stahl's note, referring as it does to Plato's *Timæus* and to a neo-Platonic tradition exemplified by Macrobius's *Commentary on the Dream of Scipio,* fits perfectly the school curriculum of the later eleventh and twelfth centuries. The *Timæus* was the sole text of Plato available (in Latin translation) to twelfth-century *clercs,* and its influence was both pervasive and fundamental during the period of Chrétien's intellectual formation and writerly activity. Indeed, as has been proved, the *Timæus,* with its explanations of the "world soul" (*anima mundi*) and its stress on the harmonization of opposites according to mathematical-musical principles, offered the great Suger, abbot of Saint-Denis and counselor to the French kings Louis VI and Louis VII, a great deal of the intellectual background necessary for his plans for the new French (now known as Gothic) architecture embodied in the mid-twelfth-century basilica of Saint-Denis.[10] Could the *Timæus* and the commentary surrounding it not have done as much for the new French literary "romance," as Chrétien understood it? Stahl's underscoring of the links connecting Martianus's poem with the neo-Platonic tradition deriving (in part) from the *Timæus* tends to reinforce even further the plausibility of Martianus's presence in *Érec et Énide*—indeed, in Chrétien's very intellectual makeup.

As Fanny Le Moine has clearly—and brilliantly—demonstrated, *De Nuptiis* operates on two levels, or in two "theaters": the upper theater comprising the fable, that is, the subject matter of the story (the "historical" past), and the lower theater corresponding to the present-tense narrative act. The work switches back and forth, from level to level, in order to accomplish precise ends. The lower theater is occupied by two characters, an old, white-haired man who defends the whole enterprise of the book against the sarcasm of his son, Martianus. The old man's enthusiasm for his story reminds one of Chrétien's fervor in the *Érec et Énide* prologue: he declares that he is working "on something that has never before been imagined or attempted," and, in response to his son's skepticism, he retorts: "Since a well-structured subject matter is addressed to Hymen (the god of marriage), is it not clear that what is being sung is a marriage?" (Book I, paragraph 2). Consequently, the fable, its meaning, its ordering (and recital), the narrator-listener relationship—all these are inextricably interconnected through the figure of the *copula*—the principle, fundamentally, of marriage. The work is no simple allegory that constructs itself through a mere display of constitutive elements. It is *informed.*

At the risk of some repetition, it may be useful to summarize in greater detail the striking correspondences between *De Nuptiis* and Chrétien's innovative romance: (1) Both Martianus's *fabula* and Chrétien's narrative recount the story of a marriage between a high-born youth (Jupiter's son; a king's son) and a socially inferior maiden (Philology, the young mortal; Énide, the daughter of a poor vavasor) who becomes the equal of her spouse (*De Nuptiis,* I, 93; *Érec et Énide,* vv. 1504–11); the consequences of both matches are described as of profound importance, and the two marriages are celebrated in greatly privileged places (Olympus, where Jupiter holds court; the court of King Arthur) among guests of the highest standing (the gods and goddesses of Mount Olympus; the knights of the Round Table and their ladies).

(2) The two couples of *De Nuptiis*—Jupiter:Juno and Mercury:Philology—correspond perfectly to their counterparts in *Érec et Énide*—Arthur:Guenevere and Érec:Énide—both in regard to their relative social standing and functions in the respective stories. (3) Chrétien's prologue appears to reply to Martianus's exordium in that his text's *bele conjointure* identifies marriage with the beautiful ordering of his tale; *bele conjointure* and *copula sacra* are, in all respects, perfectly equivalent. (4) Chrétien's *premerains vers,* to which the remainder of the romance imparts a deeper meaning, replicates Martianus's *fabula* of Books I and II; these two books will also be transformed by Books III–IX into a cosmic myth of sovereign and universal import, in which wisdom and the divine gift of intellect will combine in order to open the doors of heaven to humankind (see Le Moine, 70). Verses 1845–end of *Érec et Énide* narratively actualize the *premerains vers,* just as Books III–IX, representing in figural sequence the Seven Arts, actualize Books I and II. It is moreover probably not a pure coincidence that, in seeming imitation of Books I and II of *De Nuptiis* (which contain seven changes of scene followed by seven books devoted to the Seven Arts), the *premerains vers* of *Érec et Énide* offers seven episodes: the opening scene at Arthur's court; Guenevere's accompanying Érec and the dwarf's affront; a return to Arthur's court; the vavasor's hospitality to Érec, and the latter's falling in love with Énide; the sparrow hawk combat; Yder, vanquished, repairs to Arthur's court; Érec and Énide arrive triumphantly at Arthur's court, where Guenevere outfits Énide in splendid new apparel worthy of her new rank,[11] and where, in keeping with the Custom of the White Stag, Arthur bestows the kiss upon her. Similarly, after the wedding and the fateful "Amis, con mar fus!" (Beloved, how badly it has gone for you!) spoken by Énide,[12] the couple undergoes seven adventures, with two interludes providing moments of respite, for a total of nine episodes; these are: (1) the robber baron and his two companions; (2) the five marauding knights; (3) the amorous count; (4) an episode involving Érec's friend, Guivret le Petit; (5) the cruel giants Érec kills, and the freeing of Cadoc de Cabruel; (6) the Count of Limors, who attempts to force marriage upon Énide; and (7) the Joy of the Court.

It is plausible to conclude that these adventures reflect on the chivalric plane the intellectual and spiritual ascension symbolized by the *cursus* (curriculum) of the Seven Arts described by Martianus as female allegorical figures. At each step, helped by his wife, Érec overcomes a particular danger and goes forward, progressing in his knowledge and self-perfection. It is important to note that the lightness/darkness and slumber/awakedness motifs that are so fundamental to *De Nuptiis* find their counterpart also in *Érec et Énide* (as well as in the *Conte du Graal,* although to a lesser degree) in the numerous alternations between day and night and between vigil and sleep to be found in that text.

Many similarities of detail also link *De Nuptiis* and *Érec et Énide.* For example, Chrétien refers explicitly to the Liberal Arts (as well as to his own Latin culture) when he alludes to having learned how to "describe" from Macrobius, another late-Latin cosmologist who was very influential in the medieval schools, and to the robe adorned with the figures of the quadrivium that is worn by Érec at his coronation. In Martianus's *prosimetrum* (a work composed in both verse and prose) Apollo is the friend and brother of Mercury; he very much favors the marriage. His role is analogous to that of Gauvain in *Érec et Énide* (Gauvain, incidentally, is further associated with Apollo by being compared to the sun in *Yvain*). Juno defends Mercury's marriage (I, vv. 37–38) despite Jupiter's forebodings and fear that, once married, Mercury will neglect his godly office in order to devote himself too whole-heartedly to a protracted honeymoon (I, v. 35). Recalling the lengthy nocturnal vigils of Philology, Juno declares that Mercury's bride will see to it that her husband moves his wings and searches out the farthest limits of the world. It is impossible to believe that Érec's disregard for his knightly vocation does not derive from Jupiter's concerns.[13]

Throughout *De Nuptiis* numerical values are underscored in one fashion or another (according to certain Neoplatonic traditions, Mercury=four, Philology=three; together they add up to seven, the number corresponding to knowledge). Harmony (or Music) is given a role of honor, constituting Beauty "conjoined with" Wisdom (*bele conjointure;* and one of the meanings of *copula* is "musical chord," as well as, of course, "to unite in marriage"). By undergoing the seven adventures he experiences, Érec, with Énide's never-failing aid, reaches this kind of knowledge—knowledge of himself, the maturity that justifies his being crowned by King Arthur and his wearing the robe of the quadrivium, the Latinized Greek Arts. He comes to epitomize the chivalry to which Chrétien will allude in *Cligés* some five years after composing *Érec et Énide;* he is fit to "wear" the Arts of *clergie.* He dons the quadrivium after having lived through his personal trivium as a knight. In this way,

Chrétien's meticulously and harmoniously contrived text—a self-conscious verbal artifact—justifies Érec's putting on the Greek (or mathematical) Arts: the text of Chrétien's poem thus achieves the number seven; *chevalerie* and *clergie* are united in a *bele conjointure* of both text and marriage. The metaphor of Érec's experience fuses with the metonymy of his kingly robe just as the metaphor of Martianus's *fabula* is called upon to fuse with the metonymical procession of the Seven Arts.

The true measure of Chrétien's marvelous "invention" in *Érec et Énide* may be gauged by the manner in which the intertextual processes that he sets in motion provoke—create—the extraordinarily humane conjoining of the values he associates with *chevalerie* and *clergie*. It is in this conjoining that resides the deepest meaning of his poem. The process constitutes the touchstone of his entire œuvre. Each of Chrétien's romances offers a new meditation on the relationship of knightliness and clerkliness, and on the necessity of each to the other in a truly "courteous" society.

But why does Martianus Capella go unmentioned in *Érec et Énide* while Macrobius, the fifth-century Latin author of the *Commentary on Cicero's Dream of Scipio* and the *Saturnales*, is referred to at some length? Like Martianus, Macrobius was a "school author" who was very popular in the Middle Ages and belonged to the mythopoetic tradition we associate with *De Nuptiis*. According to Chrétien, "While reading we found in the story the description of [Érec's] robe, and I bring forth as guarantor Macrobius who put his understanding to work on behalf of the art of description and who understood it, unless I am lying," and, "Macrobius teaches me to describe [*descrivre*], just as I have found it in the book, the workmanship of the cloth and the images" (vv. 6741–43). OF *descri(v)re* conveys the notions of "demonstration," "enumeration," and "taking down," as well as our modern "describe." What does Chrétien mean by this reference?

First of all, it is important to remember that Macrobius's *Commentary* is no poem; it is not the sort of mythopoetic work that both *De Nuptiis* and *Érec et Énide* are. Rather, it is a commentary on such a work, namely, Cicero's *Dream of Scipio* (a story appended to that same author's *De Re Publica*). Thus, in explaining, or commenting upon, the *Dream* Macrobius could well have acted as Chrétien's "guarantor" and "teacher" as Chrétien, in narrative form, "explains" the story of *Érec et Énide*. Chrétien appears to be saying that Macrobius did his best in order to "understand the story," and did, in fact, "understand it." Other meanings of *descri(v)re* come to mind: "to order in proper fashion," "to tran-

scribe," "to copy." This is what Macrobius set out to do: his commen-
tary-copy reproduces an older "poem" (*estoire*) by transforming it. This
act is analogous to what Chrétien does with his subject matter to which
he imparts form and the sort of *conjointure* thanks to which his own work
(*estoire*) will become as memorable as the stories of Greek and Latin
antiquity. In this way Chrétien's *clergie* constitutes an advance on that of
Wace or the *Tristan* romancers familiar to him. Wace's *Brut* and *Rou* do
in fact transcribe the deeds of the ancients, but although he shows himself to be a master writer, he merely attaches (sometimes ambiguously)
his narrative artistry to the raw material of his narrative. Wace displays
no concern for a *bele conjointure* or a *san*.

Macrobius is significant for Chrétien in another way too. As Le Moine
points out in defining *De Nuptiis,* the term *narratio fabulosa* (fabulous
narrative) that she applies to *De Nuptiis* derives from Macrobius.[14] In
and of itself *fabula* is empty—a mere tale (the *conte* purveyed to kings
and counts by despicable minstrels from which Chrétien "derived" his
poem). However, when *fabula* is placed at the service of a spiritual or
intellectual vision through the activity of (re)writing and the application
of *estuide* (studious attention), it becomes *narratio fabulosa,* a discourse
that serves truth. As we have seen, for Chrétien the *conte,* or *fabula,* is of
far lesser value than the *narratio* or "telling," in Macrobius's sense of the
word and as exemplified by Martianus's *De Nuptiis.* Herein lies
Chrétien's "originality" with respect to the Arthurian subject matter:
Arthurian stories are neither true nor false—the *contes* merely constitute
the *clerc's* raw material. Similarly, for a twelfth-century Christian
Martianus's *fabula* could hardly be true. Conversely, the *narratio,* in the
form imparted to it by Chrétien, maintains a close relationship to truth.
Érec et Énide proves that Chrétien wished to proclaim his belief in the
myth of poetry, in the efficacy of certain self-referential poetic dictions
and configurations. *Érec et Énide* is a word-centered poem.

However, it is not only that. It invites its courtly, twelfth-century
audience to see itself at its best, as reflected in the actions and developments that the poem recounts. It is also a charming story—the story of a
handsome and worthy prince who meets, and loves, a maiden whose
husband he properly learns to become at the same time that he matures
into a worthy successor to his royal father. Énide, meanwhile, undergoes
an analogous transformation, at least in the eyes of the reader or listener. At the beginning it is her great beauty and maidenly fetchingness
that seem to be stressed; we see her largely through the effect her presence produces on Érec. She is something of a gift to him, what every

young man dreams of in an ideal woman. Interestingly, when she weeps sadly at her husband's loss of reputation, she manifests her independence in a fashion corresponding to Érec, who chose not to go along with the others and participate in the Hunt for the White Stag with the rest of Arthur's court. Both Érec and Énide have minds of their own. From the wedding-night scene, where we learn of Énide's capacity for amorous expression, through the scene of her regrets as well as her refusal to remain silent when she judges her husband to be in danger, up to the episode with the Count of Limors when she, believing herself to be widowed, is in very real danger, Énide is revealed to be more and more a genuine flesh-and-blood woman—a person. She grows in our ever-increasing understanding of her as we observe her in action. Érec, meanwhile, grows as he learns to face up to the challenges presented to him by the adventures he has undertaken. Quite literally, his maturation is a function of learning how to appreciate his wife and to value the couple that they form together. His killing of the Count of Limors proves his body-and-soul love for her.

Following upon Martianus Capella's presentation of Jupiter and Juno's "court" on Mount Olympus, Chrétien depicts the Arthurian world as the true place of *courtoisie*. It is where the best and most deserving congregate, the center of chivalry, the locus of knights and their ladies. Nevertheless, Chrétien takes pains to show us that, whatever its brilliance, the Arthurian court is hardly perfect. Indeed, he hints, its very perfection contains a dangerous flaw. Thus, despite Gauvain's wise warning, Arthur's insistence on reviving the ancient Custom of the White Stag points to a rigid formalism—a kind of chivalric estheticism—from which, one day, the Arthurian world will suffer and even fall into decay. It is precisely this formalism—chivalry for chivalry's sake—that Érec, with Énide's indispensable aid, will learn to reject. By the time the two young people are crowned king and queen at Nantes, they have outgrown the Arthurian court, just as, on the threshhold of adulthood, the adolescent comes to outgrow school. What might be tagged the authentic courtly ethic, or so Chrétien appears to be saying, is more than a mere question of rules, customs, and etiquette. True *courtoisie* is grounded in the complexity and in the free will of each individual, and, in particular, in the individual as he or she forms part of a couple. (Érec's quick dispatch of the Count of Limors illustrates just this point.) To some extent *courtoisie* may be learned as one learns to conjugate Latin verbs or to handle a sword, but it is above all meant to be experienced by each one of us in his or her own story.

Even more than contemporary romancers, Chrétien is a deft psychologist. Not only do Érec and Énide situate themselves as personalities in the society in which they live, each is endowed with a well-delineated conscience (and consciousness), which the author takes pains to reveal in a manner that is both logical and true-to-life. Although not particularly condonable, Érec's behavior toward his bride, whose tears and worries have touched him to the quick, is entirely recognizable. A proud young prince might well be expected to react as Érec reacted to this perceived criticism. Similarly, Énide's disobeying her husband in warning him of impending danger—her acceptance of the possible consequences of her lack of wifely humility—makes consummate sense in terms of her overwhelming love and respect for him. To be sure, the *romanciers antiques* and the *Tristan* romancers, following upon such thinkers as Saint Anselm, Abelard, and Saint Bernard of Clairvaux, manifested their fascination for the workings of the human soul—for questions of motivation, of conscience—but it befell Chrétien to make of these matters something quite central to his narrative fiction. Whatever our interest in the Round Table might be, *Érec et Énide* displaces our concern for King Arthur and focuses it upon the two young spouses as they construct together the harmony of their marriage in preparation for their future years as a couple in the world. Chrétien organizes things in such a way that both his characters and his narrator collaborate in the telling of this story. There is nothing didactic or moralizing in this procedure; the author does not intervene with glosses or interpretations. The reader is made to experience what the narrator tells and what the characters do and think and say.

It is consequently possible to read, enjoy, and profit from *Érec et Énide* without much—or any—prior knowledge of the history of twelfth-century French narrative, of *De Nuptiis Mercurii et Philologiæ*, or of the schools and their *artes poeticæ*. In no way is much of this chapter's analysis of Chrétien's sources and other historical-technical issues indispensable to an understanding of his enterprise. To some extent, the romance may be compared to a Gothic cathedral, the art of which was being implemented in many new structures at precisely the time Chrétien composed his works. It is well known that Gothic art is intensely bookish—indeed, the cathedral itself may be understood as a vast and ordered compendium of learning and faith—and based on fundamental philosophical and mathematical principles. Yet, miraculously, the truth and the impressive beauty of the Gothic structure are as fully available to the most humble and ignorant believer as to those who are versed in the premises of its construction. A certain perfection is involved. Just as the builders of Chartres cathedral took as much care with the adornment of the outer roof as they did with the parts of the edifice that could be seen by their contemporaries, and did so because, of course, God, if not humans, could see the roof, so Chrétien's romance seeks perfection of this sort too. *Érec et Énide* rewards readers who apply themselves to the craftsmanship that it embodies.

With *Érec et Énide* Chrétien de Troyes displays fully the artistic mastery one detects in his entire narrative corpus. It is not the work of a novice. He has assimilated the art of description as developed by earlier romancers like Benoît de Sainte-Maure and the *Énéas* author; indeed, he goes further than these predecessors in the flexibility and variety he imparts to descriptive conventions.[15] His accounts of hand-to-hand battles between knights are worthy of the great OF *chanson de geste* tradition, and surely thrilled his courtly audiences as much as they inspired his imitators; his lavishly detailed renderings of finery of dress and court ceremony must have fascinated them as well. An important feature of his originality has been well delineated by Douglas Kelly: "It is striking that, by emphasizing the knight and the cleric, rather than, say, the king, emperor or great leaders, or the ecclesiastical princes like bishops or archbishops, Chrétien is including all members of the noble classes in a common order—the order of knighthood and clergy."[16] He wrote for, and in fact helped to create, a sophisticated court-based aristocratic society; his values are personal and social, not political. Thus, his Énide, although not by birth and standing a member of the high aristocracy, is, so to speak, *naturally* noble.

Nowhere is Chrétien's poetic genius more evident than in his use of language.[17] His French is literary, of course, and conservatively so: he faithfully retains, for example, the two-case declension system even though it had begun to wane in the spoken usage of his time. His diction is largely that of the courtly love song, that is, "noble" in that he refrains from what might be regarded as vulgarisms (such as words designating certain "ignoble" parts of the body, much technical jargon). He shows a particular fondness for certain figures of speech and of sound, like rich rhyme, chiasmus, *adnominatio*,[18] alliteration, but he lightens his use of these learned, clerkly procedures through homely similes and metaphors, as well as proverbial phrases. Thus, in the *Charrette*, a pack horse is depicted as being "fat and round as an apple" (vv. 2298–99).

A certain lightness also characterizes Chrétien's syntax and prosody. Frappier has pointed out the suppleness he brought to the octosyllabic

line by his use of enjambment and midline pauses (*brisures*), thereby
stressing rhythmic and harmonic values proper to elegant speech over
purely prosodic ones (like syllable count). Similarly, he simplified such
clumsy structures as *dementres que, endementiers que*, and *parmi tot ce que*,
which perhaps had suited the "heavier" decasyllabic line of assonanced
chansons de geste but which tended to weigh down the much lighter octo-
syllable. Frappier notes that Chrétien was in all likelihood the first to use
the conjunctive *que que* in place of *pendant que* "while"; he also popular-
ized *lors que,* which would henceforth become standard in French
(Frappier, 237).

Cligés

The Story: Alixandre, heir to the throne of Constantinople but desiring to
prove himself as a knight at the court of King Arthur, leaves Greece for
Britain, where he performs many acts of chivalry in Arthur's service. He
sees there Soredamor, Gauvain's sister (and Arthur's niece). They fall in
love, but it is only after Queen Guenevere has discovered the nature of
their mutual feelings that their marriage can take place. A son—
Cligés—is born to the happy couple. The old Greek emperor dies;
Alixandre's brother, Alis, believing him dead at sea, assumes the throne.
Alixandre, accompanied by Soredamor and Cligés, arrives at
Constantinople to claim his rights. An agreement is reached with Alis,
namely, that Alis will continue to wear the crown but will make Cligés
his heir; Alis promises never to marry. Alixandre and Soredamor die.
Advised by his barons, Alis breaks his promise: he enters into negotiations with the Emperor of Germany in order to wed Fénice, the emper-
or's beautiful daughter. Cligés accompanies Alis's party to Cologne.
Fénice is overwhelmed by Cligés's handsomeness and charm;[19] he recip-
rocates her feelings. She decides that, unlike Iseut with King Mark, she
will not give her body to a man she does not love. Nevertheless, the
wedding is celebrated. Fénice's servant, Thessala, a person well versed in
magic, concocts a potion which, when administered to Alis, makes him
believe that he has enjoyed his bride's favors when, of course, he has not.
Meanwhile, Cligés distinguishes himself in combats against the nephew
of the Duke of Saxony and against the Duke himself, who was Alis's
rival in seeking Fénice's hand. Cligés and Fénice do not dare to declare
their love for one another. Only after his return from a sojourn at King
Arthur's court do the two of them confess their love. But what of
Fénice's resolution to save her body for the man she loves? Thessala
comes once again to the rescue with another potion designed to make

Fénice appear to be dead. A palatial tomb is erected for her by the master artisan Jean; in this tomb/palace Cligés and Fénice at last consummate their love. They are eventually discovered, and so take flight to King Arthur's court. Furious, Alis pursues them, but dies of spite just as an immense army has been raised to undo his usurpation. Cligés and Fénice return to Constantinople where, together as emperor and empress, they reign happily ever after. (However, from this date on, the romance informs us, Greek emperors keep very close watch on their wives!)

Artifice, especially the art of composing romance narratives, even more so than in *Érec et Énide,* provides the real subject matter of *Cligés,* along with the glorification of France and French as the place and means of artful vernacular discourse. *Cligés* presupposes on the part of its reader a sophisticated acquaintance with earlier romances—the aforementioned tales of Arthurian Britain (Wace), of Rome (*Énéas*), of Troy, and of Thebes, in addition to familiarity with the body of stories devoted to the tragic love triangle of Tristan, Iseut, and King Mark. It is likely that the OF versions of Pyramus and Thisbe and Narcissus, based on Ovid's *Metamorphoses* and perhaps even the *Lais* of Marie de France, are made use of by Chrétien de Troyes in this second of his surviving romance narratives. *Cligés,* let it be said immediately, is a work of high comedy.

The author begins his prologue by identifying himself as "he who made a poem about Érec and Énide," who provided versions of several Ovidian tales, and who told the story of "King Mark and the Blond Iseut" (v. 5). He presents himself here even more self-consciously as a *clerc* than he had done in his first romance, and virtually everything in the narrative, including its plot, may be viewed metaphorically in terms of the arts of *clergie.* These arts are defined with an emphasis on *translatio*, a term that connotes "translation" and "transfer," as well as the rhetorical figures also known as metaphor and metonymy. Thus, it is important to note, none of the titles cited in the prologue can be qualified as "original." Each one—*Érec et Énide*, the Ovidian stories, and the *Tristan* material—is "found"—"invented"—elsewhere and "transferred" by Chrétien into his own language and poetry.

These facts are essentially true, so far as we can determine: a person identifying himself as "Crestïens de Troyes" did compose a narrative entitled *Érec et Énide*; portions of the Ovid translations have survived in an early fourteenth-century work called the *Ovide moralisé.* Chrétien's version of the *Tristan* story, however, if it ever existed, has been lost. The *translatio* theme fairly pervades this prologue. We are told that the story

about to unfold is that of a youth who was born in Greece of "King
Arthur's lineage" (v. 10); the youth's father, a brave and fierce nobleman,
had left Greece in order to conquer "esteem" and "praise" at King
Arthur's court in Britain. The *translatio* is double: Greece>Britain and
Britain>Greece, with, however, the Britain of Arthur valued at a higher
level than the Greece temporarily abandoned by our hero's father.

Translatio appears once again in the prologue (vv. 30–44) when
Chrétien cites in considerable detail the old topic known as the *translatio
imperii et studii*. "Chivalry" (*imperium*) and *clergie* (*studium*) first saw the
light of day in Greece. Thence they removed to Rome, coming, finally,
to abide in France (not Britain).[20] Thus, chivalry and above all learning
now dwell in France, where the composition of the story of Cligés is taking place: the very story is as much a result of *translatio* as what the story
tells.

Transformations of the *translatio* type also characterize what Chrétien,
in *Cligés*, "does to" the list of works comprising his œuvre. *Cligés* rewrites
the works he has enumerated. How does Chrétien rework the *bele conjointure* of *Érec et Énide* in his new romance? The answer lies in his applying to the earlier work a double principle of development and of reversal.

Érec et Énide may most deeply be understood as the poetic exploration
of a marriage; and marriage itself (as Chrétien associates the story of his
protagonists with the *De Nuptiis* of Martianus Capella) incurs repercussions that at times appear cosmic in their significance. Rulership, personal growth, the harmony of Creation—all these are related to the concept
of marriage as explored in *Érec et Énide*. Énide, being both the spouse
(*fame*) and the Beloved Lady (*amie*), comes to occupy the center of Érec's
life and being. His realization of who Énide is takes place most dramati-
cally when he defends her against the Count of Limors: it is not his good
name that is at stake here, but her person and what she means to him,
and, concomitantly, his own person is revealed ("invented").

Yet, during the first section of the romance, the imperfections still
present in the *conjointure* of our protagonists have not been removed.
Though stunned to silence by Énide's extraordinary beauty, Érec fails to
ask her whether she will have him for her husband. She is merely the
object of negotiations between him, a king's son, and her father, a poor
vavasor. The wedding, of course, does take place, as does the consummation of their relationship, but Érec's attachment to his wife is uxorious, not that of a genuine husband. It is only after their adventures
together that Énide becomes genuinely Érec's *fame et amie*.

Nothing of the sort takes place in *Cligés*. Alixandre does not dare
declare his love to Soredamor, nor she to him; each undergoes long

Ovidian-style monologues with himself/herself—monologues that articulate their lovesickness and passion. No deal is proposed by Alixandre to
Gauvain (Soredamor's brother) or to Arthur through which the marriage
he devoutly wants might take place. In fact, if not for Queen Guenevere
nothing at all might have happened. It is she who intervenes, after having guessed the mutual love of the pair, and arranges the marriage
("J'assanblerai le mariage" v. 2310).

Similar shyness characterizes Cligés's love for Fénice, and hers for him.
We listen to analogously lengthy "She/he loves me, loves me not" monologues, and yet, despite Fénice's resolution not to allow Alis, her husband, to possess her body because she does not love him, nothing
happens between her and Cligés either, until Cligés's triumphant return
from King Arthur's court and his first interview with the obdurate
Fénice. When they are alone together, he starts talking to her about
Britain; she asks whether he found a love there. He replies that, indeed,
he loved, but loved from afar a person who was not there, in Britain (vv.
5157–81). His body was in Britain—an old lyric theme—but his heart
had remained behind. Meanwhile, Fénice confesses that though her body
had stayed in Constantinople, her heart went to Britain. Linguistically,
the two of them act our their feelings in terms of fashionable courtly diction. The truth of their (real) love for one another finally comes out in
this metaphorically "poetic" language.

Several options remain open to the lovers: (1) let matters rest; (2) flee
to King Arthur (this is Cligés's idea, rejected by the ever-proud Fénice);
(3) or the romance-like solution proposed by Fénice, in which she will
feign death and eventually be reunited with her lover in the tomb; however, both will be—unlike Pyramus and Thisbe, Tristan and Iseut, or
Romeo and Juliet—alive and well. Artifice, once again in the shape of
Thessala's magic potion, comes to the rescue, and things turn out as
Fénice has wished: she gives her body only to the man who possesses her
heart. Later, after Alis's timely demise, she will, like Énide, be both *fame*
and *amie* of the one she loves, and she will avoid both the fate of, and the
gossip surrounding, the unfortunate Iseut.[21]

Both couples in *Cligés* achieve a kind of *bele conjointure*; each incarnates
a happy marriage. However, whereas the achievement of this *conjointure*
takes place with considerable difficulty in Chrétien's second romance,
the difficulties are hardly the same as those facing Érec and Énide. Nor
are the results quite the same either. Within a very short time after their
marriage, Alixandre and Soredamor die; the wedding and coronation of
Cligés and his beloved Fénice marks the end, not the beginning, of their
story. Whereas Érec and Énide grow in personhood, the characters of

Cligés most decidedly do not: they remain invariable comic personages. Part of the comedy of *Cligés* resides therefore in the deliberately superficial application of what had been explored in *Érec et Énide*—another aspect of the reversal of development in this work.

But perhaps the most significant reversal of Chrétien's first romance to be found in his second lies in the manner in which *Cligés* both separates chivalry and learning and reflects a decided emphasis on learning, or *clergie*.[22] Although, as we have seen, *clergie* is present in *Érec et Énide* thematically and explicitly, the romance wears its *clergie* lightly: the emphasis is placed on *chevalerie*. The events of *Cligés* are on occasion so preposterous that, even though they occur largely in the foreign, and therefore perhaps to some degree laughable, Byzantine East, the *courtoisie* therein ostensibly celebrated is obviously open to serious questioning. In *Cligés* chivalry, construed as a system of rules and values, teeters on the brink of being a joke. After all, despite the obstacles cited, Cligés and Fénice do enjoy each other sexually. Is their pleasure—such pleasure— the true goal of *chevalerie*? The achievement of this pleasure, moreover, is dependent on the exercise of sleight-of-hand—magic potions, Jean's devoted service—and not on any vanquishing of obstacles by the protagonists.

Fénice wins the battle lost by Iseut: she has her cake and eats it too. But, in so achieving her ends, she trivializes the story of Tristan and Iseut. With this trivialization, however, *Cligés* demonstrates—and this is Chrétien's remarkable tour de force—that the story of Tristan and Iseut, like that of Cligés and Fénice, is also a romance, a story with assumptions and rules that are determined by storytelling, not necessarily by "real life." Fénice applies the story of Tristan and Iseut—in a reverse fashion—to her, and to Cligés's, life, in the story of that life. She lives out a negative romance already familiar to the audience listening to the tale of her romance.

Is, consequently, storytelling by definition mendacious? If, like *Cligés*, *Tristan et Iseut* is "merely" a romance, what are the implications of this for *clergie*? Are *clercs* but servants of untruthful, albeit entertaining, storytelling?

Cligés displays Chrétien's extraordinary honesty in regard to this question. Michelle A. Freeman, quite perceptively, has demonstrated that the potion concocted by Thessala in order to cause Alis to believe that he has indeed consummated his marriage with Fénice, as described by the narrator of *Cligés*, ought to be read as a metaphor for—a *translatio* of— romance storytelling. (By the same token, the *Cligés* potion comments on the essential nature of the famous potion in *Tristan et Iseut*: without the potion there would be no story at all.) Here, somewhat abridged, is Freeman's analysis:

> The preparation of the potion in *Cligés* is described twice: once by the poet-narrator and once by Thessala herself. The first description places the poet-narrator in a relation of service to Thessala and associates him with an object or symbol—like the cart [*Lancelot*] or the lion [*Yvain*]—namely, with the preparation of a crafted product, the potion that responds imaginatively to the *Tristan* potion. The narrator describes his artisan blending her spices into a clear, sweet potion [vv. 3251–58]. . . .
>
> The narrator qualifies Thessala's activity as *tranprer*, "to mix, to temper," and then goes on to define it more specifically as made up of three steps: the adding of an abundance of sweet spices, the beating and grinding up of these ingredients and the repeated straining of the mixture. The end product is characterized as sweet, or rather as not bitter or sour, and as *clear*. . . . None of the individual spices is mentioned by name. . . . In short, the description is not a recipe or formula that someone else—some witch not trained in the school of Thessaly—could apply mechanically to obtain the same results. . . .
>
> This description is analogous to Chrétien's own procedures in putting together [*conjointure*] his *Cligés*. He, too, uses a number of rich imported materials, such as the *Tristan* corpus, the *Roman d'Énéas* and Ovid. . . . Just as Thessala makes her mixture of imported ingredients clear, so does Chrétien have the audience recognize the clarity of his recombination of a number of textual transferences. (Freeman 1985, 112–13)

The signal importance of the potion description is underscored by the fact that it takes place at the midpoint of *Cligés*, namely at the moment in the narrative when, as in *Le Chevalier de la Charrette (Lancelot)* and *Le Chevalier au Lion (Yvain)*, and in many other courtly romances, matters of identity—title, name of protagonist, and so on—are frequently addressed. The midpoint in OF narrative is often of very great strategic significance.

Freeman has proposed that this midpoint description of Thessala's potion be construed as metaphorically indicative of the meaning of *Cligés*. She has also demonstrated that this refashioning, or *translatio*, procedure ought to be applied to Jean's seamless construction of Fénice's tomb. In brief, then, it is thanks to Thessala's and Jean's *artistry*—or craftmanship—that the story of Cligés and Fénice can occur and end so happily.

A certain realism, curiously enough, is at issue here. Psychologically—or realistically—Fénice's ideology of love, with her rules and values, are, quite simply, absurd. But the description of Thessala's potion, furnished with such consummate detail, strikes one as real. One is prepared to accept that a woman of a certain age, of Thessala's background, in fact, might well prepare such a potion, and her careful way of going about this preparation, described in full, adds weight to one's acceptance of the reality of it. (Conversely, the *Tristan et Iseut* story merely states that Iseut's mother, familiar with such potions, prepared the love drink mistakenly imbibed by Tristan and Iseut; no details are offered.) Realism of this sort pervades the actions of the authentic movers and shakers of *Cligés*. Queen Guenevere, historically very much a part of, and yet in some ways distinct from, the male chivalric world of the Arthurian Round Table, is just such a character.

Very shortly after Alixandre's arrival at King Arthur's court, he and Soredamor see each other and fall in love; neither dares declare his or her feelings, of course. The narrator describes Queen Guenevere, who is observing the strange looks and behavior of the two lovers as they cross the English Channel in a ship:

> La reïne garde s'an prant
> Et voit l'un et l'autre sovant
> Descolorer et anpalir
> Et sospirer et tressalir,
> Meis ne set por quoi il le font
> Fors que por la mer ou il sont.
> Espoir bien s'an aparceüst,
> Se la mers ne la deceüst;
> Meis la mers l'angingne et deçoit
> Si qu'an la mer l'amor ne voit;
> Qu'an la mer sont et d'amer vient,
> Et c'est amors li maus quis tient.
> Et de cez trois ne set blasmer
> La reïne fors que la mer;
> Car li dui le tierz li ancusent
> Et par le tierz li dui s'escusent,
> Qui del forfait sont entechié. (vv. 541–57)

(The Queen takes notice of it, she who sees one and the other blush and pale repeatedly; she does not know whence this behavior can come, nor does she know why they blush, except because of the sea where they find themselves [*mal de mer*; seasickness]. But the sea tricks and deceives her, so that she does not see lovesickness [*mal d'amer*]. They are at sea, and from bitterness and from love comes the illusion which holds them. And of these three the Queen knows not which to blame, except for the sea, for the two accuse the third to her, and by means of the third the other two escape detection, the two which are guilty of the crime.)

The conceit, as scholars have pointed out, is borrowed by Chrétien from the *Tristan et Iseut* narrative, and the borrowing, subjected to the preciosity of the narrator's diction—*la mer, la mers, l'amor*—with its intense use of paranomasia and other sorts of wordplay, underscores both the literariness of the passage and its intertextual essence. Michelle A. Freeman remarks that this preciosity effectively characterizes the transposition as emphasizing its very nature as a transposition. It is a pure example of poetic *translatio* (Freeman 1985, 104). Meanwhile, Guenevere's mistaking the symptoms appearing in Alixandre and Soredamor adds an element of realism to the scene, which, by the same token, underscores the literarity of the *mal de mer/mal d'amer* (seasickness/lovesickness) pun in *Tristan*. Had Guenevere guessed the truth, meanwhile, some two thousand lines of *Cligés* would have been rendered superfluous.

Queen Guenevere is present in order to serve the purposes of the romance. Her error accomplishes much of the author's agenda; but she finally gets the point of the young lovers' passion for one another, and consequently advances the plot. She no longer entertains any doubts concerning the cause of their pallor and their blushing, and declares that she will arrange matters for the wedding. In the interim, however, Alixandre has proven his chivalry in defeating, with his fellow Greeks, Arthur's wicked enemy, Count Angrés, and much lovesickness has been suffered and described. Guenevere invites Alixandre to sit beside her, with Soredamor facing them. She proceeds to lecture Alixandre on love, declaring that it can be more deadly than hatred in the pain it causes, but that, inasmuch as the two of them have "turned two hearts into one," they must no longer hide this, unless they wish to transform love into homicide. In marriage they will be able to love honorably. What she says makes sense and is in complete conformity with what we can construe of Chrétien's views concerning marriage from our reading of *Érec et Énide*. She speaks with all the authority of a courtly lady and a queen with respect to a subject in which one would expect her—like Eleanor of Aquitaine or Marie de Champagne—to be particularly expert.

Guenevere, we said, is one of the movers and shakers of *Cligés*, and in that role she shares important functions with Thessala and Jean in respect to the romance's plot. However, her service to the romance differs from theirs in that she represents a value system that may plausibly be identified with Chrétien himself. Unlike Thessala and Jean, she is not subservient to the absurdities of the sort of ideology mouthed by Fénice. She brings into the romance an external truth—good sense, genuine *courtoisie*, humane concern—according to which love, or the natural inclination of members of the opposite sex toward one another, can, indeed ought to, be "honorable." It is what she stands for in the scene just examined that the resources of authentic *clergie* are called upon to serve. She retains much of the nature attributed to Juno by Martianus Capella in *De Nuptiis*, and which she also incarnates in her welcome of Énide to Arthur's court in *Érec et Énide*. Guenevere's reality constitutes an important element in the *translatio*—in the modernity, or present-dayness—exemplified by *Cligés*.

Present-day reality also appears in what might be labeled the satiric side to *Cligés*. Thus, according to many of those who have examined *Cligés*, the "German" episodes—for example, Alis's marriage to Fénice, Cligés's defeat of the Duke of Saxony—correspond to the efforts made from about 1170 to 1174 by Emperor Frederick Barbarossa in order to secure a marriage between his house and that of the Greek emperor Manuel Comnenus. Neither the duped Alis nor the Germans are made to look other than ridiculous in these episodes, it is true; however, the satire here runs deeper than a mere passing allusion. It is indicative, and illustrative, of the mode of *translatio* which, as we have noted, pervades the entire fabric of the romance.

Whatever the attempts Frederick Barbarossa may have made to secure the alliance of the Byzantine emperor, the reality of their relationship was contentious and adversarial. Meanwhile, Manuel had married Maria (25 December 1161), the daughter of the "Frankish" Princess Constance of Antioch, a Latin princess, and he had married off his niece to the "Frankish" King Baldwin III of Jerusalem. He entertained very cordial relations with King Henry II Plantagenet, who furnished him with a corps of English bodyguards. Of still greater importance to *Cligés* is the fact that, shortly before his death in 1180, Manuel Comnenus arranged the marriage of his son and heir, Alexius, to the eight-year-old daughter of King Louis VII of France, Princess Agnès (known in Byzantium as Anne). Whether these negotiations were going on at the time of the composition of *Cligés* cannot be determined, but the fact that such negotiations did take place within the time frame of our romance is significant. It bespeaks, indeed symbolizes, the role of marriage in the complex sets of relationship between Byzantine Greece, the Latin states in the Levant, and the Latin West, and it demonstrates all too clearly the relative weakness of Byzantium with respect to the Latin Christian West.

As the daughter of Louis VII, Agnès-Anne was the sister of Marie, countess of Champagne and patroness of Chrétien de Troyes. Also, during the mid-1170s—when *Cligés* was written—both the failure of the Second Crusade and the rise of an increasingly unified Islam under Nur-ad-Din were certainly much on the minds of French chivalry, as was, one suspects, the amorous and matrimonial intrigues of the daring, though highly irresponsible, Andronicus. All these matters surely must have constituted the stuff of courtly gossip and concern in France and Champagne. The story and *invraisemblances* of Chrétien's *Cligés*, it stands to reason, were understood by his audience against the backdrop of contemporaneous historical events. It also would seem logical to assume that the French *chevaliers* and ladies for whom Chrétien wrote no longer felt absolute awe or wonderment in regard to the myths of imperial Byzantium. Indeed, what they did, thought, and believed could be considered to be superior to what was perceivable as decadence among the Orthodox Christians of the East. In other words, the myth of *translatio*—both *chevalerie* and *clergie*—might be seen as containing, and articulating, their historical sense of themselves, particularly when Chrétien's narrator speaks of the snuffing out of the burning embers of Roman and Greek power and civilization. The *translatio* topic also serves to express the sense of chivalric responsibility—a theme that will be treated in depth later by Chrétien in both *Le Chevalier au Lion (Yvain)* and *Le Conte du Graal (Perceval)*—that many in his *champenois* audience must have felt with regard to the jeopardy in which Western outposts in the Levant found themselves in the 1170s, after the setback of the Second Crusade. It was surely understood in France that henceforth Byzantium would be of little help, and possibly a hindrance, in the exhilarating crusading enterprise.

If these suppositions are accurate—and at the very least they are plausible—then *Cligés* is genuinely informed by a sense of historical reality, even by a kind of historical vision. This vision is controlled and channeled by a highly perfected comic artifice; it is so governed in order to establish a distinction between romance as pure story (that is, the *Tristan* story) and romance as serving up categories adequate to the expression of historiographical values. It is surely no mere coincidence that so many vernacular works of historiography—the *Pseudo-Turpin Chronicles* (early 1200s), the initial volume of the *Grandes Chroniques de France* (ca. 1270),

and the *Chronique de Morée* (ca. 1340), which tells of the French princi-
pality in Morea (Peloponnese)—are replete with structures and devices
of the type of romance so abundant in *Cligés*. The *Grandes Chroniques*
replicate the *translatio* motif in terms that seem virtually lifted from
Chrétien's romance. It may therefore be posited that not the least of
Cligés's merits is its role in the development of vernacular romance historiography.

It would, however, be improper to leave the impression that *Cligés* is
other than a work of high comedy—a fresh and new narrative whose
two-dimensional characters and whose twists of plot are designed to elicit the smiles of those for whom it was composed. It is a playful romance,
indeed the first in a series of humorous and wise clerkly tales that, in
later years, will come to include *Aucassin et Nicolette*, *Le Bel Inconnu*, and
many others. The story of the very young Græco-Arthurian Cligés—his
chivalric triumphs, his pains and his loves—is full of pleasant ironies,
wordplays, and jokes that must have vastly amused the sophisticatedly
self-confident, French-speaking, and courtly audience to whom it was
read. With *Cligés* Chrétien de Troyes demonstrates the sheer ingenious-
ness of *translatio* as well as some of its more serious implications. It is a
very youthful work, but not a sad one, as opposed to *Narcisus* and
Piramus et Tisbé, two Ovidian French poems that influenced it, and as
such its appeal to the youthful and proud young chivalry and ladies of its
time—to their own sense of playfulness—must have been great.

Chapter 4

Le Chevalier de la Charrette (Lancelot) and Le Chevalier au Lion (Yvain): Twin Romances

Twin Romances

Since neither *Le Chevalier de la Charrette (Lancelot)* nor *Le Chevalier au Lion (Yvain)* appears in the list of Chrétien de Troyes's works provided by the prologue to *Cligés*, it is generally assumed that these romances must have been composed after 1175 or so.[1] Meanwhile, in that the unfinished *Conte du Graal (Perceval)* was dedicated to Count Philip of Flanders (who died in 1191) and not, like *Lancelot*, to Countess Marie de Champagne, scholars believe that both *Lancelot* and *Yvain* must have been written before 1191; at some time before 1191 Chrétien must have left the service of the count and countess of Champagne before entering that of Count Philip. Both *Lancelot* and *Yvain*, it has been argued, saw the light of day at some point in the 15-year span from ca. 1176 to 1191.

Highly plausible, if not completely proven hypotheses have been advanced to situate the date of composition of the two romances more exactly. Scholars have taken stock of the cross-references *Yvain* and *Lancelot* make to one another. The fact that in *Yvain* there are three allusions to Queen Guenevere's abduction (and eventual deliverance)—the story of *Lancelot*—has led some critics to conclude that *Yvain* must have been composed subsequently to *Lancelot*. These allusions refer (1) to Gauvain's absence from Arthur's court, where he is sorely needed in order to keep his sworn promise to defend the hapless *pucelle* (maiden), Lunete, against her suitors (vv. 3698–711); (2) once again to Gauvain's departure on the quest for the abducted queen and, consequently, to his inability to rescue his own niece and nephews from the threatening giant, Harpin (vv. 3912–20)(in both cases Yvain, now known as the "Lion Knight," must stand in for him); and (3) to the queen's rescue from captivity, as well as Lancelot's imprisonment, which permits Gauvain to take up the cause of the Lord of the Noire Espine's unjust elder daughter, whose younger sister, Yvain—unbeknownst to Gauvain—will champion (vv. 4723–820).[2]

Some three decades ago Anthime Fourrier quite cogently demonstrated that certain details of *Lancelot* make sense only when referred to *Yvain*, as for example, vv. 36–37: "Aprés mangier ne se remut / li rois d'antre ses conpaignons" (after dining the king did not abandon his companions), surely an amusing—and pointed—allusion to Arthur's leaving his guests in the opening scene of *Le Chevalier au Lion*.[3] To the evidence adduced by Fourrier, Jean Frappier added that, in his view, Chrétien would hardly have depicted Arthur and Guenevere sharing the same bed had he previously told the story of her adulterous affair with Lancelot.[4] Fourrier concludes, and Frappier concurs, that in all probability Chrétien started *Yvain* first, interrupted it in order to commence work on *Lancelot*, finished *Yvain,* and left the ending of *Lancelot* to Godefroi de Leigni. What date, however, might most believably be assigned to the writing of the two romances—assuming, that is, that they were composed jointly?

Arthur's decision to arrive at the Magic Fountain on the eve of St. John's Day, "before a fortnight passes" (*Yvain*, v. 664)—a decision uttered on Whitsunday and which prompts Yvain precipitously to undertake the adventure that will lead to his marriage with Laudine,[5] the Lady of the Fountain Castle—has set scholars scurrying to discover which years during the second half of the twelfth century saw Whitsunday and St. John's Day separated by only two weeks. Fourrier determined that only 1166 and 1177 fit the bill, and for him the latter year seemed more likely than the former. Noting the presence of the word *croisié* (crusaders) in *Lancelot* (v. 5790)—the only time the term appears in Chrétien's entire œuvre—Fourrier is led to associate the use of this term with the revival of an intense crusading spirit that took place, as of 1177, at the court of Champagne. Count Henry took the cross that year, and, Fourrier reasons, Chrétien's mentioning the presence of unarmed crusader knights viewing the tournament at Noauz is perfectly natural. Furthermore, the *croisié* reference in the *Charrette* and the allusion to Nur-Eddin (a sultan whose death in 1174 was a relief to his Crusader enemies) in *Yvain* might be deemed to suggest, or reinforce, the idea of a close temporal relationship between the two romances;

around 1177 crusading was on the mind of Chrétien's noble patrons and audience.

Although none of these arguments provides absolute certainty, as at least one critic has pointed out,[6] their plausibility is high. Let us assume, then, that *Yvain* and the *Charrette* were composed at about the same time, probably conjointly, no earlier than 1177 and no later, surely, than 1181, the date of Count Henry's death upon his return home from the Crusade he had led forth in 1179, when, it has been supposed, Chrétien passed over into the service of Count Philip of Flanders.

An even more exact dating has been proposed by Philippe Ménard.[7] Agreeing with Fourrier's rationale, Ménard remarks that in order for St. John's Day (24 June) to occur between two Sundays that had elapsed after Whitsunday (see *Yvain*, vv. 659–70), Easter—like Whitsunday, a movable feast—must have taken place between 23 and 25 April, "a very rare case" (Ménard, 120). That is exactly what happened in 1177, when Easter fell on 24 April. Again following Fourrier, Ménard contends that this remarkable event is not to be set aside lightly when one seeks to determine the date of *Yvain*. It is likely, given the fact that Chrétien's chronological specificity at the start of *Yvain* is precise to the point of uniqueness within the corpus of his five extant romances, that, consequently, he is deliberately drawing on his own (and his audience's) fresh memory, or experience, of this rare concatenation of dates. It is therefore probable that Chrétien undertook the composition of *Yvain* during the Spring of 1177, or shortly thereafter.

Although I anticipate here sections of the analysis that will form the basis of this chapter, at this point I should like to declare my essential agreement, on grounds of poetic coherence, with the Fourrier-Ménard theory. *Yvain* displays a close correlation between a certain view of *clergie*, of clerkliness, and *chevalerie*: his hero, Yvain, and his "I"-saying, though anonymous, narrator "grow up" together. Each—*clerc* and *chevalier*, respectively and conjointly—learns, as it were, to master his craft and, in a sense, to fulfill himself in terms of his identity as clerk and knight. More than any other of Chrétien's narratives, *Yvain* is solidly rooted in the here and now, in reality experienced and observed. Consequently—and given Chrétien's own extraordinarily careful artistry, in which nothing is left to chance and everything has its purpose—the highly unusual and exact attention he pays to the temporal coordinates (themselves reflecting a very peculiar, but, nevertheless, authentic set of circumstances) must be significant poetically. The dates he gives, in the precision of their relationship to one another, signify a real time, albeit an unusual one, locatable in terms of his own, and his public's, experience; and, by implication, they are contrasted to what one might call the standard, or vague, romance-type references to Easter, Whitsunday, Ascension, and so on, that one finds repeatedly in twelfth-century French narrative and which generally serve either to signal that what is being read is a romance or, as in the case of the Good Friday and Easter of *Perceval*, some other iconological purpose. (It is liturgically entirely appropriate that Perceval comes to an awareness of his sinfulness on Good Friday and prepares to receive Holy Communion on the following Easter Sunday.)

In other words, then, the chronological allusions—Whitsunday, St. John's Day, a fortnight—we find in the opening scenes of *Yvain* do correspond to the typical romance temporal coordinates, but in their real, albeit exceptional, specificity, they tend to undermine the pure "romance-ness" that such coordinates normally are called upon to signal. In this manner, and in conjunction with the narrator's contrasting of the "good old" Arthurian times with the decadence of today (vv. 7–32), *Yvain* appears to be telling us that we are indeed on romance territory and in the romance time of yore. However, because of the precise specificity and the "real" memorableness of the *Yvain* dates, this territory and this time differ considerably from those of the conventional, or standard, romance world. Note, for example, the true, but odd, assertion in the rhyme words of vv. 6 and 7, where *Pantecoste* (Whitsunday) is defined as the feast that *tant coste* (is so costly); an association of this sort, involving money, is very peculiar indeed—it jars the readers in their "normal" romance expectations.

In great part thanks to the recognizable and, in all likelihood, recognized uniqueness of these real-life, present-day chronological allusions, Chrétien is setting up a deliberate and nuanced complicity with his audience, and, furthermore, this complicity is of a nature entirely opposed to that of the hyperbolic courtly rapport outlined in the prologue to the *Charrette*. In this latter poem "Crestïens" elaborately proclaims his (clerkly) devotion and service to "ma dame de Chanpaigne," a lady who was very much alive at the time *Lancelot* was composed and whose perfection is such that he will willingly undertake the mission to fulfill her *comandemanz* and make the *romanz* on the basis of the *matiere et san* she has provided him (vv. 1–29). Nothing of this sort is to be found in *Yvain*—indeed, alone among Chrétien's romances, *Yvain* has no prologue-type front matter whatsoever. In structure as in plot, *Yvain* and *Lancelot* stand in systematic contrast to one another. In this fashion, the simultaneity of their composition enters into how these two romances are supposed to be read.

Yet, to imply that *Yvain* is a kind of "anti-*Lancelot*" any more than *Cligés* is an "anti-*Tristan*" would be incorrect. Rather, the two romances interpenetrate one another on virtually all levels and they do so in a remarkably methodical manner. Based on a play of contrasts, reciprocal allusions, and shared attributes, the system serves to "pair off" *Yvain/Lancelot* against the mythopoetic and celebrative mode Chrétien illustrated in the earlier romance pair of *Érec et Énide* and *Cligés*. Each in his own way, *Le Chevalier au Lion* and *Le Chevalier de la Charrette* carry romance narrative to an extreme: *Lancelot* ostensibly exalts an ideal, a kind of impossible romance dream, which, in turn, *Yvain*, with its emphasis on such intrusive everyday concerns as marriage and even social injustice, does not so much deflate as show how quintessentially romance-like that dream is. Without ceasing to be a romance—a romance of a most unique kind—*Yvain* upends romance.

Other contrasts to be found between the two romances come to mind: love (and growth) in marriage (*Yvain*) versus a static—that is, "given"—and, in a sense, hopeless adulterous love in the *Charrette*; a completed, or closed, narrative in *Yvain* versus a far more open-ended narrative, in *Lancelot* (witness the many subsequent recastings of the Lancelot-Guenevere story; there will be no such development of an *Yvain* tradition); Yvain winds up departing, for good, from Arthur's court, while Lancelot is irrevocably tied to the court. These and many other contrasts serve, on the deepest level, to link the two texts rather than definitively oppose them; or, rather, the oppositions are contained in, and shaped by, the aforementioned systematic play. Cases in which the two romances refer to each other on the level of plot and temporality have already been cited. The story of the *Charrette* takes place, so to speak, after Gauvain's visit, with Arthur, to Laudine's castle following her marriage to Yvain and, for all intents and purposes, before Yvain's duel with Gauvain in the daughters of the Noire Espine episode. Yvain thus acquires a wife just before Arthur is about to lose his; in the one case, the husband returns to his wife (*Yvain*), while, in the other, the wife is returned to her husband. Meanwhile, interestingly enough, Yvain is mentioned, along with Gauvain and a certain "Looÿs," as one of the knights whose names Lancelot deciphers on the tombs of the "future cemetery" reserved for the Round Table (*Charrette*, vv. 1877–78); "Gauvains" and "Yvains" are in rhyme position, that is, linked in what the narrator chooses to record of Lancelot's observation.

The embedding of the *Charrette* in *Le Chevalier au Lion* is not complete, however. To be sure, Guenevere has been freed, but Lancelot himself remains imprisoned in a tower (*Yvain*, vv. 4744–45)—the very point at which, according to Godefroi de Leigni, Chrétien had abandoned further work on the *Charrette*.[8] Curiously, the two occasions on which, so to speak, Yvain's and Lancelot's personal adventures meet face to face involve, in the *Charrette*, Yvain's future demise (and prison-like resting place) and, in *Le Chevalier au Lion*, Lancelot's present, and incapacitating, tomb-like incarceration. Even more striking in this linking of the *Charrette* and *Yvain* is how sharply it focuses on Gauvain. To put it another way, the stories of Yvain and Lancelot impinge directly on one another through the presence/absence of Gauvain; he is the go-between—the emissary from Arthurian centrality to the individualized worlds of two knights who, each in his own fashion, as outcasts, or exiles, from the Arthurian world (epitomized, as we saw in our study of *Érec et Énide* and of *Cligés*, by Gauvain), and whose individuality criticizes that world. Yvain will learn to reject the Arthurian value system by essentially learning to emulate Gauvain no longer; he will go his own respectable (and perhaps somewhat dull) way. Meanwhile—and the irony is extraordinary—Lancelot, who is hardly "respectable" (but who is fascinating), will restore order to the Arthurian world by rescuing the queen, whom he loves passionately, by in fact betraying the king, his lord! But this order had first been destroyed by the foolish rash boon accorded by Arthur at the start of the poem when he agreed to grant Kay whatever he desired in order to placate him and keep him at court. Kay, who demanded the honor of defending the queen, failed to do so, and this resulted in Guenevere's abduction. Gauvain's ineffectiveness during the quest for Guenevere's deliverance is, inevitably, total.

Although *Le Chevalier au Lion* and *Le Chevalier de la Charrette* do stand on their own as independent poems, they clamor to be read intertextually, that is, in conjunction with other medieval narratives and, of course, conjointly. Gauvain, as shared attribute of the two romances, serves to indicate a certain hollowness, a certain fundamental impotence (however glorious), that seems to lie close to the heart of Chrétien's depiction of official, or codified, Arthurianism, when this Arthurianism is viewed from the diametrically opposed stories of both Yvain and Lancelot. Consequently, though independent, the two narratives must be understood as fusing together in a kind of "super romance" in which each is incomparably enriched by the other. The contrasts, or oppositions, in the two texts, as well as the reciprocal allusions and certain shared attributes, all point to and reinforce the conclusion presented here that *Yvain* and *Lancelot*, as fulfilled texts, depend on our recognizing the structural and poetic ties that bind them. The implications of such a recognition are at once important and numerous. Thus, for example, in order to grasp the sense of how the *Charrette* fits into Chrétien's ongoing meditation on the *amour passion* question exemplified in the texts concerning Tristan and Iseut, it is essential to understand the system of *Tristan* references in *Le Chevalier au Lion* as well as Gauvain's advice, after Yvain's wedding, to the effect that, in order truly to merit the love of his bride and lady, Yvain ought to leave her. Not only is intertextual reading of this sort demanded by the two romances in question, but it also protects us from the abuses of such scholar-critics as have elaborated theories concerning Chrétien's "doctrine" (or "anti-doctrine") of courtly love.

Although the term *super romance* may be deemed by some to be an anachronistic neologism, it does in fact correspond, on several pertinent levels, to medieval textual reality. As is well known, especially in respect to texts pre-dating, say, the fourteenth-century poet Machaut and, above all, post–printing press norms concerning the integrity of a given (vernacular) narrative, such supposed integrity did not—perhaps could not—prevail. Preservation of a canonical text as such was less a goal of scribes and their patrons than the meaning, or truth, of what these texts said. Fidelity to meaning entailed for them processes of transformation: amplification, abbreviation, recasting, continuation—these were the stuff of literary transmission during the Middle Ages. As was already observed in chapter 1, textual transmogrification characterizes the medieval poetic process. Jean de Meun continued *The Romance of the Rose*, which had been started, but left unfinished, by Guillaume de Lorris; yet, as has often been pointed out, his continuation constitutes in many important respects a refutation of his predecessor. Nevertheless, at approximately the midpoint of their two conjoined texts, Jean expresses great pride in the fact of his taking up where Guillaume had left off. Refutation, along with other forms of recasting or perpetuation, belonged to the storehouse of poetic creativity—techniques, possibilities—that enabled medieval writers to function as they did.

Not only authors, but also scribes took part in this creative process. A case in point is the thirteenth-century scribe of a codex containing all five romances of Chrétien de Troyes. The codex (Bibliothèque Nationale f. fr. 1450) contains a transcription of Wace's *Roman de Brut*—the story of the kings of Britain—up to the point at which Wace describes the marvels of Arthur's kingship; then (folio 139*v*) the scribe intervenes with

about 20 lines of his own to call upon Chrétien's "testimony" ("ce que
Crestïens tesmogne") concerning Arthur, and after transcribing
Chrétien's romances, he returns to complete *Brut* (and other related,
"historical" narratives). B.N. f. fr. 1450, as codex and with this specific
scribal-poetic intervention, both illustrates and justifies the concept of
super romance. To be sure, this intervention focuses on thematic issues
(such as, are the Arthurian stories true?), but such matters in the twelfth
and thirteenth centuries were not divorced from questions of form. It is
therefore by no means irrelevant that *Lancelot* was left unfinished by
Chrétien—or rather that he turned its completion over to Godefroi—
whereas, as it is stated at the end of *Yvain*, Chrétien most decidedly did
finish his *Chevalier au Lion* (vv. 6816–17). Is it too much to expect that,
in conjoining the *Charrette* and *Yvain*, and thereby poetically exploiting a
medieval literary mode, Chrétien himself understood—perhaps even
helped even invent—the potentialities of a super (that is, conjoined)
romance?

It is important to bear in mind in the following examination of the
two romances that the meaning of each depends in large part upon its
relationship at once to the other and to the new whole formed by both
together.

Le Chevalier de la Charrette (Lancelot)

In a prologue replete with hyperbolic praise of his patroness, Chrétien
declares having received the subject matter of the "Knight of the Cart,"
as well as the orientation to be followed by the story, from "my Lady of
Champagne"; he also has placed his work and his understanding totally
at the service of her bidding. What follows here is a plot summarization.

The Story: King Arthur, holding court on Ascension Day, receives the
inopportune visit of Méléagant, son of King Bademagu of Gorre, who
demands a boon of his host. Arthur rashly agrees to allow Queen
Guenevere to leave the court in the company of one of his knights, who
will be challenged by Méléagant. The winner of this encounter will be
allowed to take the queen with him. However, if Méléagant loses, he
promises to free the captives from Arthur's kingdom of Logres held in
Gorre. Seneschal Kay obtains from Arthur the honor to accompany the
queen. The two depart, followed at a distance by Gauvain, who eventually finds Kay's horse and who meets a knight (Lancelot) whom he provides with a mount. A bit later he once again encounters Lancelot, who,

after hesitating very briefly before doing so, climbs into an ignoble cart driven by a dwarf.[9] Gauvain refuses to join him there but follows along until the two reach a castle, where they are hospitably received by a young *dame*. After undergoing the dangers of the Perillous Bed, which shoots lances or arrows upon the person foolhardy enough to sleep on it, Lancelot, the next morning, views the distant procession of Queen Guenevere and her escort. The sight so moves him that he barely misses falling out of the castle window.

Lancelot (whose name has not yet been revealed in the poem and who is known, simply, as the *Chevalier* or, mockingly, as the *Chevalier de la Charrette*) meets a damsel to whom he promises to do anything she might ask of him and who shows him the two entry points to the kingdom of Gorre: the Submerged Bridge (the access eventually taken by Gauvain) and the Sword Bridge (upon whose cutting edge Lancelot will have to creep). Deep in thought, Lancelot fails to hear the challenge of the knight guarding the ford he is about to traverse, but he manages to defeat this knight anyway, sparing his life at the request of the damsel. The same evening he accepts the hospitality of another damsel (the "Immodest Damsel") whom he saves from a rape and with whom, in order to learn of Guenevere's whereabouts, he has agreed to spend the night; seeing his recalcitrance, however, she permits him to sleep alone. The next day he accompanies the damsel, finds a comb containing several golden hairs, and, when told that the comb is the queen's, worships it as though it were a holy relic. A knight (the "Importunate Lover") who lusts after the Immodest Damsel is dissuaded by his father from going through with a combat against Lancelot, although a brilliant company of damsels and knights interrupts its courtly activities at the approach of the shameful "Knight of the Cart."

Arriving at a cemetery, Lancelot hoists up a heavy stone marking the most elaborate tomb; he learns that this grave is destined to be his in that (as a hermit informs him) it is reserved for the knight who will rescue the captives from Logres now held in Gorre. That evening he is given shelter and supper by a vavasor and his family—captives from the land of Logres—who explain to him the dangers that await him. The next day, accompanied by the vavasor's two sons, Lancelot broaches the Stone Passageway and joins in a battle between people of Gorre and those of Logres. (He is given a magic ring for protection by the fairy who had raised him, the Lake Fairy.) The day after he fights a knight whom he beheads at the urging of a damsel (later to be revealed as Méléagant's sister).

Lancelot crosses the Sword Bridge after having undone the two spells protecting it; he is badly cut on his feet and hands. King Bademagu vainly attempts to convince his son, Méléagant, to return Guenevere to Lancelot and Arthur, and welcomes the knight courteously. The next morning Lancelot combats Méléagant, and when he learns that the queen is watching him his ardor redoubles. Guenevere casually reveals Lancelot's name to her damsel-in-waiting. (This is the approximate midpoint of the romance.) Méléagant is at the point of utter defeat when, persuaded to do so by Bademagu, Guenevere calls a halt to the combat. The prisoners from Logres, including the queen, are freed; Méléagant insists on a rematch with Lancelot. Bademagu leads Lancelot to Guenevere, who receives him coldly. Lancelot departs on a search for Gauvain. News of his death reaches Guenevere, whose sadness is so intense that rumors fly that she has died. These are heard by Lancelot who then tries to commit suicide. He learns she has not died and regains his courage.

The queen reveals why she had treated Lancelot so coldly: he had heeded the voice of Reason instead of that of Love, and hesitated an instant before climbing into the cart! This brief hesitation has offended her (see below). She arranges a meeting with him that night, during which they consummate their love. The following morning Méléagant discovers bloodstains on her sheets and accuses the wounded Kay, who had been sharing Guenevere's bedroom, of illicit relations with her. (In reality, the stains had come from Lancelot's hands, which he had cut while forcing open the iron bars on the window leading to Guenevere's room.) Lancelot champions Kay's innocence in judicial combat against Méléagant, but, once again, the fight is interrupted. Lancelot departs anew to find Gauvain; through the betrayal of a dwarf he falls into Méléagant's hands, while, because of a forged letter, Guenevere is led to believe he is already at Arthur's court.

A great tournament is called at Noauz (to be presided over by Guenevere), but Lancelot is imprisoned by Méléagant's seneschal and cannot participate. He is conditionally freed by his jailer's wife and repairs to Noauz, where he combats poorly in obedience to Guenevere's order. He is mocked by all (except the joyful Guenevere) and returns to his prison. King Bademagu enjoins his son to make peace with Lancelot; Méléagant refuses. Thanks to Bademagu's daughter (whom Lancelot had previously served), who discovers his whereabouts, Lancelot is freed from prison and nurtured back to health by her. For the third time Lancelot combats against Méléagant, defeats him, and cuts off his head.

A brief epilogue informs us that, with Chrétien's full approval, Godefroi de Leigni has completed the romance as of the point at which Lancelot had been imprisoned in the seneschal's castle (that is, vv. 6167–7134).

Strange as it may seem, there survives in Old French no mention previous to Chrétien de Troyes of an Arthurian knight named Lancelot. *Érec et Énide* alludes to him as third in valor of a series of knights that include Gauvain (first place), Érec (second place), and many others. "Lanceloz del Lac" is named in *Cligés* (along with "Percevaus li Gallois") as one of the champions vanquished by the young Cligés in a joust held at King Arthur's court; he is referred to in *Yvain* as "Lancelot who was traitorously emprisoned in a tower." This last allusion indicates that Chrétien's audience was familiar either with the *Charrette* or with some other version that included this episode. The existence of a *Lancelot* narrative tradition previous to Chrétien's romance would appear to be supported by our author's declaration in his prologue that he owed his subject matter (*matiere*) to the command of Countess Marie de Champagne, that she ordered him to compose a romance concerning Lancelot's adventures (probably including Queen Guenevere), but with a *san* (that is, a direction, a twist, or a meaning different from the traditional story). However, if indeed such a traditional Lancelot story ever existed in Old French, it has not been unearthed by scholars.

Two sources for the *Charrette* can nevertheless be immediately identified; both of these reappear repeatedly in Chrétien's œuvre: the Tristan and Iseut legend and the historically oriented "Matter of Britain."

The tale of a queen abducted from her husband as a result of his rashly conceding a boon to a petitioner, her subsequent recapture from the abductor by a knight belonging to the king's court, and her return to her husband can be found in an episode of the *Tristan* as recounted by Thomas (ca. 1165–70). Lancelot is in love with Guenevere as passionately as Tristan was in love with the wife of King Mark. In much-amplified form this tale underlies the entire *Chevalier de la Charrette*.

Lancelot, moreover, is suffused with Celtic myth. One need only recall the importance of fairies in the story (for example, the Immodest Damsel is surely one, the Lake Fairy another). The theme of the Land from Which No Stranger Returns—the Land of Gorre[10]—is typically Celtic. One version of the story (the *Vita sancti Gildæ*, by Caradoc de Lancarfan) tells of a certain king, Melvas, who abducts "Guennevar," the wife of King Arthur. Thanks to the intervention of Gildas and the abbot of

Glastonbury (*Glas*=Voire, Gorre?), Melvas returns the queen to her royal spouse.

A third, rather more learned Celtic tradition is perhaps still more important, for certainly Chrétien knew it well. The "historical" accounts of the kings of Britain proffered in Geoffrey of Monmouth's *Historia regum Britanniæ* and, in the vernacular, by Wace's *Roman de Brut* tell of how Guenevere (called "Ganhumara" by Geoffrey) betrayed Arthur with the latter's nephew, Mordred, who sought to gain control of Arthur's kingdom while the king was besieging Rome; this betrayal eventually caused the destruction of the Arthurian world. The clerical tradition emphasizes the equivalence of treason and adultery, which, of course, is very much downplayed by Chrétien in the *Charrette*. On the other hand, Arthur's weakness and foolishness, also stressed by Geoffrey and Wace, is one of the basic principles of the *Charrette*. For in this work it is the queen's lover who, while burning with an "illicit" passion for her, manages to display the chivalric prowess necessary to restore order in the kingdom by returning the queen to her proper place; it was the King's bumbling that disturbed this order in the first place.[11]

Until recently, relatively little attention has been paid to the possible relationship between Chrétien's *Lancelot* and a Middle High German romance, composed around 1200 (or a bit earlier) by the court romancer Ulrich von Zatzikhoven and entitled *Lanzelet*. To be sure, the similarities between the two romances have been noted—the protagonists' names, for example, the detail that Lanzelet, like Lancelot, was raised by a lake fairy, and above all the fact that on two occasions Lanzelet intervenes on behalf of Queen Guenevere, once even freeing her from captivity and bringing her back to King Arthur's court. However, these resemblances were seen to be outweighed by the obvious differences in tone, spirit, and theme separating the two romances. Moreoever, Ulrich quite explicitly names his source as being a "French book" (*welsches buoch*) brought to his German court by an Anglo-Norman nobleman, and proclaims his stringent fidelity as translator of his model. Consequently—or so it has been generally believed—his source could have been neither Chrétien's *Charrette* nor a source utilized by Chrétien.

But what is the meaning of the apparent difference between *matiere* and *san* to which Chrétien refers in the prologue to the *Charrette*? The *matiere*, or subject matter, clearly alludes to a story dealing with Lancelot and, probably, involving Guenevere too. By claiming to have received the *matiere* of his romance from Marie de Champagne, Chrétien, it may plausibly be hypothesized, is stating that she asked him to compose a romance concerning Lancelot and the queen—a subject matter presumably well known to the noblemen and women making up the court of Champagne. Still, the *Lanzelet* does not make the slightest allusion to a possible love affair between the protagonist and Guenevere. Lanzelet rescues her, to be sure, but merely in order to perform a knightly service on behalf of Arthur's court and in order to win glory for himself.[12]

Recalling the statement made by Chrétien in the front matter to his *Érec et Énide* (vv. 19–22) in which he fulminates against those minstrels and storytellers who make their living in the courts of counts and kings by "corrupting" and "fragmenting" their narratives, and remembering some of the differences between Chrétien's *bele conjointure* and the surviving thirteenth-century Welsh story of *Gereint*, it is not unreasonable to posit the existence before Chrétien's *Charrette* of an OF tale concerning Lancelot that was known to everyone in court circles as well as primitive in the manner in which *Gereint* seems to offer a primitive version of *Érec et Énide*. This early version of *Lancelot*—of which Ulrich's *Lanzelet* would be a manifestation—would constitute to Chrétien's *Charrette* something analogous to what an OF antecedent to the Welsh *Gereint* would have been to Chrétien's *Érec et Énide*. (One might call the lost OF source translated by Ulrich the "*Proto-Lanzelet*.") Although only a hypothesis, it is not an unreasonable one, and it does correspond to what Chrétien had outlined as being his practice in his first surviving romance.

Furthermore, the hypothesis presents the attractive advantage of helping to clear up the meaning of the difficult term *san*. If Chrétien's *matiere* is that of the early Lancelot story, then Marie de Champagne's *san*—her addition to this *matiere*—is the new fact of Lancelot's reciprocated love for Guenevere. This interpretation of *san* also happens to fit what we know (or presume) of the interests and character of Marie de Champagne. She was the daughter of Eleanor of Aquitaine, and she was reputed to be an expert in affairs of love and *courtoisie*.[13] There is nothing refined or courtly about the love depicted in Ulrich's *Lanzelet*: it is, rather, a boisterous and joyful physical manifestation of desire and libido. Unlike the *Proto-Lanzelet*, the *Charrette* is bathed in the soft lights of *fin'amor* and *courtoisie*; even the love scene between Lancelot and Guenevere presents a superior, ineffable joy akin to that celebrated by many troubadours and *trouvères*. To summarize, then, it is quite tempting to see in the *Chevalier de la Charrette* the subject matter of a narrative close to that of the *Proto-Lanzelet*, but transformed by Chrétien's *antancïon* and *peine* according to Marie's instructions (the *san*); as opposed to the hero of *Lanzelet*, Lancelot incarnates a pure and absolute love for the queen.

A certain absoluteness also characterizes the prologue to the *Charrette*. Without an iota of flattery, Chrétien claims, the clerkly romancer declares that "my lady of Champagne [is] the superior, even, of queens," as a "diamond gemstone is superior to lesser precious stones, like pearls and sards" (vv. 16–18). His *Chevalier de la Charrette* owes everything to her but the hard work and understanding that he employs to serve her wishes, that is, the *matiere* and *san* with which she furnishes him (vv. 21–29). What Chrétien does is at once inspired by the countess and directed to her.

In a very authentic sense, then, Chrétien's total clerkly service to the countess foreshadows, and parallels, Lancelot's chivalric service on behalf of Guenevere. Together they perform for Woman, or the Lady, and they do so in an unreasoning fashion. It is because Lancelot heeded ever so briefly the arguments of Reason that Guenevere treats him so coldly at their first meeting in Gorre. Reason tells Lancelot that the cart is shameful, that riding in it will bring to Lancelot the reproaches of everyone: his honor, or reputation, is at stake (vv. 369–73), and that causes him to fail to accept without question the dwarf's proposition. Reason, Chrétien's narrator informs us, resides in the lips, not in the heart. It is only when Love,[14] who dwells in the heart, intervenes directly in the discussion that Lancelot immediately jumps into the infamous cart. His genuine honor lies not in the respect accorded him publically, but rather in the secret recesses of his heart.

Provided the hypothesis concerning the original subject matter of the *Charrette* is credible, it is clear that just as Chrétien the *clerc* has "feminized" the masculine *matiere* of the *Proto-Lanzelet*, so his protagonist "feminizes" chivalry. Unlike Gauvain, whose principal concern is with the historical world of Arthur's kingdom and, consequently, who desires to restore Guenevere to her rightful place as the king's consort (thereby augmenting his own chivalric honor), Lancelot's overriding desire is to free and to be united with the woman he loves; his returning the queen to the Kingdom of Logres is purely incidental to his main, personal goal. Nevertheless, by remaining faithful to his purpose Lancelot does in fact achieve what Gauvain had set out to do, and Gauvain, who never betrays the slightest jealousy, is the first to admit it. To Lancelot, he declares, belongs the honor of rescuing the queen (vv. 5341–49). Thus, by ostensibly sacrificing public honors to his secret goal, Lancelot attains the respect of Arthur's court—a respect, however, which he shows himself quite willing to forfeit anew in obeying Guenevere's injunction to behave with stunning incompetence during the tournament of Noauz.

If, as *Lancelot* appears to be telling us, the service of Woman, Love, and the Heart constitutes a proper—perhaps even the proper—venue of authentic knightly prowess, so it must also follow that *clergie*, which, as the prologue to *Cligés* informs us, is also, at its best, entwined with such prowess, ought to share this same venue. Certainly the *Charrette* spares no pains in establishing the linkage. Chrétien is here proposing to us that the real, or most perfectly truthful, history of the Arthurian world lies in the *courtoisie* which it may be interpreted to represent. The Arthurian world is not in and of itself the objectively true, or historical, world of the OF *chansons de geste*, which celebrated the momentous truth of Charlemagne, the emperor of all Western Christendom, as he is aided in his imperial task by the Twelve Peers. The story of Charlemagne is *history*; it is true. In the *Charrette* Chrétien appears to be subordinating epic values of historical truth to what may be termed lyric meanings. The entire narrative is given over to hyperbole, at times even humorously, though never at the expense of our admiration for its hero. Lancelot seems to be moving within the walls of a City of Ladies, and his function is to sustain that "city." We recall that he was brought up by a lady—the Lake Fairy—who continues to protect him. It is perhaps his fidelity to that upbringing which, along with his passion for Guenevere, causes him to earn the respect, the help, and the affection of so many *dames* and *pucelles* in the romance—even those whose physical advances he spurns, and there are several. Because his love for the queen is so absolute and so pure he is able gratuitously to aid and succor with all his strength an entire sorority of women who, each and every one, recompenses his efforts with respect and, at times (as with Méléagant's sister), with devotion. Like Gauvain, none of these ladies or maidens displays the slightest jealousy.

Over the past century or so, critics and scholars alike have pointed to what has been labeled here the lyric meanings of the *Chevalier de la Charrette*. Indeed Gaston Paris, already in the early 1880s, coined the term *amour courtois* (courtly love) in order to account for the utter devotion felt by Lancelot toward Guenevere, a devotion he related to the kind of love celebrated by the Provençal troubadours of the twelfth century. Paris's *amour courtois* amounts to a kind of doctrine, or code of behavior in love, of which he declared Chrétien de Troyes to be the "epic poet."[15] The *Charrette* is shot through with typically lyric constructs. The night of love spent together by Lancelot and the queen has many of the attributes of the *alba* (*aubade*, or "dawn song"), a lyric song recounting the lovers' secret bliss together and the sadness of their early morning separation; the scene even offers a watchman, though ironically, in the figure of the sleeping Kay! The "far away love" (*amor de lonh*) motif runs through most of Chrétien's narrative: much of the time Guenevere, the object of the knight's love, is as physically inaccessible to him as the Countess of Tripoli was to Jaufre Rudel, the princely troubadour who celebrated *amor de lonh*.

Even more significant is the fact that the *Chevalier de la Charrette* is basically structured according to the lyric mode known as the song of the *mal-mariée* (the Ill-Married Wife), which Chrétien narrativizes. Lancelot, the queen, and Arthur form a triangle (like Tristan, Iseut, and King Mark); Guenevere is married to Arthur although she loves Lancelot. Her position is one of jeopardy, for acting upon her love for Lancelot entails committing not only adultery but also treason to her liege-lord. She is thus torn between her "external" duty to the masculine world—the City of Men—represented by her husband, his court, and the "historical" Matter of Britain, and the private, "internalized" feminine world of her feelings and individuality. As Reason exhorts Lancelot not to dishonor himself by climbing aboard the cart, so Reason would surely dictate to Guenevere that she not "succumb" to her passion for Lancelot, that is, to her "feminine" inclinations. The typical *mal-mariée* song depicts a beautiful young wife who suffers at the hands of an old and jealous husband, and who finds solace in the arms of a handsome young lover. However, this is not precisely the case with the *Charrette*. Although it might be assumed that Guenevere is younger than Arthur, the issue is never raised.[16] Nor, as is usually the situation in the *mal-mariée* poems, is Arthur depicted as a jealous, or suspicious, husband. (In the *mal-mariée* tradition *gilous* [jealous] is the adjective most frequently applied to the husband, and it often rhymes with *cous* [cuckold]—one of the few base words used commonly in courtly diction.) Within the confines of the *Chevalier de la Charrette*, Arthur is ensconced totally in the world of his court; Guenevere is queen, no more: she does not figure as a person in this milieu.

Chrétien transforms the lyric premises of the *mal-mariée* structure in his narrative. He splits the jealous husband figure into two characters: Arthur is the spouse, Méléagant is the *gilous*. Moreover, Méléagant's jealousy spills over to affect both Lancelot and Guenevere. Incapable of vanquishing Lancelot in a fair fight, Méléagant resorts to fraud and trickery to get his way; his angry speech to Guenevere after he discovers the bloodstains on the sheets in the queen's bedroom is exactly that of a jealous husband who has caught his wife in adultery (vv. 4774–809). Indeed, Méléagant is virtually a parody of proud knighthood and of the jealous husband. Outwardly he appears to be an unconquerable knight, inspiring trepidation in all his opponents; however, he is to knighthood what a tyrant is to the just ruler, a corruption of a noble ideal. His reputation is worse than empty because he has not interiorized what knighthood is for. Meanwhile, despite his fame and the honors almost routinely bestowed upon him, King Arthur is a bumbler. Unlike Érec with Énide, he is isolated from his wife the queen. He operates exclusively in the historically reputable City of Men—the world of the Round Table and of game-playing tournaments. He does not reign with his Guenevere (as, one is sure, Érec reigns with Énide), and can, thereby, easily abandon her to Méléagant in order to placate the sulking Kay.

The *Chevalier de la Charrette* thus presents us with an inherently defective marriage in the characters of Arthur and Guenevere when these are viewed, precisely, in conjunction with one another—in their *conjointure*. The poem seems to be arguing that the givens of the *mal-mariée* lyric lead to disasters that include the political arena usually associated with the City of Men. The conditions of the demise of the Round Table—a demise known to all those who were familiar with Geoffrey of Monmouth or with Wace's *Roman de Brut*—are posed by the *Charrette* and constitute the grounds for the sort of fictional meditation contained by Chrétien's romance. Although Lancelot, unlike Tristan, is not the king's nephew, his adulterous relationship with the queen, for whom his devotion knows no bounds, obviously also resembles that felt by Tristan for Iseut. The *Tristan* story also contains the suggestion that the lovers' illegitimate passion inspired Tristan to rescue Iseut from extreme peril and to bring her back to King Mark, her husband.

Chrétien's conjoining of the *Proto-Lanzelet* matter with that of *Tristan* furnishes him with the occasion to develop the notion that what the City of Men tends to marginalize—that is, the deeply true *conjointure* of man and woman—constitutes what in fact provides for the survival of what the City of Men ostensibly stands for: political stability and proper governance. Neither Kay nor, for that matter, Gauvain suffices to insure this stability and propriety. It is Lancelot, the knight who "betrays" Arthur, who succeeds in restoring order. In the *Chevalier de la Charrette* Chrétien both illustrates the illusory nature of what generally is accepted as being central and indicates the authentic centrality of what merely appears to be marginal, even sinful. *Chevalerie*, he seems to be affirming, must be informed by passion and a deep sense of transcendence. Lancelot's love for Guenevere is transcendental; it goes further than simply verging on worship. Genuine *chevalerie* possesses a tragic dimension. In the *Charrette* Chrétien renews the tragic knightliness of an epic Roland, but he does so, at the countess's behest, in a courtly framework.

Le Chevalier au Lion (Yvain)

The Story: The romance begins *in medias res*—there is no prologue—with the unnamed narrator speaking enthusiastically of the good old days when Arthur reigned and when knights and ladies knew how to love and to speak of love. He goes on to describe a Whitsuntide feast at court during which, to the astonishment of his guests, Arthur gets up from table, discourteously abandons his knights, and joins Guenevere in bed. Eventually the king falls asleep, but the queen, wide awake, joins a party of knights (which includes Yvain, the son of King Urien), where, after scolding the sarcastic Kay for his evil tongue, she persuades a reluctant Calogrenant to tell a story of an adventure he had undergone some seven years earlier. The adventure redounds not to his credit but to his shame, and Calogrenant has no desire to speak of it.

Calogrenant tells of his riding through the Forest of Brocéliande, meeting up with an ugly cowherd with whom he exchanges words, receiving the hospitality of a friendly vavasor and his charming daughter, and arriving at a marvelous fountain—the Magic Fountain of Barenton—located in the shade of a pine tree. He pours water on a slab of precious stone. Immediately a terrible storm ensues, and an enraged knight emerges from the nearby castle in order to challenge Calogrenant. Calogrenant is humiliatingly defeated. He returns home after once again enjoying the vavasor's hospitality.

Intrigued by this story, Yvain decides to avenge Calogrenant (who is his cousin): he will repeat the adventure before the intrigued Arthur has a chance to personally investigate Brocéliande. He leaves the court early the next morning.

Everything takes place as Calogrenant had described it, except that Yvain succeeds in defeating Esclados-le-Roux, the fearsome knight of the Magic Fountain, mortally wounding him in the process. He follows Esclados into the castle, but barely escapes with his life: his horse is sliced in two by the falling door that is closing after Esclados's entrance into the castle. Once inside the castle Yvain is aided by Lunete, a young woman whom he had befriended at some time in the past. She gives him a ring in order to render him invisible to those of Esclados's retinue who are seeking the person who killed their master. Hidden away from the others, Yvain observes Esclados's funeral procession—especially the very beautiful and grief-stricken widow, Laudine. He falls passionately in love with her. Once again Lunete comes to the hero's aid. She convinces Laudine that she ought to remarry in order to have someone to defend the terrible Fountain, and who better than the knight who defeated the redoutable Escaldos? Laudine eventually succumbs to this logic and, after meeting Yvain, consents to wed him. The wedding takes place as Arthur and his court arrive at Laudine's castle. Kay, who had disturbed the Fountain, is resoundingly defeated by Yvain.

Gauvain, Yvain's friend, interrupts his companion's bliss by warning him against the perils of losing his fame and reputation as a knight by settling down with his wife in the obscurity of Brocéliande. In order to merit the love of his lady, he tells Yvain, he must leave her and gain fame in jousts and tournaments. Very reluctantly Laudine agrees to allow Yvain to depart with Gauvain and Arthur, but for no more than one year's time. More than a year elapses and Yvain neglects to return to his wife. Laudine sends a maiden to Arthur's court in order to denounce Yvain's perfidy and to take back the love she has given him. Stricken with remorse, Yvain goes mad, wandering off into the forest. There, naked and out of his senses, he nevertheless befriends an old hermit by bringing him the flesh of animals he has hunted, in exchange for which the hermit gives him bread and water. He is cured of his madness by a magic unguent provided by the Dame de Noroison (but concocted by the fairy Morgan) and administered by one of her maidens-in-waiting. Grateful, Yvain offers his services to the Dame de Noroison, who is being attacked by an unwanted suitor, the Count Alier. After his triumph the lady offers herself to Yvain as wife, but he politely declines. He appears to understand that he must place his knightly prowess at the service of those—especially women and maidens—who are distressed.

It is at this juncture—the strategic midpoint of the narrative—that Yvain rescues a noble lion from a fire-breathing serpent; from this point on the lion will be Yvain's constant companion, and Yvain will be known to all as the Lion Knight.

Yvain returns with his lion to the Magic Fountain. Giving himself over to despair at ever recovering Laudine's love, he hears moans emanating from a nearby chapel. It is Lunete, imprisoned for "betraying" her mistress by convincing her to trust the faithless Yvain, whom Lunete now does not recognize. Only Gauvain, she says, can save her from being burned at the stake, but he is unavailable, "away" in the Lancelot story seeking to rescue Queen Guenevere, and Yvain, another possible defender, has disappeared. Without identifying himself, Yvain promises to take up Lunete's cause. That night he receives the hospitality of a noble lord whose sons and daughter are threatened by the evil designs of the wicked giant, Harpin de la Montagne; the youths are Gauvain's nephews and niece. Yvain offers to combat Harpin on the following day. With the help of his lion he vanquishes and kills the giant. He next hurries to the aid of Lunete, defeats her three accusers (once more with his lion's assistance), and returns her to the good graces of her mistress.

Yvain is received by the Lord of the Château de Pesme Aventure (the Castle of Utter Misery), who maintains a large workshop employing some 300 maidens who are forced to weave silk fabrics in dismal conditions. They are dressed in rags, hungry, and quite exhausted. Their presence at Pesme Aventure is due to the fact that the King of the Isle of Maidens requires the lord (aided by two monstrous brothers born of the union of a woman with a *netun* [monstrous demon]) to offer up as tribute to him 30 maidens each year. The lord explains to Yvain that the knight must combat the monsters on the morrow and that, if he wins, he will marry the lord's daughter and will take possession of the castle. Yvain declines the proposal of marriage, but accepts the combat. He and the lion dispatch the *fils de netun*. However, his firm refusal of marriage to the lord's daughter angers his host, and the two take leave of each other under a cloud. The 300 maidens are freed.

He returns to Arthur's court in order to defend the younger daughter of the Seigneur de la Noire Épine, whose older sister has robbed her of her inheritance. Gauvain will be the older sister's champion. Not knowing each other's identity, the two knights engage in single combat in order to decide this issue. They fight to a draw. Arthur himself resolves the inheritance question by a clever strategem through which he causes the older sister to recognize her illegitimate claim.

Thus, known only as the Lion Knight (until he and Gauvain recognize each other), Yvain undergoes five adventures that possess genuine meaning and value. He has triumphed in defense of five worthy causes, not merely in jousts designed to augment his reputation. But he has not been able to regain Laudine's love and esteem.

Once again, Lunete will come to Yvain's help. Laudine stands in dire need of a knight to defend her land against those who intrude upon the Magic Fountain; it is this need that Lunete exploits. No man in Laudine's fief is up to this essential task. What would Laudine do if she were the lady for whom the famous Lion Knight—he who "killed the giant, and vanquished the three *chevaliers*" (vv. 6605–06)—pines and who refuses to allow him to make up with her? Laudine replies that she would forgive such a knight his past sins. When Lunete presents to Laudine a kneeling Yvain, the lady realizes the implications of the situation and forgives her once-erring spouse. Yvain and Laudine are reconciled; Lunete is joyful.

The narrator ends his tale by stating that "Concerning the *Lion Knight* Chrétien finishes his narrative thus." He warns the listener not to expect more, for any addition to what has been said would be a lie. Thus, unlike the *Charrette*, *Le Chevalier au Lion* is explicitly finished by its author.

It seems probable that, like that of *Érec et Énide*, the *matiere* of *Yvain* also derives ultimately from a Celtic adventure tale more or less resembling those to be found in the Welsh *mabinogion*. Indeed, among the surviving *mabinogion* one finds a story entitled *Owein and Lunet* in which, along with other elements appearing in *Yvain*, one comes across a marvelous fountain quite similar to the Magic Fountain of Barenton. A Celtic mythological substratum clearly informs Chrétien's romance: Laudine and Lunete possess a fairylike nature;[17] water poured on the Magic Fountain's stone slab causing the terrible storm is doubtless a reference to certain Celtic rain myths; Esclados-le-Roux has been assimilated to the priest-king Nemi, who personifies the oak god, protector of fecundity and of harvests, and who is destined to be replaced by the hero who succeeds in killing him; the magic ring given to Yvain by Lunete, as well as the miraculous unguent that cures him of his madness, have Celtic analogues; the Château de Pesme Aventure would appear to be located, like Tristan's "house of glass," in the Celtic Other World. The analogies are numerous and convincing.[18] Besides, Yvain himself is named in both Geoffrey of Monmouth's Arthurian *Historia* and Wace's *Brut*, works that deal largely with "historically" Celtic matters. In the *Historia* "Iwen" is identified as the son of Urianus and as the heir to his uncle, Anguselus, King of Scotland. Wace mentions him as "Ewein, le fiz Urïen," and another time as Ewein "li curteis" ("the courtly"). In *Érec et Énide* Chrétien includes Yvain, the son of Urien, along with two other "Yvains" in the famous list of Round Table knights (vv. 1691–1750) found in that romance; Yvain's name also figures in the short list of knights whose names are inscribed on the stone grave marker lifted by Lancelot. In post-Chrétien de Troyes narratives Yvain's association with

Gauvain becomes a commonplace. His position in the Arthurian courtly world is thus a clearly established fact.

Following upon the trailblazing studies of Edmond Faral,[19] scholars have also demonstrated interest in classical influences upon Chrétien de Troyes in general and, in particular, on *Le Chevalier au Lion*. Yvain's lion is undoubtedly at least in part a latter-day avatar of the story of Androcles and his faithful lion; it is also a transmogrification of Tristan's faithful dog, Husdent. Laudine certainly owes much to Virgil's Dido, a ruler abandoned by the man she loves (although perhaps Chrétien's debt is owed less directly to Virgil than to the *Roman d'Énéas*). Frappier has pointed out direct borrowings from Ovid in *Yvain*: Yvain's pursuit of the wounded Esclados is described in words very similar to those describing, in *Metamorphoses*, I, v. 533, that of a hare by a hunting dog; one detects the presence of the *Ars amatoria* in a number of scenes in *Yvain*, for example, the aforementioned lines explaining the advantages of cemeteries for young widows seeking a new lover or husband, and the passage alluding to the rapid changes of heart to which women are susceptible (*Ars amatoria*, I, vv. 755–56; *Yvain*, vv. 1437–45).

Other classical quotations in *Yvain* refer with greater likelihood to the French *romans antiques* with which Chrétien was quite familiar than to the Latin texts upon which these were based—*Piramus et Tisbé*, for example, the *Roman d'Énéas*, and the *Roman de Thèbes*, all predating the composition of *Yvain*. Thus, the Jocaste of *Thèbes* is, like Laudine, a widow who is rapidly consoled and who marries her late husband's assassin.

Tristan et Iseut also appears in *Yvain*, although less frequently and with less emphasis than in either the *Charrette* or *Cligés*. The similarity between Yvain's exile into madness in the forest and Tristan's departure (with Iseut) to the Forest of Morois have already been noted. Yvain's encounter with a simple hermit is perhaps a reflection of the lovers' meeting the hermit Ogrin. It also would not be too far-fetched to compare Lunete's narrowly escaping being burned at the stake to Tristan's rescue of Iseut from a similar fate.

Le Chevalier au Lion is therefore as "literary" as any of the narrative compositions attributed to Chrétien de Troyes. Yet, perhaps because of the absence of a prologue, it appears far less literarily contrived than *Cligés* or *Lancelot*, or, for that matter, *Érec et Énide*. Readers of these last romances must see themselves as guided by the set of instructions explicitly spelled out in the front matter to each: we are to pay attention to the *bele conjointure* governing *Érec et Énide*; the relationship of *clergie* and *chevalerie*—and the special importance of *clergie*—stands at the center of

Cligés; and service to one's Lady informs *Lancelot*. Nothing of this sort is spelled out in *Le Chevalier au Lion*. Nor is Chrétien even named in *Yvain* until the very end of the narrative. All this is quite disconcerting.

"Literature" makes its presence felt in the opening lines of our poem:

> Artus, li boens rois de Bretaingne,
> La cui proesce nos enseigne . . .

(Arthur, the good king of Britain, whose prowess is instructive to us . . .)

The couplet is reminiscent of the noble opening to the Oxford *Roland*: "Carles li reis, nostre emperere magnes . . ." (Charles the king, our great emperor . . .). A few lines later our narrator contrasts the present day and its abasement of love with the "good old times" of King Arthur, when knights and ladies knew the true meaning of love—a use of the "Good-old-days" topic reminiscent of the initial stanza of the *Life of Saint Alexis*, where, it is asserted, during the Roman days of yore faith, justice and charity received their proper due, while in our own time these have severely weakened.

With these very charged literary allusions, the narrator, who is expressing his opinion and judgment, links the Arthurian world—its history—to the profoundly truthful history of hagiography and the *chanson de geste*, a linkage no twelfth-century reader would fail to grasp. Is this narrator the mouthpiece of the author of the *Chevalier de la Charrette*, whose King Arthur, as ruler and husband, leaves so much to be desired? And what is one to make of the very accurate, but surely misplaced statement, in the rhyme position, describing Whitsunday, as an especially *costly* feast (". . . cele feste qui tant coste, / Qu'an doit clamer la Pantecoste" [vv. 5–6])? This tiny, realistic detail detracts from the celebrative generalizations described. Money should not be an issue in the world of *courtoisie* and knightly flowering.

The discrepancy between the narrator's willingness to praise the courtly idea associated with the Arthurian world and his honest reporting of what he knows to be accurate grows sharper as he reports what happened on that Whitsunday. To the utter confusion of his guests, the king leaves the table in order to spend some time in the bedroom with the queen; there he eventually falls asleep, leaving Guenevere wide awake. To say the very least, Arthur has behaved impolitely. When the queen leaves the nuptial bed, she happens upon a group of knights chatting among themselves and telling stories. Several rise in respect at the sight of her, others who had not noticed her presence fail to stand. This gives way to bickering and sarcasm, especially on the part of Kay, whom Guenevere winds up comparing to a poisonous snake because of his venomous tongue. Arthur's discourtesy is fairly closely matched by that of his Round Table entourage, even that, perhaps, of his consort.

A pattern seems to be established in these opening lines and scenes. Our narrator's opinions are belied by what he sees, yet he reports honestly what he witnesses despite the contradiction. His *clergie*, though not perfect, is genuine, and it seems to be associated with truthful witness. He refuses to permit his (deficient) ideology to stand invariably in the way of accuracy and truth. Yet, the narrator does not switch abruptly from his ideological eulogizing of Arthurianism because what he witnesses and reports contradicts that ideology. The process of change is slow. For example, when Gauvain and Yvain are about to begin their fierce combat, the narrator protests that neither wishes to harm the other—their great friendship would not permit it. However, as he views the two champions come to blows, he confesses that "or ai manti molt leidemant" (now I have lied most horrendously), and he goes on to describe the ferocity of their combat (vv. 6075–96). In this passage, however, he appears to realize that a discrepancy prevents the ideology of courtly friendship from prevailing in this precise, real instance—a realization that he does not articulate in the opening scene, when he shows Arthur behaving discourteously.

To put the matter another way, the narrator undergoes a process of growth as the events of the romance unfold. And this process culminates at the very end of the work when, with gentle irony, Yvain is "re-conjoined" with his wife, Laudine, thanks to the good efforts of Lunete, and without commentary of any sort the narrator states the joy of Yvain and Laudine as well as the great contentment felt by Lunete at this turn of events. It is also at this juncture that the romance, so to speak, "generates" its author: the narrator names "Crestïens" as he who "finishes" his narrative thus.

As already mentioned, a charming figure of speech—an example of *adnominatio*—underscores the presence of *clergie* in this ending. It now deserves quoting in full:

> Et Lunete rest mout a eise;
> Ne li faut chose qui li pleise,
> Des qu'ele a fet la pes sanz *fin*
> De monseignor Yvain le *fin*

Et de s'amie chiere et *fine*.
Del *"Chevalier au Lyeon" fine*
Crestïens son romans ensi.

(vv. 6812–17; emphasis mine)

(And Lunete remains very happy; nothing is lacking to her pleasure, since
she has created the endless peace of the gentle Lord Yvain and of his dear
and gentle beloved. Concerning the Lion Knight Chrétien finishes his
poem thus.)

The masculine rhyme words *fin* (the noun meaning "end," and the adjective signifying "genteel, polished") are followed by the feminine rhymes
fine ("genteel, polished" and the verb "ends"), and, taken together, constitute both an example of *adnominatio* and chiasmus. The grammatical
parts of speech are conjoined, as are the two genders, and the notion of
"end" is placed in conjunction with the concept of "refinement." The
narrator proves here his genuine mastery of *clergie*, and this permits his
being associated with the "Crestïens" who is at last named as author.
Meanwhile—and this is of the greatest importance to an understanding
of the romance—Lunete, the traditionally literary feminine go-between
here transformed, is identified as she "who made" (*a fet*) the peace that
constitutes the fount of Yvain's and Laudine's joy. Her "work" is assimilated to that of the poet, the *faiseur*, to use twelfth-century vernacular
terminology. The feminine Lunete forms an authentic couple with the
masculine *clerc(s)* consisting of "Crestïens" and his narrator.

This structure depends of course on the "growing up" experienced by
the romance's protagonist. After the terrible disorientation he felt upon
incurring the loss of his lady, Yvain remakes himself: he becomes the
Lion Knight and performs chivalric works in the service of others, with
no thought for his personal fame, any immediate gain, or for reasons of
ambition. He does not (at least consciously) perform these works in
order to regain Laudine's favor. It consequently appears reasonable to
associate Yvain's maturing as a knight and as a man with analogous
transformations occurring in the narrator. By the end of the poem the
narrator is free from all reliance on the ideology of Arthurianism.
Recounting what happens as it happens suffices; he no longer feels the
need to link the deeds of his characters to what, for him, has become the
pseudohistorical world of the Round Table society. He accomplishes this
transformation just as Yvain learns that, *pace* Gauvain, a husband's place
is at his wife's side, not elsewhere earning fame in order to merit better

her esteem. The Forest of Brocéliande and Laudine's castle are far from
Arthur's court—a good two weeks' journey—but however marginal this
place may be in the eyes of a Gauvain it is, Yvain learns to realize, his
proper place, he will stay there and he will protect this place against
those who disturb its peace by upsetting the tranquility of the Magic
Fountain. Analogously, it may be argued, *Yvain*'s "twin romance," *Le
Chevalier de la Charrette*, also depicts a knight who learns his place.
Lancelot's comes to dwell exclusively in the space occupied by his and
Guenevere's love. However, whereas the implications of Lancelot's
choice, like those of Tristan, will possibly lead to tragic consequences, it
is hard to see Yvain living other than a rewarding—albeit somewhat
obscure—future.

Like Thessala in *Cligés*, the most interesting character in *Le Chevalier
au Lion* is probably Lunete. (Laudine's presence in the romance is shad-
owy; she is essentially an important background figure, the character
around whom the events turn.) Whereas Thessala's powers reside in her
ability to combine things (such as herbs and spices) in order to achieve
certain ends, Lunete's medium is, of course, language. Her achievements
are due to her natural command of rhetoric—a rhetoric that she places
at the service of what can only be described as superior understanding.
Thus, she immediately grasps the appropriateness of bringing together
Yvain and her mistress, Laudine; she gauges the sincerity of Yvain's passion for Laudine and she recognizes both her mistress's need for a knight
to defend the Magic Fountain and the likelihood of her responding affir-
matively to Yvain's love. In short, Lunete's talent serves what she knows
to be right. Her pleasant dalliance with Gauvain—she plays the moon to
his sun—after King Arthur's arrival at Laudine's castle proves her virtu-
osity in the language and behavior of *courtoisie*. It is the desperation of
her plight after having been accused of treason by Laudine's evil-minded
courtiers that provides one of the fundamental ideas expressed in *Yvain*,
namely that *clergie*—a specifically feminine *clergie* at that—requires, and
by so requiring furnishes a *raison d'être* for the dedication and the protection of *chevalerie*. In accepting to defend Lunete, with no thought of personal gain involved, Yvain, the Lion Knight, demonstrates his
acquisition of authentic chivalry. Without *clergie*, or so the romance
appears to be saying, chivalry would be a dead letter, would exist in a
meaningless void.

The verb *faire*, as applied to what Lunete accomplished, is particularly apt in that it is she who sets up the structure of the events that
Chrétien's narrator relates. She is responsible for both the poem's begin-

ning and its end. What precedes her intervention in first helping the lovesick Yvain constitutes the work's front matter—its background, a subject that merits further examination.

It is fair to say that initially the readers of *Yvain* are confused—indeed, they are supposed to be confused, and even bewildered, in their expectations. The disjunction between the reputation enjoyed by Arthur's court and what actually happens at the Whitsunday feast is overwhelming. Then follows Calogrenant's story. What is striking about this tale is its absolutely perfect—even classic—romance form. It starts out with a proverb (something recommended by contemporary works dedicated to the poetic arts); it is dedicated to a high-born lady, Queen Guenevere; learned literary allusions may be detected;[20] at the precise midpoint of the story we find a very interesting passage:

> — Je sui, ce voiz, uns chevaliers
> Qui quier ce que trover ne puis;
> Assez ai quis, et rien ne truis.
> — Et que voldroies tu trover?
> — Avanture, por esprover
> Ma proesce et mon hardemant.
> Or te pri et quier et demant,
> Se tu sez, que tu me consoille
> Ou d'aventure ou de mervoille.
>
> (vv. 356–64)

("I am, as you can see, a knight who seeks what I cannot find; I have sought long and hard, and found nothing." "And what would you wish to find?" "Adventure, in order to test my prowess and my bravery. Now I beg you, and ask you, and demand of you that, if you know how, you advise me concerning adventure or marvels.")

Calogrenant is seeking chivalric adventure—some memorable occasion to test his knightly abilities. That is his purpose, as he explains to the churlish cowherd. However, the verb *trover* that he employs, meaning "find," also means "to make poetry" (compare *trobadour* and *trouver*). Calogrenant's chivalric failure—after all, he is soundly defeated by Esclados-le-Roux—is counterweighted by his clerkly perfection: his story obeys all the rules of sophisticated romance narrative as set out in contemporary literary handbooks. Or should the matter be turned around, so that Chrétien is suggesting here that the outward formal perfection of Calogrenant's *clergie* matches his chivalric imperfection? If such a reading is correct, then it follows that Chrétien is informing his readers that his story concerning Yvain will be based on structural principles not brought to bear from the outside—from rule-books—but, rather, will derive from the inner requirements of his story. Yvain, it is true, will relive Calogrenant's story, but he will transcend it by defeating Esclados, by falling in love with Laudine, and by meeting Lunete. These events constitute the beginning of his history, a particular history unlike any other. Thus, just as the general history, or reputation, of King Arthur and his court is belied by what really happens on the specific day being recorded here, so Yvain's story is that of an individual, not a symbolic fiction designed to articulate general truths. It is in this way that Chrétien decides to reveal (and criticize) the dangers and the untruth of historical Arthurianism. In *Yvain* the general value of what Arthur represents proves to be wanting when this value system is confronted by a "real" case; it simply fails to work.

The front matter to the romance thus sets up a confrontation between what might be tagged as the ideological and the real, which is the basic theme of the entire narrative. Small wonder then that scholars have found *Yvain* to be the most "realistic" of Chrétien's romance narratives. Jean Frappier has put the issue very well: just as the presence of marvelous fountains, magic rings, and faithful lions appears to locate the events of the romance in an "imaginary world inherited from a distant mythology, . . . all of a sudden, in a surprising contrast, Chrétien's readers find themselves in a land well known to them—they are at home, in twelfth-century France and Champagne; a multitude of concrete details, sketches, and tableaux injects a familiar, quotidian reality into this fairy story" (Frappier 1969, 119; translation mine). *Yvain's* realism goes much further than the sort of realistic adaptation one discovers in many *romans antiques* (such as Dido summoning the fleeing Énéas back to Carthage by gesturing "hundreds of times" with her "ermine sleeve"), or the appearance in translations from the Latin of customs and values appropriate not to antiquity but, rather, like *courtoisie*, pertaining to the twelfth century. Realism in *Yvain* signifies what Frappier defines simply as "interest brought to bear on real things and beings, along with the art of depicting these with exactness and relief" (Frappier 1969, 120). This interest corresponds to the poetic and thematic purposes alluded to in the proceeding discussion.

A brief selection of examples will illustrate the realism of *Yvain*. When Lunete introduces the lovesick but bashfully terrified Yvain to Laudine, she has outfitted him with elegant new clothing—so new, in fact, that the tailor's chalk marks are still visible on it (v. 1887). The author, clearly, is smiling both at his characters and at his narrator's predilection for reporting all the details of what he witnesses. In the scene in which Yvain, having gone insane, meets the hermit living in the forest, emphasis is placed not on the hermit's spirituality or superior wisdom (as is the case with Tristan's hermit, Ogrin), but, instead, on the difficulties he faces in keeping body and soul together—his meager rations and cheap, sour-tasting bread—and on his generous sharing of what he has with Yvain.

The description of the horrible conditions under which the 300 captive *pucelles* work the silk at the Château de Pesme Aventure also surely owes much to contemporary reality—the new silk workshops being established during the second half of the twelfth century in Champagne and their exploitation of cheap feminine labor. The *pucelles* receive but four pence while their boss earns 60 times as much for their work. The injustice that Yvain will repair by defeating the two *fils de netun* is consequently a real injustice, not merely the "symbolic" injustice of employing noble maidens at tasks beneath their social standing.

The voice of realism in the romance is, of course, that of Lunete, allied, as has already been suggested, to that of a narrator whose *clergie*, at its best, consists in reporting what he "sees." Lunete understands that Laudine requires a successor to Esclados-le-Roux, and who better than the knight who has succeeded in defeating him and who, moreover, is head over heels in love with Laudine? Next to this genuine need, the fact that Yvain is Esclados's killer and that very little time elapses between Laudine's widowhood and her remarriage is unimportant. Lunete is unmoved by these ideological considerations, and she succeeds in convincing Laudine of the rightness of her viewpoint. Lunete's realism is hardly cold-blooded, however; she wants to repay Yvain for the kindness he once showed her, and she certainly has her mistress's interests at heart. Nothing is mentioned of her standing to gain anything personally from her action. It may in fact be reasonable to conjecture that the increased confidence with which the narrator gives free rein to his reporting proclivities is inspired by the sympathy that the readers, and the entire romance, feel for Lunete's realism and for her character as a person.

In several important respects, Lunete plays a role in *Le Chevalier au Lion* analogous to that played by the Countess Marie in *Le Chevalier de la Charrette*: she inspires the narrator by her example. She is first named in the romance during the flirtation scene with Gauvain, when the narrator compares her to the moon: "I do not say this / Merely because of her great renown, / But because her name is Lunete" ("little moon") (vv. 2414–16). She is described as an "attractive brunette," "wise and learned" (*sage*), as well as "shrewd" (*veziee*) and "knowledgeable" (*cointe*) (vv. 2417–19). Later (v. 4394), she is identified as one "whom Yvain had much loved" (for whom he had had great esteem); v. 4576 describes her as "joyful and happy" (*baude* and *liee*) at being reconciled with her lady. However, unlike the historical Marie de Champagne, the fictitious Lunete exists totally within the romance whose principal agent she becomes; Marie is the agent responsible for the inception of *Lancelot*, while Lunete bears responsibility for the carrying out of *Yvain*, and for its meaning.

Despite its apparently lackadaisical attention to the strict conventions of romance narrative construction—no prologue, no *sententia*-like initial statement, no authority or source cited—*Le Chevalier au Lion* has often been described as Chrétien's most carefully contrived romance. In addition to what Frappier and others have referred to as its stylistic harmony and beauty of language, *Yvain* (along with *Cligés*) is Chrétien's most self-contained narrative. It has a beginning, a middle, and an end: we are in no doubt that Yvain's story is over, that he and Laudine will live happily ever after. (Interestingly, Ulrich von Zatzikhoven's *Lanzelet* has a similar ending.) In contrast, *Le Chevalier de la Charrette*, *Yvain*'s "twin," not only was left unfinished by Chrétien, the story of Lancelot and the queen is itself by no means finished; what the *Charrette* recounts is merely an episode in a much longer story whose ending nobody can foretell. Formally, then, *Yvain* focuses on the ending (where Chrétien's name is finally revealed), whereas *Lancelot* emphasizes the beginning, with the involved prologue describing Chrétien's clerkly service to his patroness.

Other contrasts suggest themselves: the *Charrette* constitutes a lengthy meditation on *fin'amors*, the consequences of which it brings to their final conclusion. The story of Lancelot investigates—exemplifies—*fin'amors*, and, in the last analysis, describes how the values it contains are assimilated by its protagonist. It is the history of Lancelot's inner understanding. Both *Lancelot* and *Yvain* distinguish between vain public reputation and genuine chivalry, with the latter presented as flourishing only within the bounds of a couple united in love. Both knights have their hearts in the right place, but they must undergo a series of experiences in order fully to fathom the proper nature of the love they feel for their respective ladies. The fulfillment of Lancelot's love, however, depends entirely on his lady's dispensation of a sort of grace; Yvain's salvation is rather more a matter of his works. What his error and his madness teach him is that his knightly prowess, in order to be genuine and of real moral worth, must be gratuitous: it is to be put at the service of those who need and deserve it. The Lion Knight does not stand to gain anything from his acts of prowess, at least not immediately. Indeed, Lunete's final intervention is required in order for his reconciliation with Laudine to take place.[21]

Taken together, in their complementarity and in their differences, these two romances constitute Chrétien's most profound statement on the nature and the power of human love. They reaffirm the centrality to human experience of the couple of Man and Woman; they underscore the intimate linkage of *chevalerie* and *clergie*. Along with the *Conte du Graal*, the two romances are also very human—even humane—creations. Each is replete with humor and delightful linguistic play. History, *Yvain* seems to say, resides in the particular, in the real; meanwhile, the *Charrette* explores our capacity for transcendence, our longing for the absolute despite—perhaps because of?—the inevitability that this yearning will bring down upon our heads the full weight of tragedy.

Chapter 5

Myth and Spirituality: *Le Conte du Graal (Perceval)*

This romance opens with a 68-line prologue, the initial part of which contains a *sententia* ("He who sows little, reaps little, / but he who wishes to reap plentifully / casts his seed on ground / that will increase his fruit a hundredfold").[1] "Crestïens" sows his seed "in such a good place / that it cannot fail to be bountiful" (vv. 9–10), that is, for Count Philip of Flanders, his patron, a man more worthy than Alexander.[2] Unlike that of Alexander, Philip's generosity responds to the Gospel's command, "let not thy left hand know what thy right hand doeth" (Matthew 6:3). The left symbolizes vainglory, whereas the right hand stands for charity (*caritas*, "love"). Chrétien incorrectly attributes the identity of God and *charitez* to Saint Paul (v. 49)—the statement that "God is Love" was actually made in John's first Epistle (4:8)—but, assuming this was no blunder, his reason for doing so remains unclear. Count Philip, not Alexander, is the true practitioner of charity, and it is at his command that Chrétien has undertaken "to rhyme the best story / that has ever been told in [a] royal court" (vv. 64–65). This "is the *Story of the Grail*, / whose book was given him by the count" (vv. 66–67). *Sententia*, patron, authoritative source, author's name and his pride in his clerkly art—all the elements of the classic romance-type prologue are present here. To these, however, Chrétien adds a dimension hitherto unexplored by him—that of spirituality and of the Christian faith.

The Story: It is a beautiful spring morning in the Waste Forest (*Gaste Forest*)—a lyric time of birdsong and the awakening of life. A young man has decided to visit some harrowers working in his mother's freshly seeded fields. While he is busy practicing throwing javelins, he hears the clanking of armor and the beat of horses' hooves. The young man thinks that the noise they make must be of the devil. However, he is not afraid; he prepares to defend himself. Five knights pursuing another group of knights and three maidens suddenly appear. When he sees the maidens he finds them so beautiful that he believes they must be angels. And isn't the handsomest of the group God Himself? He falls to his knees, recites the Credo and all the other prayers he has been taught by his mother. The leader of the knights treats the innocent lad with courtesy. He wants to ask him directions, but the young man pesters him with wide-eyed questions about chivalry. Their conversation is both comic and touching. As soon as possible the lad wants to find the great king who dubs knights: his vocation is born. He may be boorishly innocent (*nice*, in Old French), but his sole ambition is to become a knight. He runs to tell his mother of his decision. She, who has lost her husband (the boy's father) and another son to chivalric combat, is distraught. Despite all her efforts to isolate her one remaining son, he too will take up knightly arms!

The lad barely consents to remain three more days with his mother; she prepares clothing for him (a simple shirt made of hemp and breeches cut in the Welsh manner). The young man leaves, after hardly paying attention to the last words of advice given to him by his mother, which can be summarized as (1) Help ladies and maidens in distress, but do nothing to displease them. If a maiden grant you a kiss, do not try to take more; if she wishes to make you a present of a ring, you may accept this present; (2) If you accept someone's hospitality do not tarry in asking your host's name; seek out the company of *prodomes*, that is, men of experience and wisdom, and heed their counsel; (3) Frequent churches and chapels in order to pray to Our Lord (to which the young man, who does not even know his own name, asks ingenuously: "Mother, what is a church?" (v. 555). As he rides off, he looks back and sees his mother fall down in a faint "as though she had died."

The aspiring knight's first adventure is called the "Tent Maiden." After riding for an entire day and spending the night in the forest, he continues his journey and spies a splendid tent that, because of its beauty, he thinks is a church. After dismounting, he enters the tent and he finds a sleeping maiden. She awakens, sees him, and, shivering with fear, begs him to leave immediately before her *ami* returns. "Not before you give me a kiss," he replies, and he forces her to kiss him, and finds her kisses far more pleasant than the bitter-tasting mouths of his mother's chambermaids; he also takes possession of an emerald ring. (He is merely following his mother's advice!) Hungry and thirsty, he gobbles down a meat pie and drinks a goblet of wine before taking his leave. The jealous *ami* returns, accuses the maiden of infidelity, and cruelly punishes her by forcing her to accompany him on foot, dressed in rags.

Our hero meets a charcoal-burner (whom he addresses as a nobleman!) who directs him to Carduel, where Arthur is holding court. Upon his arrival he encounters a knight in red armor; this knight had just come from the king, whom he had insulted before the count. Fascinated by the striking armor, the young man nevertheless hastens into the castle where he seeks out Arthur, who is lost in his thoughts over the recent intrusion of the Red Knight, who had behaved insultingly in the presence of the court and who had spilled a *coupe* of wine on Guenevere as he made off with this precious object. He demands to be knighted; Arthur does not respond. The youth betrays his impatience, but he finally gets the king's attention. Ever impatient, the young man demands to be dubbed a knight, and also to be granted permission to take possession of the Red Knight's arms. Kay intervenes with one of his sarcasms. As the new knight departs he salutes a lovely young maiden who smiles at him (she had never been known to smile before this time) and declares that no knight will ever surpass this young man in knightliness. Furious, Kay slaps her and kicks a jester into the burning fireplace. The youth does not react to these angry acts. He rides out of court; once again he encounters the Red Knight, whose armor he demands. The Red Knight strikes the young *valet* with his lance, and the younger man responds by throwing a javelin that pierces the Red Knight's eye, killing him instantaneously. Aided by the squire Yonet, he puts on the dead knight's armor and learns the rudiments of riding a horse fully armed. The grateful youth gives Yonet his first horse and asks him to return the king's *coupe*, as well as to inform the Smiling Damsel that he will avenge the insult inflicted by Kay. Meanwhile Arthur, pleased at being rid of the Red Knight, is disappointed that he did not succeed in keeping the new knight at his court for a longer time. He may be *nice*, but there is something extraordinary about him.

The *valet* rides until he reaches an estuary on the other side of which stands a magnificent castle; a *prodome* welcomes him, recognizing that he has still much to learn about knighthood. The *prodome* teaches him the art of knightly combat, and finds in his pupil a willing and naturally able subject. The young man, remembering his mother's advice, asks the *prodome* his name. It is Gornemant de Goort. The next day the youth thinks about his mother, worrying if her fainting had been caused by his departure (this is the first time he thinks about someone other than himself); he even considers leaving Gornemant's castle. However, he remains and is armed *chevalier* by his host, who proceeds to give him wise advice, which consists of not killing a defeated adversary if the adversary cries out for mercy; being courteously discreet, that is, holding his tongue; and avoiding ridicule by not quoting what his mother has told him at every opportunity. In essence, Gornemant seeks to inculcate in his young *protégé* the values and rules of manly *courtoisie*. The *prodome* superimposes upon the maternal principles taught to him by his mother a kind of masculine set of virtues. He has Perceval replace the rough clothing given to him by his mother with finer and more fashionable apparel.

Planning on returning to see his mother, the *valet* rides through the forest, where he comes upon another castle, located near the sea, at Beaurepaire. He decides to request hospitality there for the night. He pounds on the castle door, which is finally opened by four men-at-arms who lead him through the deserted streets and among the ruined houses of the fortified place, to the palace, where he is welcomed by a marvelously beautiful *châtelaine*. She seats him beside her on a bed draped in brocade and waits for him to speak. But, remembering Gornemant's advice, he keeps silent. Breaking with convention, she speaks to him; he learns that she is Gornemant's niece. Supper is served, but because of the dire straits in which the castle and its inhabitants find themselves, there is very little to eat. He goes to bed and sleeps soundly; meanwhile, his hostess, Blancheflor, is unable to rest. Her castle is besieged by Anguingueron, the seneschal of Count Clamadeu des Îles, who desires both Blancheflor and her lands. Unless the situation changes, she will have to surrender on the morrow. What if this newly arrived knight were to help her?, she asks herself.

Desperate, Blancheflor goes to the young knight's room; her tears dampen his face and he awakens. He learns of his hostess's plight, hugs her, and promises to help. He invites her to stay with him the night. She joins him in his bed, and "side by side, mouth to mouth" (v. 2045), they remain together until morning. The scene is tenderly *courtois*. (Chrétien is deliberately ambiguous as to whether the couple made love or merely indulged in bundling.)

Anguingueron is duly vanquished, and the victor sends him to the Smiling Damsel at Arthur's court, to be in "her prison" until such time as he will avenge her. Clamadeu is defeated in turn, and a merchant ship arrives with provisions for Beaurepaire; the inhabitants' joy is immense. Clamadeu joins his seneschal in the Smiling Damsel's "prison." Our victorious knight spends some time with Blancheflor, but the memory of his mother causes him to depart, not without promising, however, to return to Blancheflor whether he finds his mother living or dead.

While riding in the direction of home, our young knight never stops praying that he will find his mother in good health (vv. 2946–50). However, on the shore of a dangerously rapid stream he spies a boat carrying two men, one of whom is fishing. The fisherman offers him lodging, which he will find once he has climbed up a rock overlooking the river. At first our hero sees nothing, but then he makes out a tower, and at last an entire great castle. He hurries inside the courtyard, is relieved of his arms and horse, and is dressed in a costly mantle. Taken to the castle's hall, he discovers a white-haired *prodome* half-reclining on a bed: it is the same fisherman he had seen earlier in the day. The youth sits down beside his host, who presents him with a splendid sword—the gift of a "blond maiden" to her uncle, the Fisher King, the master of the castle.

A marvelous scene ensues. In the brightness of torchlight, a *valet* enters the hall carrying a radiantly shining lance from the tip of which there falls continuously into the *valet*'s hand a single drop of blood. The young knight desperately wants to ask his host the meaning of this wondrous spectacle, but remembering the advice of Gornemant de Goort, he refrains from doing so. Next comes a lovely young maiden carrying in her hands *a* "grail" (*graal*[3]); she is preceded by two male servants who carry candle-holders of "at least ten candles each," and a second maiden who conveys a carving platter (*tailleor*). The grail is of fine gold, ornamented with precious stones; it sheds a brightness that outshines all the other lights. Both lance and grail pass by the bed on which our knight is seated and head for a neighboring room. Despite his growing curiosity, our knight continues to heed Gornemant's advice to keep silent. A glorious meal is served to our knight and his host; the Grail Procession returns from the neighboring room. The young *chevalier* retires to bed, his questions neither posed nor resolved. He awakens the following morning to a deserted castle; the drawbridge is opened to him but nobody answers his shouted questions. After he leaves it, the castle disappears into the mists, as mysteriously as it had originally appeared.

Our knight meets a weeping damsel, who explains to him that her *ami* had been killed that very morning by a *chevalier*. She also tells him that the Fisher King is a maimed king (*mehaigné*), for he had been wounded years ago in a battle by a javelin that had pierced him between his haunches (or thighs—the manuscripts differ) and that is why, unable to ride or to hunt, he amuses himself by fishing. After listening to the young knight's tale of what happened in the castle, she scolds him for not inquiring about the Bleeding Lance or the Grail. His silence, she explains, is due to his sin in causing his mother's death. She turns out to be our hero's cousin. Furthermore, his new sword will break in battle and can only be repaired by a certain Trabuchet, who lives in a far-off land. When the maiden asks him his name, he guesses that it is Perceval the Welshman (*Percevax li Galois* [v. 3541]).

Saddened by the news of his mother's death, Perceval decides not to return to the Waste Forest; remorse is useless; he will embark on a course of action.

He meets a thin, wasted maiden, whose clothes are ripped and torn, and whose palfrey, obviously starved, is on its last legs. She advises Perceval to flee before the return of the Orgueilleux de la Lande, who is strong and will surely kill him. She is none other than the Tent Maiden from whom the naive young *valet* had stolen kisses and who is being punished by her jealous *ami*. The terrible *ami* appears suddenly, speaks most discourteously, and engages in combat with Perceval. Naturally, our hero wins, and sparing his adversary's life, enjoins him to make up for his cruelty to his *amie*, and to repair with her to Arthur's court. The defeated Orgueilleux de la Lande obeys these instructions scrupulously.

King Arthur, the queen, and their entire retinue leave Carlion to go in search of the mysterious knight who has sent so many vanquished opponents to the court. They set up camp in a field. Early the next morning snow covers the area. Perceval is nearby. As he rides toward the king's camp, he notices a flock of wild geese being chased by a falcon. One of the geese is wounded by the falcon and momentarily falls to the ground; three drops of blood trickle from her wound onto the snow. Perceval rushes to the site, but the goose has resumed her flight. He contemplates the three blood-drops on the snow; transfixed, he thinks of the coloring of Blancheflor,[4] and spends the entire morning in contemplation. Several squires from Arthur's camp notice him and inform one of the Round Table knights, Sagremor li Desreez, of his presence. With the king's permission Sagremor ventures forth to speak with Perceval, but, irritated by Perceval's failure to respond, seeks to unhorse him. It is Sagremor who meets with that fate. Next comes Kay, threatening Perceval. Coming momentarily to his senses, Perceval spurs his horse and meets Kay's challenge, unhorsing him too and causing him to break a shoulderbone. He plunges anew into his meditation on the blood-drops. Gauvain, Arthur's nephew, criticizes Kay for his discourtesy in disturbing the unknown knight so violently, and, despite Kay's sarcasm, undertakes to meet the new arrival. By this time Perceval has begun to come to—the sun has evaporated two of the three drops of blood—and he is able to respond positively to Gauvain's invitation to return with him to Arthur's court. Everyone is overjoyed, especially the Smiling Damsel, who has finally been avenged of Kay's insulting and painful slap. For the first time Perceval speaks with undisputed *courtoisie* in his exchange of compliments with Queen Guenevere. He has attained the status of a *chevalier courtois*—the level epitomized by his new friend, Gauvain; but, of course, we also remember that he is also something other than Gauvain.

That very evening everyone, including Perceval, accompanies Arthur back to Carlion. A brilliant and festive celebration takes place, contrasting with the former morosity of the court. However, on the third day the festivities are interrupted by the arrival of the Hideous Damsel, who does not mince her words in condemning Perceval for not having asked any questions at the Grail Castle. Had he done so, the *roi méhaignié* would have been cured and the king's land would have known a new peace and prosperity. Perceval's failure will surely bring about the death of many husbands, the orphaning of numerous maidens, and the devastation of much of the country. Perceval thereupon swears that he will not sleep two nights in the same place without first having solved the mystery of the Grail and of the Bleeding Lance. With this oath he forswears the worldly chivalry of Gauvain—the chivalry of tournaments and amorous dalliance—and he does so despite the Hideous Damsel's having told him that he has already lost his one and only chance. Perceval's knightly career will henceforth take place at least partially outside of the Arthurian world of the Round Table. The Hideous Damsel had proposed several "adventures" worthy of the best knights (Gauvain will choose to rescue the besieged Maiden of Montesclere, the most prestigious of the adventures described; Girflet will go to the Château Orgueilleux [Proud Castle]; Kaherdin will climb the Dolorous Mountain), but none of these interests Perceval.

At this point Perceval's story is interrupted by that of Gauvain (vv. 4715–6180).

Before Gauvain can leave for Montesclere, Guinganbresil bursts into the court, accusing him of having killed his lord by unchivalric means (that is, not properly challenging him). A duel between accused and accuser is arranged to take place within 40 days. Gauvain is thus sidetracked from going to Montesclere; he is also detained en route at Tintagel in order to participate in a joust on behalf of a very young, but flirtatious, maiden (the Maiden with Short Sleeves) to whom he swears (as he does to so many maidens and ladies) eternal service and affection. He wins and takes his leave. After spending the night in a religious retreat and hunting down a white doe (which he is prevented from killing), he arrives at a castle where a young knight invites him to stay, adding that he has a beautiful sister who will be very pleased to meet him. Gauvain is unaware that his host, the King of Esclavon, is the son of the man whom he is accused of killing traitorously; he is surrounded by people unfriendly to him. But the sister receives him well; he promises her his heart and his knightly service. While dallying with her and enjoying her kisses, Gauvain is recognized by a vavasor who denounces him. The whole town is up in arms. Gauvain and the sister prepare to defend themselves. Gauvain uses well his marvelous sword, Escalibor, and the maiden throws chessmen at the intruders! The situation is saved—somewhat humiliatingly for Gauvain—by the arrival of the defiant and insulting knight Guinganbresil, who challenges him to an individual combat; finally it is decided that a guest must never be mistreated by his host, no matter who he may be. Gauvain is freed, but only on condition that within one year's time he return to the king with the Bleeding Lance of the Grail Castle, for it is predicted that the Bleeding Lance will one day destroy the kingdom of Logres. Gauvain's hesitation at this point is understandable: Logres is Arthur's kingdom, and Arthur is his uncle. He accepts the condition, though, because it does not specify in his oath that he must present the Bleeding Lance to the king; he swears only that he will do his best to find it.

The tale now returns to Perceval. Five years have gone by, we learn, since he has been in a church "or adored God or His Cross" (v. 6189). However, nothing has interfered with his practice of chivalry; he has sent 60 knights as prisoners to Arthur's court during these five years. Then he encounters a party of knights accompanied by 10 ladies. They are walking barefoot and are wearing hairshirts. They are surprised to find Perceval fully armed and on horseback, and one asks him whether he believes in Jesus and in the "New Law." Perceval does not realize that it is Good Friday, "when one should weep for one's sins" (v. 6234). He asks the knights and ladies where they are coming from, and they tell him of a saintly Hermit who lives in this forest. Perceval weeps at this news; he too wishes to confess his sins.[5] Perceval arrives at the hermitage and a nearby chapel just as mass is starting. The Hermit hears his confession, which is detailed in the text and which includes his attribution of his failure to ask the proper questions during the Grail Ceremony to his sinful state. After learning Perceval's name, the Hermit explains that he has sinned by causing his mother such great sorrow at the time of his departure from her; the only reason he has so far been kept alive is due to his mother's having commended him to God. Perceval also learns that the Hermit is his mother's brother, as is the Fisher King; they are his uncles. He is told that the Grail serves the Fisher King's father, who is "so *espiritax* [spiritual, holy]" that his life is sustained by his eating a single Host. The Grail itself is a *sainte chose* (holy thing). Perceval's penance is (1) to attend mass daily; (2) to believe in God, love God, worship God; (3) to honor noble men and women, for respect is a sign of humility; and (4) to use his knightly talents in order to come to the aid of maidens, widows, and orphans. The Hermit asks him to spend the next two days with him, eating only what the Hermit eats—"chervil, lettuce, watercress, and barley and oat bread, with clear water" (vv. 6464–66). Perceval comes to understand the meaning of Good Friday; on Easter he attends mass and receives Holy Communion.

At this point the romance leaves off speaking about Perceval: "You will have heard a great deal / about my lord Gauvain / before I speak of Perceval again" (vv. 6476–78).

Verses 6479–9184 recount Gauvain's adventures. There is something pagan—mythologically "other-worldly"—about these strange and somewhat chaotic episodes through which Gauvain, perfectly *courtois* as usual, moves. After meeting up with a grieving *pucelle* and her seriously wounded *ami*, he crosses over into the dangerous Land of Galvoie, from which no stranger has ever returned. He reaches the outskirts of a castle, where he finds a damsel sitting under an elm tree. After a witty exchange of words, he agrees to fetch the maiden's palfrey from a near-by orchard. (He is told by a crowd of people that he has engaged himself in a pretty risky business.) He brings the horse back to the *pucelle* and tries to help her mount, but she refuses all aid, covering him with sarcastic remarks, and all the while showing off to him her tantalizing beauty. She tells him she seeks his shame; it is clear that she dislikes enterprising knights like Gauvain. Understandably, she is usually referred to as the *Male Pucele* (the Evil Maiden). Gauvain and the *Male Pucele* return to the damsel and her wounded *ami*. A villainous squire appears, full of insults; Gauvain takes his *roncin* (nag) away from him. After curing the knight's wound, Gauvain helps him on to his (Gauvain's) own horse, at which point, instead of gratitude, the knight—who, it turns out, is Greoreas, a *chevalier* whom Gauvain had humiliatingly defeated earlier—hurls insults at Gauvain and rides off, leaving Gauvain with the squire's nag. It is not difficult to imagine the sarcasms bestowed on him by the *Male Pucele*! The damsel and Gauvain reach a beautiful château whose 500 open windows reveal the presence of as many ladies and maidens. The *Male Pucele* invites Gauvain to get aboard a boat tied up to a stone pillar, declaring that his fate will be sealed if he fails to do so. Greoreas returns at this point; he and Gauvain join battle, and Gauvain wins. He takes back his noble horse. Meanwhile, the *Male Pucele* and the boat have disappeared.

Gauvain succeeds in bargaining his way to the beautiful castle; he exchanges his prisoner for passage across the river. The boatman offers him hospitality. The next morning Gauvain asks his new friend the name of the castle's lord, but the boatman does not know. He explains that in the castle there lives a very great queen, accompanied by her daughter (who is also a queen) and her lovely granddaughter. The castle was built especially for the queen; in it no knight may reside if he is cowardly, disloyal, or avaricious. It also shelters 500 *valets*—some of them rather old to be called *valets*—who are learning the martial arts. A number of widows and orphan damsels also dwell there. Everyone awaits the arrival of a knight who will find husbands for the orphans, who will restore their lands to the impoverished widows, and who will makes knights of the *valets*. Gauvain thinks he might just be the man to accomplish this marvelous adventure. He has the somewhat recalcitrant boatman lead him to the castle. They meet a rich and powerful one-legged man who is whittling a stick of oak with a penknife. After entering the splendid castle they come to a room that contains a magnificent bed—the *Liz de la Mervoille*—from which no person who sits or lies on it can ever get up. Despite the boatman's warnings, Gauvain, still fully armed, sits down on it. All of a sudden the windows open up and a torrent of arrows falls upon the bed and on him; he is wounded. Next, a fearsome lion comes to attack him; Gauvain slays the lion, cutting off his head and two paws. He returns to the bed. The boatman joyfully comes back to tell him that he has successfully undergone the required tests. The *valets* come into the room and offer Gauvain their services; a multitude of lovely damsels arrives, headed by a *pucelle* more beautiful than the others. They bow before him and, in the name of the queen, they render homage to him: he will be their lord and master. Gauvain is delighted. He has done well so far, but as matters turn out he fails to achieve any of the goals desired by the castle's inhabitants. He becomes a kind of prisoner, unable to leave the castle, surrounded by charming women.

When once he realizes the loss of his freedom, Gauvain is saddened. The beautiful *pucelle*—her name is Clarissant—takes pity on him and tries to cheer him. She informs her grandmother the queen of Gauvain's state of mind. The queen, dressed beautifully and with flowing white hair, visits him, inquires about King Lot and his sons (Gauvain is the eldest of these), about Arthur, Guenevere, and the knights of the Round Table. His mood improves. Festivities—a brilliant supper, dancing, flirting—ensue until Gauvain feels tired and goes to sleep in the Marvelous Bed.

Early the next morning, Gauvain looks out over the river and spies the *Male Pucele* followed by an armed knight. The white-haired queen reluctantly allows him to leave the castle, provided he does not reveal his name for eight days; he must return to the castle by nightfall. He and his horse cross the river with the boatman. Immediately he is attacked by the knight accompanying the *Male Pucele*; after a hard-fought combat he wins and sends the defeated knight—who had described himself as the guardian of the "ports of Galvoie" and who was probably the same man who had wounded Greoreas—to the care of the boatman. True to her character, the *Male Pucele* spares him none of her sarcasm. She defies him to accomplish what her defeated friend regularly did on her behalf, namely, to leap over the Perilous Ford on horseback in order to pick some flowers for her. Gauvain tries, but falls into the middle of the ford. His sturdy steed saves the day by swimming over to the other side, but exhausts himself in the process; Gauvain is forced to groom him (a task ill-befitting a knight). He then resumes his ride, but slowly, and encounters a handsome young *chevalier* with whom he participates in a very "courteous" conversation. The young knight tells him that the *Male Pucele* had lied in recounting to him how her *ami* had regularly jumped over the ford: no man has ever before come out alive from this test. He continues to speak ill of the devil-like *Male Pucele*. "I once loved her," he reports, but she did not reciprocate; "I loved her against her will, after having taken her from a lover [whom] I killed" (vv. 8520–23). Her real name is the *Orgueilleuse de Logres* (the Proud Maiden of Logres), and her intention was to have Gauvain die in attempting to leap over the ford. A frank and pleasant conversation between the young knight, whose name is Guiromelant, and Gauvain ensues. We learn that the beautiful château is called the *Roche de Champguin* (the Rock of Champguin), and that the main business of its inhabitants is the dyeing of textiles. The white-haired queen is Ygerne, Arthur's mother and Gauvain's grandmother. The other queen is Gauvain's mother; Clarissant is his sister. Gauvain is astounded; he had thought that his grandmother had died 60 years ago, and that his mother had died over 20 years ago. Guiromelant is in love with Clarissant, although he has never spoken directly with her. He hates her father, though, because he killed his own father; he also hates Gauvain because Gauvain killed one of his first cousins. Not knowing that he is talking to Gauvain in person, he confides a ring for her to Gauvain, with the message that he is confident in her love for him, and that were he to kill her brother, she would prefer that to his being even slightly wounded. Gauvain accepts to be the messenger. But then, at

Guiromelant's urging, he reveals his name. A duel between the two of them is arranged for one week hence.

This time Gauvain and his horse succeed in leaping over the ford. He meets a newly chastened *Male Pucele*, who tells him her story—a story of hatred for Guiromelant, who pressed her for her love after killing the knight she really loved. She confesses the anger and the violence of her language, and repents. She begs Gauvain to avenge her. Gauvain takes her with him back to the castle, where she is well received and soon joins the coterie of beautiful ladies and maidens there. He remits the ring and its message to Clarissant, who clearly is fond of Guiromelant. Meanwhile, the two queens, not knowing that Gauvain and Clarissant are brother and sister, seek to arrange a marriage between the two. Gauvain sends a message to King Arthur urging him to come with his full court to witness his upcoming duel with Guiromelant.

Gauvain dubs the 500 young and old *valets*. His messenger reaches Arthur's court. However, the king, who had just summoned all his barons, is so saddened that Gauvain is not there that he faints away; he does not hear a word of the message.

Chrétien's romance ends at this point.

It has been necessary to summarize *Le Conte du Graal (Perceval)* in greater detail than the romances we have studied previously because it is far more complex than the others, and because, just as *Érec et Énide* and *Cligés* both respond to one another as well as to the later romances of *Lancelot* and *Yvain* (and these two, in complementing one another, also respond to the first couple of romances), *Perceval* may be said to respond to the entire body of Chrétien's previous œuvre, in part by containing within itself the two stories of Gauvain and Perceval. One cannot hope to analyze *Le Conte du Graal* without first having mastered what is going on in the story. It is by far the most open-ended and the most intricately profound of Chrétien's narratives.

As is apparent from the discussions of the romances preceding *Le Conte du Graal*, Gauvain plays a significant role in all of them—the only one of Chrétien's *chevaliers* to do so. In *Érec et Énide* it is he who warns Arthur of the consequences of reviving the Custom of the White Stag; in *Cligés* he is the eponymous hero's uncle and the knight who jousts with him, proving Cligés's valor by fighting him to a draw; in the *Charrette* he is Lancelot's amiable rival in the quest for Guenevere; in *Le Chevalier au Lion* he is Yvain's closest friend and the person Yvain wants most to emulate, at least during the first half of the romance. (Also in the

Charrette, although it is Gauvain who accompanies the queen back to court, he claims none of the glory for himself in this exploit, even though Lancelot is not present at the time.) In both the *Charrette* and *Yvain*, despite his numerous virtues, Gauvain is depicted not so much as a failed knight as somehow wanting, especially when matters of love are involved. One cannot imagine Gauvain able to experience passion as Lancelot does; nor could he aspire to the sort of total union that Yvain desires with Laudine.

Le *Conte du Graal* carries this notion even further. Gauvain remains ever the perfect knight—worldly, well-spoken, handsome, and capable both in combat and in conversation with ladies or maidens. In a very real sense it is Gauvain that Perceval aspires to become after his initial encounter with the party of knights in the Waste Forest, and Perceval does not conceal his delight at meeting Gauvain after the episode of The Three Drops of Blood on the Snow. He willingly lets himself be led by Gauvain back to Arthur's courtly camp. For Perceval, clearly, Gauvain's example goes beyond mere ability to fight; in other romances by Chrétien, Gauvain stands for an ideal—the ideal of an essentially world-ly *courtoisie*, of a certain ideal of *courtoisie* about which Chrétien himself remains ambivalent. The term and some of the values it represents merit closer scrutiny.[6]

Like many other OF words containing the suffix -*ois(e)*, *cortois(e)* and *corteisie* have to do with behavior and, especially, with language. Like the English suffix -*ese,* as in *journalese*, -*ois* could be joined to virtually any adjective or noun in order to designate a peculiar jargon or type of behavior. Although we normally associate *cortois* with mid-twelfth-century attitudes toward love (as in *amour courtois*) or with the refined diction of courtly romance and courtly love lyric, the term occurs several times in such early documents as the *Song of Roland* (in the Oxford version, commonly dated around 1100), where it signifies "noble and genteel behavior and/or speech."

Being associated with speech and behavior, *courtois(e)* is to be identified with an individual's relationship to the Other: one speaks, or behaves, courteously, or, conversely, *dis*courteously. What one says and how one says it, like what one does and how one does it, may be judged positively or negatively, or (more exactly) *read*, by those to whom this speech and action are directed, as well as by those who are in a position to witness it.

Of course, what is read can also be misread, either deliberately or naively; furthermore, one can feign courtly speech and behavior in order to deceive the reader-interlocutor-witness. In numerous romances and love poems, ladies quite rightly often attempt to decipher whether the knight who seeks their love—speaking and behaving accordingly—is sincere or false. Discrepancies between what is said and what is genuine are not unusual. Ambivalences and ambiguities seem to characterize the courtly world and those who populate it. The world of *courtoisie* is a world subject to interpretation, with all the dangers and soul-searching and heartbreak that interpretation seems inevitably to entail.

However, despite the railings and the invectives of churchmen and other moralists who decried the mendacity of courtly lyric and romance narrative—especially the rhymed, poetic variety—it may safely be generalized that the Middle Ages in France, from the time of the establishment of the Capetian dynasty down to the decline of the Valois kings in the sixteenth century, constitute a period dominated by faith in *courtoisie* as a noble value—as something inherently *meaningful*, the achievement of which was to be striven for by those making up the aristocratic governing classes. *Courtois* diction and behavior were not invariably a mere parlor game; ramifications of courtly behavior and speech affected such matters as one's sense of identity, one's relationship with one's peers, one's nation, one's capacity for love, one's sense of mission in life. Also, courtliness furnished a marvelous place in which individuals and those who wrote poems and works in prose could study and celebrate human behavior at its most complex and significant, as well as its capacity for *dépassement*, or self-transcendence. This area is exquisitely explored by Chrétien in *Perceval*.

As was already noted, to understand properly this capacity would require a massive study of book-length proportions; merely touching on several significant points will have to suffice here. Before discussing Chrétien de Troyes's œuvre and, more particularly, *Le Conte du Graal*, it might be helpful to focus on *courtoisie* in another seminal OF work: the mid-twelfth-century *Roman d'Énéas*, a poem looked at earlier in this study, and one that was designed in part to deal with the historical transfer of political legitimacy and power from ancient Troy to Rome to Britain through the agency of Æneas's great-great grandson, Brutus. Like the *Perceval* which, like all of Chrétien's romances, it influenced, the *Énéas* is a rhymed romance narrative; and both possess an important historiographical dimension. Each is designed to appeal to an aristocratic public made up, presumably, of men and women; this audience is called upon to recognize itself in the characters whose actions and sentiments are deployed.

Readers familiar with the *Æneid* will recall that three major female characters play substantial roles in Æneas's story. These are Dido, queen of Carthage, whom Æneas surreptitiously abandons after enjoying her hospitality and love because his historical mission cannot be sacrificed to what is seen to be merely a dalliance, however deeply felt, and who commits suicide; Camilla, the warrior-princess (or *bellatrix*), Turnus's confederate, who, after effectively aiding her ally, is traitorously killed by one of Æneas's warriors; and Lavinia, the daughter of King Latinus, whom Æneas weds and with whom he founds the dynasty that will preside over the foundation of Rome. Virgil deems it essential to kill off both the passionate woman ruler (Dido) and the woman warrior (Camilla), whereas in Lavinia he retains, and celebrates, the prototype of the Roman *matrona*.

The *Énéas* poet neglects none of these three women. However, he endows each of them with characteristics that call upon his audience to recognize their autonomy as women and also their function, as individuals, in the various couples they form with, in the case of Dido and Lavine, Énéas and, in that of Camille, her ally Turnus. Thus, Dido's suicide is portrayed as pitiable because Énéas has behaved discourteously by jilting her in stealth; in large part he is to be blamed for her sad demise. But even more interesting to the present purpose is the character of Camille, the proud princess and warrior.

To be sure, the mid-twelfth-century audience was not unfamiliar with the ancient tribe of Amazons, nor are ladies entirely absent from the textual corpus of *chansons de geste*. In the *Song of William* (ca. 1100–50?), Guiborc, wife to Count William of Orange, mounts the barricades with her army of ladies to defend the city against Saracen attacks when William is detained in battle elsewhere. By and large, however, it is true that the idea of a woman knight—like the *Énéas*'s Camille—was fairly novel around 1150 or so. (Camille is an early literary forerunner of the historically "real" fifteenth-century Joan of Arc.) It was *courtoisie*, as well as certain interesting implications, that allowed this idea to be explored.

Let us take a brief look at the text in which, in typical OF *chanson de geste* fashion, Camille is being insulted and harangued by her adversary Tarcon; before coming to blows epic antagonists usually riled each other up by a series of violent insults:

> Vers Camille se retorna,
> molt fierement l'araisona.
> "Dame," fait il, "qui estes vos,
> qui ci vos anbatez sor nos?

Noz chevaliers vos voi abatre.
Feme ne se doit pas combatre,
se par nuit non tot an gisant;
la puet fere home recreant;
mais ja prodom o les escuz
par feme ne sera vencuz. . . .
Venistes ça por vos mostrer?
Ge ne vos voil pas acheter;
portant blanche vos voi et bloie;
quatre deniers ai ci de Troie,
qui sont molt bon de fin or tuit;
çaus vos donrai por mon deduit
une piece mener o vos;
ge n'en serai ja trop jalos,
baillerai vos as escuiers."
    Camille ot honte et molt grant ire
de ce que el li oï dire;
lo bon cheval broche et point,
vers Tarcon let aler, s'i joint.
Ele le fiert par grant vertu
desoz la bocle de l'escu;
d'or an altre li a brisié
l'auberc tresliz et desmaillié;
mort lo trebuche del destrier,
puis li a dit an reprovier:
"Ne ving pas ça por moi mostrer
ne por putage demener,
mais por faire chevalerie.
De voz deniers ne voil ge mie,
trop avez fait fole bargaigne;
ge ne vif pas de tel gaaigne;
mialz sai abatre un chevalier
que acoler ne dosnoier;
ne me sai pas combatre anverse."
                              (vv. 7061–125)

(He turned to Camille and addressed her very haughtily: "Lady," he said, "who are you, that you do battle against us here? I see you striking down our knights, but a woman should not do battle, except at night, lying down [on her back]; there she can defeat any man. But a bold man with a shield will never be defeated by a woman.

    "Let this arrogance be. Put down the shield and the lance and the hauberk, which cuts you too much, and stop exhibiting your prowess. That is not your calling, but rather to spin, to sew, and to clip. It is good to do battle with a maiden like you in a beautiful chamber, beneath a bed-curtain. Have you come here to show yourself off? I do not want to buy you. But nevertheless, I see that you are fair and blond. I have here four Trojan deniers, all of very good fine gold; I will give you these to have my pleasure with you a little while. I will not be too jealous of it, but will share you with the squires. . . ."

Camille was full of shame and very great anger at what she heard him say. She dug and spurred her good horse, letting it charge at Tarcon, and attacked him. She struck him with great strength below the boss of the shield. She shattered it from one side to the other, tore his hauberk, and stripped off its mail, throwing him dead from his charger. Then she said to him in reproach, "I do not come here to show myself off, or to indulge in debauchery, but to practice chivalry. I want none of your deniers: you have made a most foolish bargain. I know better how to strike down a knight than to embrace him or to make love to him; I do not know how to do battle on my back."[7]

Tarcon's behavior and his speech (though not his vocabulary) are utterly discourteous. No woman, least of all a woman of noble lineage,[8] ought to suffer such insults, even though she has taken up the manly profession of arms. To be offered money in return for her sexual services, to be told what her place is, and to be the object of scorn in this manner cannot be tolerated, either by Camille herself or by the audience listening to the story. In this fashion the idea of the *bellatrix*—an idea that was anathema to Virgil and perhaps somewhat strange to the *Énéas*'s audience—is rendered entirely acceptable, and we all cheer when Camille puts a definitive end to Tarcon's ranting. Meanwhile, by deserving to die at Camille's hands, Tarcon authenticates her knightliness. And if this notion is acceptable in a noble romance narrative like the *Roman d'Énéas*, the same notion acquires a certain legitimacy in its own right.

What was hinted at in the last passage is further developed in a second text from the *Énéas*. Here, Turnus, Camille's ally and friend, is lamenting the death of his former companion.

> *Tant estïez cortoise et bele,*
> *tant amïez chevalerie,*
> vos an avez changié la vie.
> *Ne fu femme de nul parage*
> *qui anpreïst tel vasalage,*
> ne qui de ce s'antremeïst.
> Molt m'a fet qui vos ocist;

> perdu an ai, por vostre mort,
> a toz tens mes joie et deport.
> Vos venistes por mon servise,
> si vos i estes del tot mise;
> males soldees an avez. . . .
> D'autres fames estïez flor;
> unques [N]ature, ce me sanble,
> dous meillors ne josta ansanble:
> si grant proëce o grant ce o grant bialté.
> Qui an voldroit dire verté,
> il sanbleroit que ce fust fable,
> tant par estoient dessanblable
> vostre valor et vostre aage,
> vostre avis de vostre corage.
> Vos estïez une donzelle
> *cortoise et avenanz et bele,*
> *si estïez hardie et forte.* . . .
> Ge ne sai mes que ge vos die,
> mais dolanz sui de vostre mort,
> ja mais ne quit avoir confort."
>
> (vv. 7365–426; emphasis mine)

(*You were so courteous and beautiful, and you so loved chivalry,* that you have lost your life for it. *There was never a woman of any lineage who did such heroic deeds or who so gave herself to chivalry.* The man who killed you has hurt me grievously. By your death I lost my joy and my pleasure. You came to serve me, and now are cut off from everything: you have been badly paid for your service. . . .You were the flower of all women; never, I think, did nature join together two better qualities: such great prowess with such great beauty. If anyone would tell the truth about it, it would seem like a lie, so wholly different was your valor from your youth, your judgment from your heart. *You were a courteous and gracious and beautiful damsel, and you were also brave and strong.* . . . I do not know what more to say to you, but I am so sorrowful over your death that I never expect to take comfort.")

The lament is couched in the purest sort of courtly diction. In fact, it comes close to replicating the language of the lover's lyric *planctus* (lament) on the death of his beloved. Language of this sort in the voice of a man underscores the feminine nature of Camille. She is *bele, avenanz,* and *cortoise*—the "flower of women." Turnus's words emphasize the deeply felt character of his grief. It is within this indisputably feminine context that, as Turnus puts it, Camille "loved chivalry." Never was woman born who was of such loyal *vasalage*, nor did Nature ever create so perfect a blend of *proëce* and *bialté* (qualities not usually associated with one another, of course). It is Turnus's *courtoisie*—especially when contrasted with Tarcon's *dis*courtesy—that allows the poem to resolve what in Virgil is presented as a contradiction, namely the young woman's physical charm and her proclivity to exercise the manly art of chivalric arms; and to elaborate a concept of friendship—*amitié*—between Man and Woman (a new form of couplehood) that is every bit as deeply felt as a love passion, but that does not involve a sexual attachment. This is a wonderful, and powerful, idea, of course, and, it is a new idea in the ongoing Western fascination with what constitutes the parameters of male-female relationships. Friendships of this sort—even as passionate as this one—had hitherto been pretty much the province of relationships between men.

There is, moreover, something androgynous in the description offered of Camille in Turnus's lament: Camille contains within herself fundamental traits normally associated with the masculine and others usually confined to the feminine: "Vos estïez une donzelle / cortoise et avenanz et bele, / si estïez hardie et forte." What is novel and significant here is that, in addition to offering the first example (to my knowledge) in a Western vernacular literature of the androgyne figure, these two sets of traits are neither mutually exclusive nor contradictory. Nor, as Camille represents them, are they in any manner reprehensible. Also, the conventions of romance *courtoisie* require a man like Turnus to speak in these terms of a woman like Camille; but it is this very requirement that engenders these interesting concepts.

The third text comes from the lengthy exchange between Lavine and her mother concerning love and, eventually, Lavine's preference for Énéas over Turnus. The mother, to whom the daughter appeals for instruction in the nature of love, plays out a power trip. She wants Lavine to choose Turnus over Énéas for reasons political and personal to her; she displays no interest in her daughter's feelings.

When it becomes clear that Lavine is not about to be convinced by her mother's admonitions and "logic," the mother reveals in full blaze her discourteous fury. She has recourse to rumor and slander in order to vilify, in the basest possible language, Énéas's sexuality and reputation.

> La reïne se porpensa
> et les sillebes asanbla.

—Tu me diz "E" puis "ne" et "as";
ces letres sonent "Eneas."
—Voire, dame, par toi, c'est il.
—Se ne t'avra Turnus? —Nenil,
ja ne avrai lui a seignor,
mais a cestui otroi m'amor.
—Que as tu dit, fole desvee?
Sez tu vers cui tu t'es donee?
Cil cuiverz est de tel nature
qu'il n'a gaires de femmes cure;
il prise plus lo ploin mestier;
il ne velt pas biset mangier,
molt par aimme char de maslon;
il priseroit mialz un garçon
que toi ne altre acoler;
o feme ne set il joër,
ne parlerast pas a guichet;
molt aime fraise de vallet;
an ce sont Troïen norri. . . .
Fille, molt as lo sens perdu,
quant de tel home as fait ton dru
qui ja de toi ne avra cure
et qui si fet contre nature,
les homes prent, les fames let,
la natural cople desfait. . . .
Se tu joïr vials de m'amor,
donc lesse ester lo traïtor
et t'amor torne vers celui
dont je te pri, se lai cestui;
cil te seroit toz tens estrange.
—Ge ne puis pas faire cest change.
—Ce que ge voil ne doiz amer?
—Nel puis an mon cuer atorner.
                    (vv. 8557–624; emphasis mine)

(The queen thought and assembled the syllables.
    "You tell me *E*, then *ne*, and *as*; these letters spell *Eneas!*"
    "True, mother; in faith, it is he."
    "And you will not have Turnus?"
    "No, I will never have him as my lord [husband], but I grant my love
to the other."
    "What have you said, foolish madwoman? Do you know to whom you

have given yourself? This wretch is of the sort who have hardly any interest in women. He prefers the opposite trade: he will not eat hens, but he
loves very much the flesh of a cock. He would prefer to embrace a boy
rather than you or any other woman. He does not know how to play with
women, and would not parley at the wicket-gate; but he loves very much
the breech of a young man. The Trojans are raised on this. . . . Daughter,
you have completely lost your senses, since you have taken as your love
such a man, who will never have a care for you, and who acts so against
nature that he takes men and leaves women, *undoing the natural union.* . . .
If you wish to enjoy my love, then let this traitor be. Turn your love
toward him of whom I spoke, and leave this other one, who would be a
stranger to you."
     "I cannot make this change."
     "You would not love him whom I wish?"
     "I cannot persuade myself to it in my heart.")

This attack on sexual activities that could well be considered as
against nature (*contra naturam*) and that incurred the full reprobation of
the church are here expressed as the articulation of a power-hungry
woman's spite, and consequently engage our sympathies on behalf of the
person attacked, namely Énéas, whether or not the charges are true!
This fact is all the more interesting in that the mother's accusations are
not entirely without foundation: Énéas's behavior with his friend Pallas,
like that of Achilles and Patrocles, is, so to speak, suspect. However, as
matters turn out, Énéas is genuinely in love with Lavine. His possible
homosexual behavior does not, finally, seriously conflict with his hetero-
sexuality. The poem raises in this fashion the issue of bisexuality, which,
of course, in terms of the either/or morality prevalent in the "official"
rule systems of the time becomes interesting and worth pondering. But
it is only the mother's total lack of *courtoisie*, as evidenced both in her
patronizing attitude toward her daughter and in her language, that permits this issue to be at all brought to the reader's attention.

     Clearly, it can be concluded—at least provisionally—that the exam-
ple of the *Roman d'Énéas* proves the existence of the closest possible affin-
ity between romance-type narrative and the ideal of *courtoisie* that does so
much to inform it. It may also be argued that Virgil's *Æneid* was palat-
able to a mid-twelfth-century French-speaking aristocratic audience only
to the degree that Virgil's poetic history could be plausibly recast into a
courtly mold.

     The narrative mode initiated by the *Roman d'Énéas* pervades most
subsequent medieval vernacular storytelling, including such works as

purport to be essentially historiographical in nature—that is, chronicles, biographies, genealogies, and the like. Without the courtly values they articulate, the *Grandes Chroniques de France* (begun in 1270 at the instigation of King Louis IX, and including a prologue that virtually replicates the *translatio imperii et studii* topic found in the front matter to Chrétien de Troyes's *Cligés*), Jean de Joinville's *Histoire de saint Louis* (1309), the undeservedly little-known fourteenth-century *Chronique de Morée* (ca. 1330), and the *Chronicles* of Froissart (ca. 1370–1400) would hardly have been conceivable. Indeed, at times it seems that the articulation of *courtoisie* is accorded greater importance by the authors of these historiographical works than fidelity to what actually took place. The question of historical accuracy deserves to be looked at; and *Le Conte du Graal* offers an indispensable development within this process.

It would useful at this juncture to record several uses to which Chrétien puts *cortois* and its congeners in his later romances. Verses 41–42 of the *Charrette*, for example, link *courtoisie* with praiseworthy language: "Mainte bele dame cortoise, / Bien parlant an lengue françoise" (Many a beautiful, courtly lady, / Speaking well in the French language). Elsewhere in that poem, being *cortois(e)* is associated with *sagesse*, with loyalty, proper upbringing, and nobility. Certain actions freely performed on behalf of others—some quite specific, others more adequately described as behavior—are identified as manifestations of *corteisie*. *Corteisie*, like *amor*, is identified as a "pure value" in vv. 4377–78: "Einz est amors et *corteisie* / Quanqu'an puet feire por s'amie" (It is, rather, love and courtesy, / Whatever one might do on behalf of one's beloved lady). A passage from the *Charrette* describing the (false) news of Lancelot's death to Queen Guenevere provides an interesting use of *cortois*. The news is identified as "not courteous," but her innately noble courtesy seems to provide her with the wherewithal to behave in public, at least for a while, as though this sad news did not affect her. Chrétien utilizes the conceit in order to underscore, litotes-fashion, the depth of the queen's passionate feeling for Lancelot:

> Et s'i estoit li deslëax
> De traïson plains et conblez,
> Qui molt laidemant a troblez
> Por Lancelot toz ces qui vienent.
> Por mort et por traï se tienent,
> S'an font grant duel, que molt lor poise.
> N'est pas la novele *cortoise*
> Qui la reïne cest duel porte;

Neporquant ele s'an deporte
Au plus belemant qu'ele puet.
(vv. 5204–13; emphasis mine)

(And among them there was also this wicked man / Full of betrayals, / Who has so much troubled / All comers about Lancelot. / They consider themselves to have been fatally betrayed, / And they lament their fate, for their anxiety is great. / The news is not *courteous* / That is brought before the queen; / Nevertheless, she behaves / As pleasantly as she can.)

The queen's self-possession thus allows her simultaneously to mask her grief (in public) and to express it inwardly, that is, *truthfully*, as the narrator relates it to us. The inwardness and the outwardness of *cortoisie* thus do not invariably mesh. Tensions result, and these are meaningful to *Perceval*.

At first glance it might seem odd that the *Charrette*, the so-called epic poem of courtly love, should contain but 15 instances of the words *cortois(e)* and/or *corteisie*, whereas *Yvain* offers 30 such instances, and *Perceval* some two dozen. These numbers are significant, but they must be understood, as in the *Roman d'Énéas*, within the context of a reading of the poems involved. Thus, *cortois* and *corteisie* appear six times in the initial hundred lines of *Yvain*, during the narrator's description of the "good old days" when, during Arthur's reign, love and courtesy prevailed, as they do no longer, in present times, and during the spiteful scene between Guenevere and Kay that gives the lie, in fact, to what the narrator had asserted. The narrator is very much under the sway of the courtly reputation of the Arthurian world—a reputation belied, of course, by what actually transpires after Arthur's surprising abandonment of his guests at table, and by the subsequent events leading up to Calogrenant's story. Enjoying the reputation for *corteisie* is consequently not the same as truly being *cortois*. As the romance progresses, however, *cortois* and its congeners more frequently come to bear upon the character trait that prompts a given character to say or do something admirable: the disjunction typifying the first part of the romance is replaced increasingly by the conjunction of courtliness with an example of courtly behavior. *Cortois* and *corteisie* are thus words (and values) utilized by Chrétien in *Yvain* in order to reflect the progress made by the narrator in both lucidity and honest reporting, and to differentiate between mere public reputation (which may mask falsehood, hypocrisy, or limitedness on the part of a given character) and the "real thing," which is not necessarily known and celebrated. This usage parallels beautifully, and exactly, the deportment of *messire* Gauvain, Yvain's friend and symbolic opposite. Thus, in *Le Chevalier au Lion*, while Yvain, known merely as the "Lion Knight," defends Lunete (whom Gauvain had sworn to protect), Gauvain is away, off in a storybook, participating quite ineffectively in the rescue of Queen Guenevere. Gauvain is but "famously" *courtois*, whereas, at this juncture, Yvain's real name is unknown and his *courtoisie* is a matter of various characters interpreting what the man whom they do not know as Yvain does.

Meanwhile, in the *Charrette*, Gauvain's *courtoisie* also possesses a skin-deep profundity. He would not be caught dead climbing aboard the cart. For him *courtoisie*—as reputation—constitutes an end in itself; it is consequently quite ineffectual when the chips are down. In contrast, Lancelot's unique fault lies in his residual concern for the reputational side to *courtoisie*; what is labeled *Raison* causes him to hesitate ever so briefly before getting into the cart. *Raison*, it may be concluded, argues the case for public renown and esteem, for *courtoisie* of the Gauvain type. Interestingly, the various *dames* and *puceles* whom Lancelot meets during his quest—including the Immodest Damsel with whom he had promised he would spend the night—and to whom he speaks quite bluntly, at times with an apparently studied indifference to the finery of courtly diction, all, without exception, appreciate his authentic devotion to womankind, which, in turn, has its source in his unswervingly faithful love for Guenevere, not in any recognizable courtly ideology. Lancelot's authentic and effective *courtoisie* thus corresponds to the values represented by *Amors*, not by *Raison*. It is significant that, in the *Charrette*, *Amors* is invariably depicted as feminine, while in *Yvain* the personification is at times feminine, at times masculine (Venus/Cupid). *Le Chevalier au Lion* comes very close to identifying the appearance (rather than the reality) of *courtoisie* with what is "reasonable," whereas genuine *courtoisie* (the hidden or not-always-apparent kind), deriving from Love, is not reasonable.

While not appearing once in *Lancelot*, the term *nice(s)* (boorishly innocent) occurs three times in *Yvain*. In two cases it is directly associated with *folie* (madness).[9] Its value is entirely negative. In *Le Conte du Graal*, meanwhile, the term (alongside *nicemant*) occurs on five occasions, and when applied to Perceval, it is three times associated with *folie* and once with *bestiax* (animal-like). His odd behavior is ascribed to the apparent fact that he is *fos et nices*; he embraces a damsel *nicemant*, and so forth. The word is used twice by the narrator and twice by Arthur; in both these last cases the king, admonishing Kay, explains that but for his being *nices* and ignorant of chivalry, the youth (Perceval) would be a fine knight[10]. *Niceté*, it would seem, is not a terminal, incorrigible defect. What Perceval lacks turns out to be a kind of social correctness.

Meanwhile, as in both *Yvain* and *Lancelot*, Gauvain virtually embodies social correctness; Perceval aspires to emulate him, although it is never stated that he wishes to learn *courtoisie*. However, his language has become *courtois* when, led to the royal court by Gauvain after the Blood Drops on the Snow episode,[11] he addresses Queen Guenevere:

> "Dex doint joie et enor
> A la plus bele, a la mellor
> De totes les dames qui soient,
> Tesmoinz de toz ceus qui la voient
> Et toz ceus qui veüe l'ont!"
>
> (vv. 4553–57)

("May God give joy and honor / to the most beautiful and best / of all the ladies in the world, / as all who see her or who / have ever seen her bear witness.")

What has happened here, and how has it happened? Clearly, Perceval is no longer *nice*. Has Gauvain's *courtoisie* rubbed off on him, like the lessons given to him earlier by his uncle, Gornemant de Gohort? But no hint is provided to support the assertion that Perceval is applying here courtesy lessons given to him by Gauvain or by anyone else. Nor is it anywhere stated that this *courtoisie* has entailed the abandonment of *all* the characteristics of *niceté*. On the contrary, Gauvain's desire to serve the maiden whose father has just described her as *nice chose et fole*—alleging that failing to do so would be churlish (v. 5326)—would seem to recognize that *courtoisie* and *niceté* are not on all counts to be opposed to one another. And if what is signified in Perceval's courtly speech to Guenevere is merely that he has attained Gauvain's "level" of courtly manners and language, then why do Gauvain and he diverge so totally in what occurs after each departs on his chosen quest—Gauvain, eventually, on that of the Bleeding Lance, Perceval on that of the Grail Mystery? To be sure, the romance is unfinished, but the reader is nevertheless left with the impression that Perceval will succeed in his mission while Gauvain will remain sidetracked. To adopt the terminology of the *Charrette*, Gauvain's *courtoisie* is reasonable; *niceté* and *folie* are totally eliminated in him—everything, including love, is game-playing.

Unlike Yvain, Lancelot, and Perceval, Gauvain has no history; he functions as a kind of reagent, or catalyst, in certain episodes, making up the story of others. In *Le Conte du Graal* Chrétien performs the tour de force of creating a series of Gauvain-centered episodes in which Arthur's noble nephew plays out adventures while retaining his catalyst-like nature. Chrétien composes a Gauvain-focused antihistory, which functions as a backdrop to the story of Perceval's painful growth in spirituality—the Good Friday episode at his uncle the Hermit's, his confession and absolution, and his solitary departure on his quest. Gauvain is a character in whom courtesy and prowess reside, whose very reason for being consists in incarnating these values in a platonically absolute manner. Therefore, as in the *Charrette* where he is contrasted with Lancelot, in the *Graal* he is frequently distinguished from Perceval in such a manner as to make him an essentially comic figure. He is "Mr. Courtesy." Meanwhile, Lancelot's *histoire d'amour* allows him to reach a level of *courtoisie* which, on occasion, appears to negate certain courtly values; and Yvain's arduous recovery of Laudine, his wife, causes him to abjure the seductions of Arthur's world in order to perform anonymous good deeds in a genuine service to women.

Like the seed referred to in the initial *sententia* of *Le Conte du Graal*, Perceval grows. The simile of growth, however, does not entail on the maturing plant's part an abandonment of its initial seedly nature. In the seed there exist potentialities that come to fruition without the seed's contents necessarily being shucked off. Perceval's *niceté* and *folie* are not so much replaced by his newly found *courtoisie* as they are subsumed into it, informing it, and stamping it as properly Perceval's—as an indispensable ingredient of his history. Furthermore, the young hero's attainment of *courtoisie* is not merely a prerequisite to his later spiritual conversion according to some kind of preestablished way: it is, rather, the prerequisite to his, quite personal, conversion. Perceval's *courtoisie* is decidedly not a game, whereas, in comparison, Gauvain's is perfectly gamelike. Perceval's history recounts his struggle to achieve the potential that he contains. For him, unlike for Gauvain, it is not simply a matter of being (or representing); it is a question of self-construction. He attracts our interest and sympathy in part because he is *nices et fos*. Furthermore, he listens and, especially in consequence of the Blancheflor episode, he reveals himself as capable of responding to what he hears. (In this fashion he resembles somewhat the Yvain of the second half of *Le Chevalier au Lion*, who also undergoes the experience of *folie*.) Perceval's *courtoisie* thus resides in his learned ability to respond to the Other—chiefly the feminine Other. His embarking on the Grail Quest is no more and no less than his response to what he now understands as the sense-filled mystery of that spiritual object.

In several significant ways, then, *Le Conte du Graal* constitutes a response to—or, a re-writing of—the anonymous *Roman d'Énéas*. Perceval resembles, yet is very different from, Énéas. Both heroes are engaged on an extraordinary quest, or mission: the founding of New Troy, the spiritual Mystery of the Grail. Both are the guests of beautiful, queenly hostesses—Dido and Blancheflor—who, to all appearances, love them and need them. However, whereas Énéas enjoys the pleasures of Dido's bed and her munificent hospitality only to slip away from her during the night in order to continue on his quest, Perceval's courteous response to Blancheflor's plaintive state brings about the restitution to her of her domain and, indeed, of her life. To be sure, Énéas is *courtois* to Dido, but only up to a point; his priorities are such that he cannot fully mean his *courtoisie*. Conversely, Perceval's courtesy to Blancheflor is genuine;[12] and consequently his acts of *courtoisie* with respect to her become inextricably woven into his quest for knighthood and for the solution of the Grail Mystery. That is why he sees Blancheflor's face mirrored in the three drops of blood on the snow in the episode just preceding his second introduction to Arthur's court and to Queen Guenevere.

There is something Gauvain-like about Énéas; Énéas is the actor whose job is to act out his peculiar historical role: Énéas is the founder of Rome much as Gauvain is Arthur's nephew—the paragon of knighthood, and the bearer of chivalric standards for the sake of the brotherhood of the Round Table. Nowhere is Gauvain's status—his mission—more completely delineated than in *Cligés,* whose eponymous hero is not only the son of Gauvain's sister but gains recognition of his own merit by measuring himself in a tournament during which he combats to a draw against his maternal uncle. Just as Gauvain is the Arthurian knight par excellence so Énéas is the founder of Rome, the New Troy. Because Gauvain is the exemplar of Arthurian knighthood, he, quite literally, is unable to accept the dwarf's invitation to climb aboard the infamous cart (as Lancelot, albeit after briefly hesitating, had done). Analogously, Énéas's mission required him to abandon Dido most discourteously, and even in a cowardly fashion, causing her unspeakable misery and leading her to suicide. And, unlike Turnus grieving over Camille's death, Énéas never repents—never even realizes—the horrible extent of the damage that his pursuing his cause has inflicted. Meanwhile, to be quite blunt about it, although no doubt sincere,

Énéas's love for Lavine turns out to be quite convenient for him: his eventual marriage to the daughter of King Latinus serves his mission. Chrétien's Gauvain, however, in *Yvain*, in the *Charrette*, and also in *Perceval* is consistently depicted as ridiculous when matters turn serious: (1) Yvain must learn not to emulate the Gauvain who, in a kind of parody of *courtoisie*, convinces his friend that in order to merit the love of his new wife he must leave her and gain fame in tournaments; (2) it is most decidedly Lancelot, the adulterous lover, who rescues the queen and restores order to the Arthurian world by bringing her back from the Kingdom of Gorre; (3) Perceval, we are sure, has grown sufficiently in knightliness and spirituality to resolve the Grail Mystery, whereas we doubt on the basis of what we learn during the Gauvain episodes closing the romance, whether this peerless knight will get very far in dealing with the Bleeding Lance, for he is too busy being the perfect knight. For Chrétien de Troyes, Énéas's Rome mission and Gauvain's model chivalry would seem to be perfectly equivalent: both—to quote the prologue to *Cligés*—are embers that have ceased to burn.

Of course, what is at issue here is a question of conversion—its presence in the character and chivalry of Perceval, its absence in Gauvain. *Le Conte du Graal* recounts the story of Perceval's education, and in telling this story Chrétien takes great pains to utilize the resources of the romance narrative form in order to distinguish between "outer" forms of learning and interiorized forms—appearances and realities. Thus, when Perceval applies literally what he has learned, say, from advice given to him by his mother or by Gornemant de Goort, he behaves laughably. It is only during his encounter with Blancheflor that his courtly chivalry begins to take on a reality that may properly be identified with him as a person, something akin to the experience of Yvain's madness. His *courtoisie* toward Blancheflor is not merely outwardly impeccable, it corresponds to something deep inside himself. It is a means, not an end, not a constraint, but a new freedom. Yet, viewed objectively, Perceval's service to Blancheflor is an act of folly.

In conclusion then, again with reference to the *Roman d'Énéas*, it is clear that just as the anonymous romancer to whom we owe this poem "translates," and reshapes, the *matière de Rome* provided by Virgil, Chrétien reworks, in *Perceval*, the *translatio* initiated by his romance forerunner. The example standing behind Chrétien's protagonists—and Perceval in particular—is provided by Turnus who, unlike Virgil's personage, undergoes after Camille's death a change so dramatic it deserves to be called a conversion. The death of his friend, who had united in her person the values of *bialté* and *proëce* and who was "une donzelle / *cortoise et avenanz et bele*, [and]. . . hardie et forte" (vv. 7409–11), situates whether he will succeed, or fail, in defeating Énéas in an entirely new perspective. He no longer truly cares. Serving his historical mission has entailed the loss of his *amie*, and this loss can never be made right. To be sure, on the morrow he will do what he can, but if he fails he will freely "surrender entirely the inheritance and the possession of it" (v. 7751). Paradoxically, Turnus's great loss has made him a stronger, more whole person, and these words articulate this new wholeness. Turnus has become profoundly *courtois*.

Is it not with this example in mind that we might better understand a line from the Crusade song by Conon de Béthune? I refer to the song "Ahi! Amours, con dure departie," in which the poet laments his having to leave his lady in order to serve the Lord in the Holy Land. He says, however: "Pour li m'en vois souspirant en Surie, / car je ne doi faillir mon creatour" ("For her I go off, sighing, to Syria, / for I must not fail my Creator"). He must not fail his Creator; consequently it is for her, his lady, that, truly, he departs, sighing, for Syria.[13] In the same sense, I believe, the *courtoisie* elicited in Perceval by Blancheflor marks the starting point of that process of authentic self-knowledge that will lead him back once again, after he has confessed his sins on Good Friday and attended mass, to the Grail Castle. From the Blancheflor episode on through Perceval's initial failure at the Grail Castle to the Blood Drops scene to the Hermit Episode, Chrétien amplifies on Turnus's conversion to authentic *courtoisie*. However, he endows it with specifically Christian values and depth, and, by a magnificent development, he invests Perceval's newly achieved *courtoisie* with spiritual resonances of world-historical significance that far surpass Énéas's mere founding of New Troy.[14]

The central meaning of OF *corteisie* is "gift," or "action freely performed on behalf of another." If we bear this definition in mind, certain lines of the prologue to *Le Conte du Graal* become clearer—specifically, the lengthy section comparing Alexander the Great with Count Philip of Flanders. Alexander was celebrated for his liberality and generosity (like Gauvain for his *courtoisie*), but Count Philip (like Perceval) is more authentically generous because in giving he is truly charitable. Alexandrine liberality is vainglorious—it serves the giver's reputation— whereas charity is hidden from the public view:

> Donc sachoiz bien de verité
> Que li don sont de charité

> Que le bons cuens Felipes done,
> C'onques nelui n'an areisonne
> Fors son franc cuer le debonere
> Qui le loe le bien a fere.
> Ne valt mialz cil que ne valut
> Alixandres, cui ne chalut
> De charité ne de nul bien?
>
> (vv. 51–59)

(Know truly therefore that the gifts / given by the good Count Philip / are gifts of charity; / for he consults no one / except his noble, honest heart, / which urges him to do good. / Is he not more worthy than / Alexander, who cared not / for charity or any good deeds?)

"Yes! Do not for a moment doubt it," says the narrator. Chrétien de Troyes's *Conte du Graal* embeds *courtoisie* in the fertile soil of Divine Love, and by so doing renews totally the romance of the Arthurian kingdom and, very importantly, its history.

The Perceval sections of *Le Conte du Graal* take the reader up to, and through, his conversion, that is, from his first seeing a party of knights in the fields belonging to his mother up to his post-Easter departure from the Hermit's refuge in the forest. Both the first and the last of these sections involve his meeting a party of knights. The first of these two parties is thus described: "He heard five armed knights / coming through the woods, / in armor from head to toe. / And the approaching knights' armor / made a great racket, / for the branches of oak and hornbeam / often slapped against the metal. / Their hauberks all clinked, / their lances knocked against the shields, / and the metal of hauberks and / the wood of shields resounded" (vv. 100–110). Perceval did not yet see the knights; he heard them. "But when he caught sight of them / coming out of the woods, / he saw the glittering hauberks / and the bright, shining helmets, / the lances and the shields, / which he had never seen before, / and he beheld the green and the vermilion / glistening in the sunshine, / and the gold, the blue, and silver: / he found it most fair and noble. / Then he said: 'Lord God, I give you thanks! / These are angels I see before me. / Ah! in truth I sinned grievously / and did a most wicked thing / in saying they were devils'" (vv. 127–41). In order to expiate this "sin," Perceval throws himself to the ground, quotes his mother as to one's duty to believe in God, and to adore, worship, and honor him (vv. 150–52). This is Perceval the *nice* whose actions and words are being reported. We, on the other hand, know better: these are but five knights riding through the forest together, all decked out in their armed splendor—impressive, to be sure, but decidedly not angels. It is amusing to us, and perhaps a bit touching, to witness the young Perceval responding in religious awe to this sight.

This initial encounter with knights begs to be contrasted with what happens during Perceval's second solo encounter with a party of knights (vv. 6204–97). We recall that five years have gone by during which our hero, quite alone,[15] has been accomplishing acts of chivalric prowess, sending "sixty worthy knights / as prisoners to King Arthur's court" (vv. 6199–6200). During this period, however, he had "so totally" lost his memory "that he no longer remembered God" (vv. 6183–84).[16] He had neither entered a church nor "adored God." While riding fully armed (like the knights of his first encounter) through a deserted area, he meets three "knights / and, with them, as many as ten ladies, / their heads covered by hoods; / they were all walking barefoot / and wearing hairshirts" (vv. 6208–12). The situation of the first episode is reversed here: it is Perceval, not the knights, who is dressed up in his knightly garb; it is the knights who wear, to say the least, substandard clothing, not befitting their station. Meanwhile, unlike the exclusively male company of the first episode, these knights accompany ladies dressed as they are, in sackcloth, one presumes, and hairshirts. Moreover, they are on foot, and barefoot at that, whereas both Perceval here and the knights of the first episode are on horseback. Also, in this second episode it is the party of knights and ladies—and they are authentic knights and ladies, despite their outwardly miserable appearance—who expresses astonishment, not the rustic-looking (but noble) youth of the first episode. They are "quite surprised / to find him [Perceval] fully armed / and bearing his shield and lance" (vv. 6212–13), since, for the salvation of their souls, they are doing "penance on foot / for the sins they had committed" (vv. 6217–18). They explain to Perceval that it is Good Friday, a day in which one does not venture forth armed. And then, in a beautiful turnabout of the roles played during Perceval's first encounter with knights when he prays and recites the Credo, here it is one of the knights who articulates the Credo, in vv. 6241–57, quite literally and almost completely.[17]

There can be no doubt that these two scenes are meant to be read against one another; they constitute both a parallel and a contrast. The Perceval of the second episode is (at least superficially) no longer *nice*. He has learned to be like Gauvain, so much so that the circumstances involved in his sending back 60 prisoners to King Arthur's court are not really worth telling—they would be boring, and, worse, irrelevant to his

history. He speaks with courtesy. Yet, just as in the first episode when the
youth understood that something was lacking—that, in other words, he
wanted to be a knight—so here too, in the second scene, he realizes an
insufficiency in himself. And he associates this insufficiency with sin, particularly with the sin of which he had been previously accused by his
cousin after leaving the Grail Castle, the sin of abandoning in so egotistical a fashion his mother to her death. But whereas he had been told by
the Hideous Damsel that he would never be given a chance to redeem
himself—he had let pass the occasion to ask the proper questions at the
Grail Castle—he had determined to try anyway. When Perceval learns
that this second party of knights (and ladies) had just come from the
dwelling of a saintly Hermit in order to ask forgiveness of their sins, the
news, we recall, makes him weep tears of contrition: his heart is ready to
receive God, a distinct parallelism is established between the Hermit's
refuge and the revelation in the initial episode of Perceval's encounter
with the five knights of the "king who makes knights" (v. 333), King
Arthur and his chivalric court at Carduel. As he had once before request-
ed directions to Arthur's court, so he asks here for directions to the
Hermit. But instead of embarking on an adventure, that is, *adventura*,
looking for things to happen (like the Tent Maiden), he has before him a
path—a goal and a way to reach it—with signs pointing out the correct
way. All he has to do is follow this path.

From a state of aimlessness and insufficiency—a state of being reflecting the vaguest sort of notion that all is not right—Perceval passes into a
condition of hope, of repentance, and of openness to God's love:
"Weeping he went toward the thicket, / and when he came to the hermitage / he dismounted and removed his armor" (6303–5). He is con-
scious of having sinned. His confession covers the following two points:
(1) his having not loved God nor believed in Him, and for having done
only evil; and (2) his failure to ask about the Bleeding Lance or who was
being served by the Grail, or to make amends for not having done this.
At the Hermit's request Perceval reveals his name, at which the Hermit
reiterates what had been told to him by his cousin, namely, that this failure was caused by the sin of his causing his mother to die of sorrow. The
Hermit further explains that it has been because his mother had prayed
to God to protect him that Perceval has been able to survive until now.
We are to understand that her love for God and for her own son prompted God to shower his love and protection upon Perceval. The Hermit
knows all about the nature of Perceval's folly because the rich king
served by the Grail is his brother and Perceval's mother was his sister.

The Grail, he adds, is a "sainte chose" and his brother is "so spiritual" that he requires no more nourishment "than the Host that comes in the [G]rail" (v. 6394).

Chrétien's Grail constitutes already the fairly advanced Christian-iztion of an item of Celtic mythology. As far as scholars have been able to determine, the Grail's capacity to provide abundant nourishment for the saintly recluse relates this household object to Bran's Horn—the Horn of Plenty.[18] We know moreover that this process of Christianization will undergo further developments in later works concerning the Grail: it will become specifically the Holy Grail; it will assume the (essentially feminine) vaselike shape of a chalice; it will be identified with the recep-tacle in which Joseph of Arimathea collected the blood of Christ. In short, the Grail will take on characteristics linking it specifically to the celebration of the Eucharist. These later developments render explicit what is, in large part, already present in the functions ascribed to the Grail in Chrétien's romance. Nevertheless, it is important to remember that in Le Conte du Graal, the Grail is not merely Christianized: it retains much of its Celtic mythological aura, and it applies brilliantly to the motifs of plenty versus famine, of nourishment versus starvation, of growth versus sterility, of sowing and reaping that permeate the romance. Chrétien makes sure that his reader/listener remains in the domain of narrative fiction, and to do so he retains, and utilizes, modern, that is, nonclassical, Celtic story material. This retention permits him to situate Perceval's conversion within the context of a chivalric story of adventure—the Adventure of the Grail; Perceval's coming to grips with his sinfulness and his reliance on God recharges his strength as a knight. Nowhere does the romance or, for that matter, the Hermit suggest that knightly prowess is futile. On the contrary, one leaves Perceval after his sojourn with the Hermit even more convinced that now his prowess has become, unlike that of the purely worldly Gauvain, genuine.

Perceval accepts the Hermit's strictures, which are: (1) he must start every day by doing penance in church, as early in the day as he can; (2) if mass has begun he must stay until it is completed, and in this way he will win "honor and paradise" (v. 6424); (3) he must actively believe in God, love God, and worship God;[19] (4) he must respect gentlemen and ladies, "because it is a sign of humility" (v. 6430); (5) he must be pre-pared to offer succor to maidens, widows, and orphans. These, of course, are all values of courtoisie, but of an informed courtoisie. These courtly val-ues are in and of themselves perfectly reasonable, but, in Perceval's case, they depend on an act of faith—in other words, on an act of folly, in the

positive sense ascribed to "folly" by the very model of one who has experienced conversion, namely, Saint Paul, the underlying spiritual presence
in *Le Conte du Graal*.[20]

Two Pauline texts bear quoting at this point in order to illustrate
what seems to me to be Chrétien's linking of Perceval's innate *niceté* with
folly. Thus, 1 Corinthians clearly distinguishes between nefarious worldly wisdom and affirmative folly:

> Nemo se seducat. Si quis videtur inter vos *sapiens esse in hoc sæculo, stultus
> fiat ut sit sapiens*; sapientia enim hujus mundi stultitia est apud Deum.
> Scriptum est enim: Comprehendam sapientes in astutia eorum. Et
> iterum: Dominus novit cogitationes sapientium, quoniam vanæ sunt.
> Nemo itaque glorietur in homnibus. (1 Cor. 3:18–21)

To be worldly wise requires an undoing—an active return to *stultitia*, or
foolishness—in order to become *sapiens*, that is, wise in the ways of God.
As has been noted repeatedly, Gauvain's worldly knightliness and *courtoisie* are ultimately vain, like Alexander's liberality, whereas Perceval's
natural *niceté*, combined with the maturity he learns from experience and
from the teachings of Gornemant de Goort (evidenced already in
Perceval's response to Blancheflor), must be recognized as the foundation
of the humility required to free himself from the trap of *astutia*.

The positive value assigned by Saint Paul to *stultus* and *stultitia* is
determined by its being placed in a context of worldly *astutia* or *sapien-
tia*. This valuing parallels the value attributed to Perceval's *niceté* as
opposed to Gauvain's worldly *courtoisie*. Negative "foolishness" is also
alluded to in 1 Corinthians (15:35–47, 51), as in the following passage,
which merits citation also for its explanation of spirituality (important
for the meaning of the Grail) and its use of seed/growth/fruit imagery:

> But some man will say, How are the dead raised up? and with what body
> will they come? *Thou* fool, that which thou sowest is not quickened,
> except it die: And that which thou sowest, thou sowest not that body
> that shall be, but bare grain, it may chance of wheat, or of some other
> *grain*: But God giveth it a body as it hath pleased him, and to every seed
> its own body. All flesh *is* not the same flesh but *there is* one *kind of* flesh of
> men, another flesh of beasts, another of fishes, *and* another of birds. *There
> are* also celestial bodies, and bodies terrestrial; but the glory of the celes-
> tial *is* one, and the *glory* of the terrestrial *is* another. *There is* one glory of
> the sun, and another glory of the moon, and another glory of the stars:
> for *one* star differeth from *another* star in glory. So also *is* the resurrection

of the dead. It is sown in corruption; it is raised in incorruption; It is sown in dishonor; it is raised in glory: it is sown in weakness; it is raised in power; It is sown a natural body; it is raised a spiritual body. There is a natural body, and there is a spiritual body. And so it is written, The first man Adam was made a living soul; the last Adam *was made* a quickening spirit. Howbeit that *was* not first which is spiritual, but that which is natural; and afterward that which is spiritual[?] The first man *is* of the earth, earthy: the second man *is* the Lord from heaven. . . . Behold, I shew you a mystery; We shall not all sleep, but we shall all be changed.

Sameness, difference, change—body and spirit—these are the themes touched upon here, in the context of life and death. Born in sin, all humans are flesh, but each person, like each star differing from other stars in glory and light, differs from all others. Each of us has been sown as a natural body; we are raised, through the grace of God, to being a spiritual body; our weakness is thereby transformed into strength. However, nowhere here is it suggested that our nature is discarded, or shed, like the snake's skin. As described here, our transformation—our conversion—consists in our "putting on" (*possidebit*) incorruption. This transformation, in life, signifies that we must be "steadfast, unmoveable, always abounding in the work of the Lord, forasmuch as [we] know that [our] labor is not in vain in the Lord" (1 Cor. 15:58).

Rather than renouncing his chivalric history, Perceval is enjoined by his uncle the Hermit to labor, as a knight, in the name of the Lord; his penance is designed to give him practice in doing so properly.[21] He is required to understand that although his sinfulness is part of his human condition, his sin with respect both to his mother's death and to his failure at the Grail Castle is not irrevocable, as he had earlier been told. He can undergo the strengthening of spirit of which Saint Paul has written, and for which, as we have stressed here, his *niceté* constitutes a native resource—to be integrated as a constitutive part of his newly mastered *courtoisie*, his chivalric prowess, and of his spiritual awareness. In a very real sense Perceval comes to know a new and genuine freedom.

The transformations under discussion in connection with Perceval are also applicable to the evolution in *clergie* that the *Le Conte du Graal* illustrates in respect to Chrétien de Troyes's narrative art and scope. The transformations may be indicated at many levels. Thus, the extraordinarily beautiful human *amor* felt by Lancelot for Guenevere, which that protagonist learns to understand in all its implications during the history of his rescue of the queen, is, in *Le Conte du Graal*, transformed into the *caritas*—the highest form of love—according to which Perceval learns to govern his life. The true sense of knightly mission, which Yvain finally grasps after his earlier worldliness and his madness, is transformed by *Le Conte du Graal* into a veritably cosmic chivalric goal that is intimately linked to the story of human redemption. Chrétien prepares the way here for subsequent romance developments of that story which, through the Adventure of the Holy Grail, the Arthurian world and all romance history will be vindicated.

Pervading *Le Conte du Graal*, as it does the entirety of Chrétien's œuvre, is Chrétien's overriding interest in two basic matters: the education and development of the youth to manhood;[22] and the mysteries surrounding the—to him—essential relationship of Man and Woman, or, as the issue is put today, the "masculine" and the "feminine." These are fundamental romance issues; consequently they entail the overriding question of the suitability of romance narrative for their examination and exposition. For, despite our emphasis on moral and spiritual themes, Chrétien was essentially an artist. Thus, *Érec et Énide* already explores in romance form the education-in-marriage, and the renewal-strengthening of love, of a young prince who, with his wife, receives a royal crown inherited from his deceased father at the conclusion of the narrative. *Cligés* analyzes the extraordinary transformative power of art, exalting the *translatio* of *clergie* from Greece to Rome to France. Here again Man and Woman are depicted in their relationship to one another and to this art: the narrator of *Cligés* can be said to mirror the power of Fénice's loyal servant and confidante, Thessala. His verbal artistry corresponds—even responds—to her magical illusionary powers. *Yvain* illustrates the married couple as the place where authentic *chevalerie* can be deployed; the knight achieves full and independent selfhood as a knight when he willingly quits the unreal world of Arthurian games and comes to dwell in the City of his Lady. All of these young romance heroes—and Lancelot may be included among them—learn to be what they become, largely through the agency of their relationship to a woman.

As we have observed, fertility and fecundity—associated with the sowing of seeds and growth—constantly reappear in various episodes and images in *Le Conte du Graal*. In a quite genuine sense Perceval restores a kind of fertility to Blancheflor's lands in ridding them of the dangerous Count Clamadeu des Îles and his wicked seneschal. Abundance for the inhabitants of Blancheflor's castle is the result of his intervention. We are inevitably reminded of Yvain, who, after his reconciliation with Laudine, will, surely, reinstate peace to her land and subjects by defending them properly against those who dare disturb the cursed Magic Fountain. The springtime planting and harrowing with which *Le Conte du Graal* opens suggests the return of the fertile season—of growth and a future harvest. Perceval learns that the knight who resolves the mystery of the Grail will restore the health of the wounded monarch and, in so doing, bring back fertility to the Grail kingdom. There exist clear analogies between this restoration of fertility to a kingdom deprived, so to speak, by accident of it through the crippling of its reigning monarch and, in the *Charrette*, Lancelot's restoration of a proper order to an Arthurian kingdom dispossessed of its queen because of the king's bungling. Thanks to Lancelot Guenevere returns to where she belongs, and order is restored. Finally, common to *Perceval* and all the previous romances of Chrétien de Troyes is the notion that the knightly hero learns to accept freedom and to take charge of—as well as responsibility for—his own destiny. This is what, with Énide's help, Érec does; it is true of Cligés (although in many respects *Cligés* too remains a special case), it is true of both the protagonist and the narrator of *Yvain*. This is perhaps the principal meaning of Lancelot's finally grasping the totality of Love; he becomes a kind of outlaw. And this is very specifically the case of Perceval as he rides off, away from his uncle's hermitage. Nowhere, however, in Chrétien's œuvre does fecundity loom so large as in *Le Conte du Graal*. One merely takes for granted that the union of Érec and Énide, of Cligés and Fénice, and of Yvain and Laudine will be blessed with children; offspring, however, will hardly be the fate of Lancelot and Guenevere, an issue to be profoundly explored later on in the *Prose Lancelot*. *Perceval*, consequently, constitutes a departure from Chrétien's earlier production.

The children to be born to the aforementioned couples obviously concern those couples, or at most, from a "historical" point of view, possess a dynastic importance. Their significance is lesser than the cosmically relevant motif of fecundity developed in the *Graal*. It is therefore legitimate, especially in consideration of Chrétien's proclivity to write responses to other works, to make new poems out of old poems, to renew the *matières* that provide him with "inventions," to wonder as to what text or body of texts Chrétien might have had in mind with respect to the issue of fertility. I believe that *Le Conte du Graal* constitutes Chrétien's final, and most profound, response to the *matière* of Tristan and Iseut.

The circumstances of Perceval's childhood and youth resemble in some respect those of Tristan: both are fatherless; both stem from noble roots; both live in isolation far from civilization. Both have immense natural talent and are amenable to training. Both are, and to a considerable degree remain all their lives, outsiders—Tristan resides at King

Mark's court, but he never becomes of this court, despite the fact that Mark is his dead mother's brother and that he loyally serves his uncle. The *Tristan* story is not, properly speaking, Arthurian, although some versions (such as Béroul's) have King Arthur appear in Cornwall, at Mark's court, for example, on the occasion of Iseut's judgment.

In the Béroul *Tristan et Iseut* fragment there is, as in both *Yvain* and *Perceval*, a hermit, Ogrin, who lives, like Perceval's uncle, far from the madding crowd, and who has a reputation for holy wisdom. But Ogrin, whom the lovers visit twice, once before the effects of the Magic Potion which caused their passion for one another to wear off, the second time afterwards, becomes essentially the means by which the lovers, who wish to return to the courtly life, succeed in their purpose. To be sure, Ogrin speaks to them of repentance, but, unlike in *Le Conte du Graal*, one has the impression that his words constitute a mere formality. In essence, the lovers never change; they remain stuck in their situation—a situation that leads them irrevocably to their deaths.

The great Middle High German romancer Gottfried von Straßurg, whose *Tristan* is presented as a "translation" of the OF version attributed to Thomas,[23] makes much of the association, in the lovers' story, between love and death.[24] Two brief quotations from Gottfried's prologue will suffice to establish this connection:

Now we hear too much of one opinion, with which I all but agree, that the more a love-sick soul has to do with love-tales the more it will despond. I would hold with this opinion but for one objection: when we are deeply in love, however great the pain, our heart does not flinch. The more a lover's passion burns in its furnace of desire, the more ardently will he love. This sorrow is so full of joy, this ill is so inspiring that, having once been heartened by it, no noble heart will forgo it! I know as sure as death and have learned it from this same anguish: the noble lover loves love-tales. Therefore, whoever wants a story need go no further than here.—I will story him well with noble lovers who gave proof of perfect love:

A man, a woman; a woman, a man:
Tristan, Isolde; Isolde, Tristan.

And:

This is bread to all noble hearts. With this their death lives on. We read their life, we read their death, and to us it is as sweet as bread.
Their life, their death are our bread. Thus lives their life, thus lives their death. Thus they live still and yet are dead, and their death is the

bread of the living.
   And whoever now desires to be told of their life, their death, their joy,
their sorrow, let him lend me his heart and ears—he shall find all that he
desires![25]

   The world of *Tristan et Iseut* is for all intents and purposes godless; it is
unrelentingly Celtic—Cornwall, Ireland, Brittany—in geography,
topography, and mythology. It is replete with potions, charms, dragons,
and various forms of magic which retain their power and which exercise
the imagination. Although Thomas and others attempted to import this
Celtic world into the courtly milieu of later twelfth-century England and
France, it remained far less domesticated, say, than the legends concerning Arthur and the Round Table. Iseut, quite clearly, belongs to a lineage
of druid-style sorceress-princesses and queens exemplified by her mother. The couple of Man and Woman, which had so fascinated the twelfth
century and vernacular literature from at least the times of the *Life of
Saint Alexis* and the early troubadours, is here bound to a destiny of passion and suffering marked by an unremitting fatalism. As Denis de
Rougemont has pointed out, it was with the *Tristan* story that the irre-
sistible myth of romantic love—the term he gave to the kind of love
unbreakably linked to death—crashed like a tidal wave upon the
Western consciousness, where it lives, commanding as ever, in our nov-
els, films, and soap operas.[26]
   In this type of *amour passion* the Self loves itself as it pleases to see, or
find, itself reflected in the Other. One is reminded of Érec's stupefaction
at first viewing Énide in her father's courtyard—the exact point at which
the sort of self-indulgence that will eventually lead to the criticism levied
against him by his fellow knights for his loss of *chevalerie* commences.
This brings about Énide's sorrowful and guilty lament, as well as Érec's
eventual redemption.
   Whereas in the first four romances of Chrétien de Troyes heroes and
the couples of which they are a part work their way out of the *Tristan*-
like situation in which they find themselves—even Lancelot, who brings
Guenevere back to Arthur, and does not run off with her, as Tristan and
Iseut do, to some distant forest retreat—in *Le Conte du Graal* what
Gottfried had called the breadlike sweetness of *amour passion* is revealed
to be a handful of bitter-tasting ashes. What Perceval learns is, to
rephrase Shakespeare, that love is not love which is not infused with the
transformative, life-giving power of charity—that is, with the love of
God. Whereas *Tristan* is a depiction of the unavoidable omnipotence of
fatality, *Perceval* constitutes a paean to the freedom which God in his love

has granted us. The *Graal* rejects the celebration of death, especially the kind of "immortality" which, as Gottfried has put it, was enjoyed after their death by the "perfect" lovers, Tristan and Isolde, in the memories of those who live now, and suffer, as they did. As I have tried to show here, *Le Conte du Graal*, Chrétien's greatest masterpiece, composed in all likelihood in the last years (or perhaps months) of his life, when the author himself was not far from death, is a hymn to life. It is a serious work, and a funny work too, one full of tears and of smiles—a work of very great artistry by an artist in full possession of his art and wits. The *Graal* overflows with mystery, but it eschews the tricky obfuscation that is necessary to make the *Tristan* story work; it is a supremely wise poem.

Appendix

A Note on *Philomena* (*Ovide moralisé*) and the Lyric Poems

Philomena

In the prologue to *Cligés*, Chrétien de Troyes lists, in addition to *Érec et Énide*, a number of titles of works that he says he composed before undertaking the romance at hand. Among these works is one to which he gives the title "de la hupe et de l'aronde et del rossignol la muance" (vv. 6–7; "the transformation of the hoopoe, the swallow and the nightingale"), a short narrative poem adapted from Ovid's *Metamorphoses* (VI, vv. 426–674). This is the only apparent one of Chrétien's several adaptations of Ovidian texts into the vernacular to have survived.

It does not exist, however, as an independent work, as do certain other brief OF Ovidian-type narratives like *Piramus et Tisbé* and *Narcisus*. "De la Hupe"—or, as it is more commonly known, *Philomena*[1]—was incorporated into a vast compilation of shorter fictions known as the *Ovide moralisé* (end of the thirteenth century, or more probably from the very beginning of the fourteenth century).[2] The attribution of *Philomena* to Chrétien de Troyes has been disputed, but since both before and after providing the text of this poem in his *Ovide moralisé* the compiler/author declares quite firmly that he is doing no more than "translating" Chrétien, it seems likely that the work mentioned in the *Cligés* prologue is substantially what he provides.[3] In fact, such revisions of Chrétien's original as can be substantiated are rather slight—some changes in vocabulary, a few examples of retouching—especially when one thinks, say, of the prose recasting of the *Charrette* inserted at the midpoint of the *Prose Lancelot*. Medieval notions of fidelity to texts being copied or reworked differ totally from our post–printing press values: more often than not, fidelity to one's model required drastic revision.[4]

The Story: Pandion, the king of Athens, has two beloved daughters, the eldest of whom, Procne, he gives in marriage to Tereus, king of Thrace. After a wedding in which numerous signs of misfortune manifest them-

selves, Tereus takes his wife home. Itis, their son, is born. Five years go
by. Procne wishes to see her younger sister, Philomena, and, in order to
bring this sister back with him, Tereus sets sail for Athens. He meets the
young woman and falls madly in love with her. Pandion regretfully gives
permission to Philomena to depart with Tereus. As soon as his ships
arrive at the shore of Thrace, Tereus convinces Philomena to accompany
him to a lonely house in the midst of a forest. There he declares his love,
and, paying no attention to Philomena's refusals, he rapes her, and cuts
out her tongue so that she might not tell what happened. He leaves her
in the house, under the guard of a peasant woman. Returning home,
Tereus, feigning grief, announces to Procne that her sister has died.
Grieving mightily, Procne sacrifices a bull to Pluto in order that her sister's soul rest in peace. Meanwhile, Philomena weaves the tale of her
misfortune in a tapestry and, eventually, succeeds in conveying her message to Procne. The older sister takes vengeance on her husband by hid-
ing Philomena in the palace and by serving up to Tereus the decapitated
body of their son, Itis. Philomena appears, hurling the bloody head at
the rapist. Deprived in this way of any vestige of humanity, the three
characters at this point are transformed into birds: Tereus, a hoopoe,[5]
Procne, a swallow, and Philomena, a nightingale.

   In retelling this Ovidian tale, Chrétien is undoubtedly putting into
practice what he had learned to do in school: imitate the ancients
according to certain canonized rules of imitation in favor in medieval
cathedral schools from the later eleventh century down to his own day.
He puts his "art," that is, his mastery of the craft of *clergie*, on display for
all to admire. Thus, at the instant in which Tereus falls prey to his passion for Philomena, whereas Ovid had been satisfied to compare her
beauty to that of nymphs, Chrétien furnishes a canonical description of
the girl's charms, beginning with her hair and continuing down to her
feet. Chrétien compares the arduousness of his literary task with those
faced by the great *clercs* of antiquity: Plato, Homer, and Cato. Not only
is Philomena physically perfect, she possesses a truly aristocratic taste for,
and mastery of, such games as chess and the art of falconry. She is an
accomplished musician, and a writer of verses. She excels so wonderfully
in literary composition that she would be qualified to open a school! In
refusing to accede to Tereus's advances, Philomena employs to perfection
the arts of *disputatio* and dialectic.
   Two points deserve to be made with respect to this youthful work of
Chrétien. The first is that *Philomena* illustrates fully Chrétien's proclivity

to provide a narrative setting for the articulation of values he holds dear. Rendering Ovid's tragic story into Old French also furnishes him with the opportunity to speak the praises of the clerkly arts. Philomena's mastery of these and other noble arts forms part of her beauty, her attractiveness, and the sympathy she is meant to elicit in Chrétien's public. Already in this early schoolbook-like exercise, Chrétien is giving voice to a value—a kind of narrative *san*—which remains invariably present throughout his vast œuvre: the essential nobility of *clergie*. One remembers: (1) Érec's donning a robe decorated with the figures of the *quadrivium* at his, and Énide's, coronation, as well as Chrétien's celebration of *conjointure* in the prologue to *Érec et Énide*; (2) the proud articulation of the *translatio* topic in the prologue to *Cligés*, and that romance's consistent praise of the values of *clergie*; (3) Chrétien's declaration of clerkly service on behalf of Countess Marie de Champagne in the Prologue to the *Charrette*—a service paralleling Lancelot's chivalric service to Guenevere; (4) Yvain's defense of Lunete against her evil-speaking detractors, along with the narrator's growth in clerkly reporting; and (5) Perceval's deepening abilities in the use of language, his gradual assuming of responsibility for his own story, and his spiritual maturation.

The second point is also significant. In *Philomena* the values of *clergie* are associated with a woman. Philomena is consequently a forerunner of such indisputably clerkly figures as *Cligés*'s Thessala and *Yvain*'s Lunete. (In several important respects she also foreshadows such "doctors of love" as Énide, Guenevere, and Blancheflor.) In its feminine shape *clergie* requires the protection and love of male *chevalerie*; this lesson is most forcibly put in *Le Chevalier au Lion* when Yvain, in Gauvain's absence, successfully takes up Lunete's cause, with the satisfying result that, in so doing, he prepares the way for his reconciliation with Laudine. Tereus, of course, is the knightly betrayer of women, with disastrously tragic results; he fails to live up to the ideals of *chevalerie*, and hence totally disturbs the order of things. He does what Méléagant would have done had Lancelot not been there to stop him.

Reading *Philomena* after having familiarized oneself with Chrétien's subsequent romance œuvre is convincing of the steadfastness of his beliefs and values. *Philomena* possesses a certain programmatic character with respect to what will come. In Chrétien de Troyes we have not only a supreme artist in romance narrative, but also we find manifest in him a keen critical consciousness, a powerful defender of the sort of enterprise for which he engaged his life. Only the *Lais* of his probable contemporary, Marie de France, approach the work of Chrétien de Troyes in its near-perfect blending into a new *san* of storytelling and a critical sense of the importance of clerkly activity in the vernacular.

The Lyric Poems

About all that seems to be certain in the case of the attribution to Chrétien de Troyes of several lyric poems (or *chansons courtoises*) is that the likelihood of his having composed some of these is quite high. Until fairly recently, most scholars agreed that only two surviving poems could be assigned to Chrétien with any certainty. The most recent editor, Marie-Claire Zai, has suggested that four such songs might plausibly be attributed to him.[6]

The fact that Chrétien did compose courtly songs has considerable historical interest. Given the time frame of his poetic flourishing, his having done so would make of him one of the first, if not the first writer in Old French to imitate the Old Provençal lyric troubadours—a courtly *trouvère*. And since courtly songs typically involve love—*fin'amors*—and constitute instruments for the analysis of the poet-lover's feelings both toward his beloved and toward those who stand in the way of his fulfillment (the *losengiers*), his early interest in troubadour lyric announces his lifetime fascination with the wellsprings of the human heart, particularly in the domain of love. One may also rightfully link the utilization of lyric motifs and sentiments in *Le Chevalier de la Charrette*, which depicts the ineffable consummation of Lancelot's and Guenevere's love according to the format to be found in the lyric *aubade* (or *alba*),[7] to his experience as a lyric *trouvère*. It is important to remember that Marie de Champagne, his patron, was the daughter of Eleanor of Aquitaine, herself the granddaughter of the first known troubadour, William IX, duke of Aquitaine; Eleanor was steeped in Old Provençal culture, especially poetry, and her court was famous for its hospitality to troubadours. She transmitted these tastes to her daughter, Chrétien's patroness.

Both poems of certain attribution are composed according to techniques frequently used by troubadours. Thus, the first ("Amors, tençon et bataille") comprises six stanzas of eight heptasyllabic lines, rhyming *a b a b b a b a* (the shape is that of a chiasmus, an ornamental figure much used by Chrétien); the second ("D'Amors, qui m'a tolu a moi") is made up of six stanzas containing nine octosyllables each. Both adopt the Old Provençal *cobla doblada* form, that is, stanzas 1 and 2 form a pair, rhyming identically, followed by stanzas 3 and 4, and so on. Echoes of the great troubadour Bernard de Ventadorn ("Quand vey la lauzeta mover"), have been detected in the second of Chrétien's songs. The compositional art is thus fairly sophisticated, if not particularly inspired. Both poems develop, as would be expected, lyric commonplaces. "Amors, tençon et bataille" laments that Love unjustly wars against his "champion," the poet-lover, but expresses the latter's resolve to continue loving despite this injustice, even though no recompense can be expected. "D'Amors, qui m'a tolu a moi" is also a complaint: the Lady remains cold to the poet-lover's feelings, and yet he will remain faithfully in love with her.

An interesting allusion to the *Tristan* story is made in stanza 3 of "Amors, tençon et bataille."[8] Even though such allusions are hardly uncommon in the troubadour and *trouvère* lyric, its appearance here tends to support the hypothesis of the veritable obsession felt by Chrétien for the story of Tristan and Iseut, especially given the likelihood that Chrétien composed his songs during the "experimental" days of his youth. One is struck by the somewhat didactic, or clerkly, tone of this stanza: the kind of philtre-induced passion enjoyed (and suffered) by Iseut and Tristan is not to be associated with the genuinely felt, nonnarcotic kind of love felt by the poet-lover. His love is predicated on his "refined" (that is, tender and "courteous") heart and on his "good will" (that is, discriminating freedom and resoluteness)—elements opposed to what caused the downful of Tristan and his paramour. If, as at least it seems possible, Chrétien wrote this song at about the time he was working on the Ovid translations, it could be said that what he means by *fins cuers* and *bone volentez* is precisely what is is lacking in the violent, destructive passion characterizing Tereus's attraction to Philomena. Tereus is entirely bereft of a refined heart and of good will. He behaves like a rutting animal while he wears a king's crown and possesses the human ingenuity necessary to be deceitful.

Fins cuers and *bone volentez* continue to be constitutive of love as expounded in Chrétien de Troyes's romances. Each of Chrétien's protagonists undergoes a process of deepening his understanding of truly courteous refinement and good will. And, as in *Le Conte du Graal*, this understanding eventually acquires an important spiritual dimension. No two knights could be more unlike each another than Tereus and the Perceval who takes leave of his Hermit uncle.

One is strongly tempted to see in this extraordinary contrast—and the aforementioned reference to *Tristan*—an important feature of the *translatio* so fulsomely praised by Chrétien. Great ancient and master though he was, Ovid was a pagan poet from Rome, the "live coal" of which has long since burned itself out; *clergie* is at present to be found in (Christian) France, where may God grant her a long and happy sojourn (*Cligés*, vv. 40–44).

Another lyric commonplace—that of resolute chivalric service without a hope of recompense—which is articulated in "Amors, tençon et bataille"—also becomes one of the central themes of Chrétien's narrative work, in *Lancelot* and *Yvain* especially, and also, centrally, in *Perceval*. Whereas the "normal" Arthurian knight seeks renown and glory, the three knights just named must learn that worldly renown cannot be the goal of genuine *chevalerie*. Even Lancelot must do penance for having tarried ever so briefly before getting into the infamous cart. Yvain and Perceval learn to rid themselves of the Gauvain model of knightliness. Perfection in chivalry is attained by the knight who acts not only in accordance with God's will, but who acts, finally, for God.

The surviving minor works of Chrétien de Troyes thus constitute useful and, if they are as youthful as they appear to be, prescient commentaries on the values explored and proclaimed by the five great romances. They consequently deserve something more than purely bibliographic mention in a study of Chrétien's narrative creativity.

Notes and References

Chapter 1

1. I have chosen the Modern French form of his name in preference to the Old French "Crestïen(s)," or the anglicized form, "Christian." American scholars appear to prefer "Chrétien," while their British counterparts tend to use "Crestïen" (often without the diæresis).

2. In large part the person of the twelfth-century vernacular writer was less interesting to contemporaries than the processes of composition and writing (*clergie*) within which he or she functioned. This is why writers like Wace, Chrétien, and Marie de France define themselves above all in terms of their craft in whatever autobiographical statements they choose to make.

3. For three and one-half decades the standard study of Chrétien's background and work has been Jean Frappier's *Chrétien de Troyes: l'homme et l'œuvre*, Connaissance des Lettres, no. 50 (Paris: Hatier, 1957; rev. ed., 1968); I refer to the 1968 edition, hereafter cited in text as Frappier 1968. This work is translated by Raymond Cormier under the title *Chrétien de Troyes, the Man and His Work* (Athens: Ohio University Press, 1982). A more recent synthesis is Douglas Kelly, ed., *The Romances of Chrétien de Troyes: A Symposium*, The Edward C. Armstrong Monographs on Medieval Literature, no. 3 (Lexington, KY: French Forum, 1985); hereafter cited in text as Kelly 1985. This work is written jointly by D. Kelly, Edward J. Buckbee, Michelle A. Freeman, Matilda T. Bruckner, Karl D. Uitti, Rupert J. Pickens, and Alfred Foulet. For other studies of Chrétien and his work, see the Bibliography.

4. For example, during the 1950s and early 1960s, interpretations of the Grail Procession in Chrétien's *Conte du Graal (Perceval)* led several scholars on both sides of the Atlantic to posit that Chrétien was a converted Jew; this position was forcefully combated by scholars unconvinced by the reasoning employed. Tempers rose and much ink was wasted during this controversy.

5. Chrétien de Troyes, *Le Chevalier au Lion (Yvain)*, ed. Karl D. Uitti (with Modern French translation by Philippe Walter), in Daniel Poirion, ed.; *Œuvres complètes de Chrétien de Troyes*, Bibiothèque de la Pléiade (Paris: Gallimard, 1994), v. 6820; hereafter cited in text by verse number. Translations mine unless otherwise noted.

6. There has been some discussion as to whether *Del roi Marc et d'Iseut la blonde* might not correspond to the now-lost *Ur-Tristan* whose existence, which at present seems to many quite doubtful, was proclaimed by nineteenth- and early twentieth-century scholars. It is true that Chrétien's entire œuvre betrays a virtual obsession with aspects of the *Tristan* story, but that very fact,

it would seem, militates against his having composed a "complete" version of that story. More logically, his *Del roi Marc* constituted the first of his many commentaries on the implications of the *Tristan* legend. It would appear more likely that *Del roi Marc* was a short narrative poem, perhaps only somewhat longer than the *Chèvrefeuille* of his great contemporary, Marie de France. It might have told, for example, how a bird carried to King Mark a strand of Iseut's blond hair.

7. Each of these narratives has been preserved in a number of thirteenth-century manuscripts; some codices contain the entirety of Chrétien's œuvre, as we will discuss later.

8. Interestingly, Chrétien never provides the title of *Cligés*. His prologue tells us that he will recount the story of a "young man who in Greece was of the lineage of King Arthur," that is, Cligés, the protagonist. In this otherwise very literarily explicit tale, the absence of a title verges on being a provocation!

9. *Erec und Enide*, vol. 3 of Christian von Troyes, *Sämtlichen erhaltene Werke*, ed. Wendelin Foerster (Halle, Germany: Max Niemeyer, 1890; Amsterdam: Éditions RODOPI, 1965); *Cliges*, vol. 1 of Christian von Troyes, *Sämtlichen erhaltene Werke*, ed. Wendelin Foerster (Halle, Germany: Max Niemeyer, 1884; Amsterdam: Éditions RODOPI, 1965); *Le Chevalier de la Charrette (Lancelot)*, ed. Alfred Foulet and Karl D. Uitti (with facing page Modern French translation), Classiques Garnier (Paris: Bordas, 1989); *"The Story of the Grail,"* or *"Perceval"*, ed. Rupert T. Pickens (with facing page English translation by William W. Kibler), Series A: Garland Library of Medieval Literature (New York and London: Garland, 1990). These editions are hereafter cited in text by verse number. Unless otherwise noted, English translations are mine.

10. "Crestiiens," with two *i*'s, is the same as "Crestïens." Foerster's double *i* and the diæresis used by other editors merely mark the syllabic, vocalic quality of the *i*; the name is trisyllabic.

11. *Li Torneimenz Antercrit*, ed. Georg Wimmer, *Ausgaben und Abhandlungen aus dem Gebiete der romanischen Philologie*, 76 (Marburg: Elwert, 1888), v. 1339; hereafter cited in text by verse number. English translation mine unless otherwise noted.

12. Enemies of courtly romance narrative—and there were many of these, especially during the opening decades of the thirteenth century—also referred to Chrétien or to his work as to be avoided. One sage adviser writes (as quoted by Kelly 1985, 24): "Leissiez Cligés et Perceval, / Qui les cuers tue et met a mal, / Et les romanz de vanité" (Set aside *Cligés* and *Perceval*, / For they kill hearts and corrupt them, / And all romances of vanity).

13. Countess Marie was well known as a participant—indeed, as a leader—in the courtly circles of her time. She figures as an important character in Andreas Capellanus's *De Arte honeste amandi* (ca. 1180s), a treatise on noble love, and in a lyric song by the aristocratic *trouvère* Conon de Béthune. Her maternal great-grandfather was William of Aquitaine, the first-known troubadour.

14. Benoît de Sainte-Maure, *Le Roman de Troie*, ed. Léopold Constans, vol. 1, Société des Anciens Textes Français (Paris: Firmin Didot, 1904), vv. 13; Wace, *Roman de Rou*, ed. A. J. Holden, vol. 1, Troisième Partie, Société des Anciens Textes Français (Paris: Picard, 1970), vv. 1–6; Chrétien de Troyes, *Cligés*, v. 28.

15. A not infrequent topic in twelfth- and thirteenth-century debate poetry is that articulated by two ladies who are loved, respectively, by a *chevalier* and a *clerc*. Which of the two has the better lover? Since the composition of poetic debates was largely the province of clerics, it is not difficult to guess which one most commonly wins the contest. The very terms of the debate reinforce, however, the connection between *chevalerie* and *clergie*.

16. For a pioneering study of Chrétien's critical terminology, see F. Douglas Kelly, *"Sens" and "Conjointure" in the "Chevalier de la Charrette"* (The Hague: Mouton, 1966); hereafter cited as Kelly 1966.

17. The terms *Franceis* (French) and *Franc(s)* (Frank[s]) are used interchangeably in the *Song of Roland*; Charlemagne is depicted there as the (i.e., "French") king and "our great emperor" (MS Digby 23, line 1). The "Charles" of the *Roland* thus "comprises" both the Carolingian dynasty and its Capetian successor.

18. Marie de France also distinguished between *sen* and *sens*; compare vv. 16 and 20 of the prologue to her *Lais*. In v. 16's "lur sen," *sen* refers to the "meaning" or "direction" placed by the ancients in their works; the moderns have the job of glossing the ancients in order to restore what is present but not understood in their works. *Sens* in v. 20 refers to the moderns' "subtlety" of "understanding," which stands them in good stead as they attempt to undo the damage to ancient works caused by the ravages of time. Later writers and scribes, for grammatical reasons and because of the semantic closeness of the two nouns, frequently conflated, or otherwise confused, them. (Kelly 1966 does not distinguish between these terms.)

19. Marie de France is quite explicit in this latter regard. Her prologue to the *Lais* begins by citing the obligations placed upon those whom God has endowed with "good eloquence." Later on (vv. 23–27), she speaks of the benefits of study (that is, Chrétien's *painne*) and of willingly undertaking a serious clerkly job of work ("entendre / A grevose ovre comencier"); her *entendre* is closely related to Chrétien's *antancïon*.

20. *Adnominatio* is a rhetorical figure that repeats the root part of a word but varies its desinence, for example, *Romam vado, Romanus sum, Romæ cor meum est*, "I am going *to* Rome, I am Rom*an*, *to* or *of* Rome is my heart." Chrétien employs this figure frequently, as he does, also, other figures like chiasmus. See chapter 3 for further discussion on this topic.

21. Chrétien seems here to be echoing Heloise in one of her personal letters to her lover-husband Abelard, when she declares that she would rather be Abelard's harlot (*meretrix*) than wife to the emperor of Rome. Marriage as contract or as political alliance was abhorrent to Heloise. In Chrétien's romances—

except for Fénice's union with Alis—marriage is invariably a matter of love between the spouses. Thus, Énide is designated as Érec's "wife and beloved" (*espouse et amie*).

22. Also, in this romance Arthur's worth as a chivalric husband is, at best, highly problematic; he blunders repeatedly, to a virtually criminal degree.

23. Clairvaux, the site of the abbey founded by Saint Bernard, is located in the *département* of Aube, of which Troyes is the prefecture. Bernard was very active throughout eastern France, especially in Champagne, attending synodical and other meetings at, among other locations, Troyes and Rheims.

24. A dimension of sanctity adheres to "coupling." Here are some words attributed to Christ by a late-twelfth-century metrical version of the Bible: "Dicit enim quod carne duo reputantur in una, / Dimittique patres, *copula sancta facit*" (He says that the two be recounted as forming one flesh, that he renounce his parents, that he constitute a *holy coupling*), in *Evangelium Ægidi* (vv. 1679–80): *Aurora Petri Rigæ: A Verse Commentary on the Bible*, ed. Paul E. Beichner, Publications in Medieval Studies, no. 19, pt. 2 (Notre Dame, Ind.: Notre Dame University Press, 1965), 576. One finds no mention of "*copula sacra*" in Matt. 19:4–10, or Mark 10:7, where Jesus is depicted as quoting Gen. 2:24–25 on the marriage of man and woman.

Chapter 2

1. The vital importance of medieval copyists and commentarists in the preservation of Latin antiquity has not always been adequately acknowledged by post-Renaissance scholars who all too often describe themselves as diligent restorers of proper texts—texts "corrupted" by their medieval predecessors. Yet, the preservation of much of the classical corpus is owed to the handiwork of medieval scribes and commentarists.

2. Quoted by Edmond Faral, *Les Arts poétiques du XIIe et du XIIIe siècle: Recherches et documents sur la technique littéraire du moyen âge*, Bibliothèque de l'École des Hautes Études, Sciences historiques et philologiques, 238 (Paris: Champion, 1923), 99–101. Note that this passage does not call attention to specific canonical writers, but focuses instead upon writing itself as the product of eloquence.

3. By and large, scholars of the eleventh, twelfth, and thirteenth centuries made little or no distinction between poetics and rhetoric. The arts of grammar and of rhetoric formed the basis of medieval poetic practice as well as theory. Poetics per se did not constitute one of the curricular arts.

4. Thus, while Continental Europe underwent the violence of invasion during the centuries preceding Carolingian times (eighth and ninth centuries) and literary culture suffered an almost mortal decline, ancient learning was preserved, largely, first in Ireland and then in Britain. Charlemagne's invitation to English and Spanish scholars was of enormous significance to the Carolingian Renaissance of the late eighth century.

5. Numerous books and monographs have been devoted to twelfth-century Latin literature and its many representatives. A useful general study is that of J. de Ghellinck, S. J., *L'Essor de la littérature latine au XIIe siècle*, 2 vols., Museum Lessianum (Brussels: L'Édition Universelle, 1946; Paris: Desclée de Brouwer, 1946); hereafter cited in text. On the general issue of the cultural and historical importance of medieval Latinity, see Ernst Robert Curtius, *European Literature and the Latin Middle Ages*, translated by Willard Trask (New York: Pantheon, 1953). Alongside the de Ghellinck essay, the standard reference work on twelfth-century Latin literature is the monumental *Geschichte der lateinischen Literatur des Mittelalters*, vol. 3, *Vom Ausbruch des Kirchenstreites bis zum Ende des zwölften Jahrhunderts*, by Max Manitius, revised by Paul Lehmann (Munich: C. H. Beck'sche Verlagsbuchhandlung, 1931). Of general use also for English-speaking readers is F. J. E. Raby, *A History of Secular Latin Poetry in the Middle Ages*, 2 vols. (Oxford: Clarendon Press, 1934).

6. J. de Ghellinck points out that many of Alain's arguments contain the expression "quibus auctoritatibus et rationibus probatur quod . . ." (by which authorities and reasons it is proved that . . .), that is, by a double appeal to a literary-styled "authority" and to a more Scholastic kind of "reason" (de Ghellinck, vol. 1, 83).

7. Like the *trivium* itself, logic followed grammar, the basic subject. R. W. Southern's characterization of Berengar of Tours, who, like Bernard of Chartres, would have described himself as a grammarian, bears quoting here: "He was interested in the meanings and derivations of words, in the relation between language and reality, and in the rules of eloquence. . . . That he was a fanatical speculative grammarian, anxious to push the conclusions of his subject as far as possible and to apply them to the clarifying of dogma, there can be no doubt" (*The Making of the Middle Ages* [New Haven and London: Yale University Press, 1953], 198–99; hereafter cited in text). Berengar may be seen, then, as a kind of transitional figure between the literary-minded Bernard and the logician Abelard.

8. The term *amour courtois* was coined by the French philologist Gaston Paris in the early 1880s, in a three-part, lengthy essay on the *Chevalier de la Charrette*, entitled "Études sur les romans de la Table Ronde" (in *Romania*, 10 [1881]: 465–96; 12 [1883]: 459–534; 16 [1887]: 100–101). He goes as far as to characterize Chrétien in this romance as "the epic poet of courtly love." Gaston Paris documents his argument with numerous references to Andreas Capellanus, whom he sees as having codified the "rules" of courtly love. Since his day, the debate over the supposed "reality" of courtly love has engaged the attention of many scholars, for and against. Was Andreas serious in his treatise, or was he ironic? Much of Andreas's work appears to have been composed tongue-in-cheek, and it does not seem right to read into it a modern ideological, or programmatic, statement. Nevertheless, in the refined, courtly circles of Marie de Champagne, love, and woman's importance to its definition, were of primary importance; and what those of the twelfth century called *fin'amors*

(refined love) was undeniably present as an ideal both of sentiment and behavior that deserved to be striven for, along with the attention and respect of noble gentlemen and ladies.

9. In the *Historia calamitatum* Abelard uses precisely these metaphors. He describes himself as quitting the service of Mars for that of Minerva, as "arming himself" with the weapons of dialectic, and as "winning trophies" in diverse arguments and disputes. He understood the *disputatio* as a variety of tournament. See *Historia calamitatum: Texte critique avec une introduction*, ed. J. Monfrin (Paris: Vrin, 1978), 63–64; hereafter cited in text.

10. The motif of lovers/spouses united in the same tomb after their death is not infrequent in twelfth-century OF literature. Certain versions of *The Life of Saint Alexis* mention that the saint and his bride, who had not consummated their marriage in life, shared a common bed in the tomb and enjoyed "great joy" in heaven. The *Liebestodt* of Tristan and Iseut is recognized by King Mark, who orders that the dead lovers be buried together; he plants a rosebush at their grave. The OF *Piramus et Tisbé*—a translation from Ovid's *Metamorphoses* composed during the 1160s—also tells of the youthful lovers who are entombed together by their repentant parents.

11. Peter the Venerable articulates this joy to the disconsolate Heloise in his beautiful letter of condolence: "Therefore, my illustrious and most dear sister in the Lord, this man to whom you joined yourself after your bodily union, with the more powerful and the better bond of divine love, this man with whom and under whom you have served God—I declare—is now cherished by God in His lap, in place of you, or like a replica of you, and at the Coming of God, to the sound of the trumpet and the voice of the archangel proclaiming God's descent from Heaven, God will restore him to you, through His grace, having reserved him for you" [translation mine] (from *The Letters of Peter the Venerable*, ed. Giles Constable, vol. 1 [Cambridge, Mass.: Harvard University Press, 1967], 307–8).

12. Given the extraordinary proximity of the Paraclete to Troyes (less than a dozen kilometers), and the fame of Abelard and Heloise (a fame, or notoriety, that resulted in the continued destruction of Abelard's writings), it is quite inconceivable that Chrétien de Troyes did not know their story. Peter Dronke has adduced convincing evidence that the story had already made its entry into twelfth-century Latin literature through a dream-vision poem composed ca. 1142 and entitled *Metamorphosis Golie episcopi* (in imitation of Martianus Capella's *De Nuptiis*) with which Chrétien might have been familiar. See Dronke's *Abelard and Heloise in Medieval Testimonies* (Glasgow: University of Glasgow Press, 1976), 16–31.

13. It is worth noting that also by around 1100 the Old Provençal tradition had begun to define itself; narrative works like the *Boethius* fragment and the extraordinary *Life of Saint Fides*, both dating from the middle of the second half of the eleventh century, survive. Presumably as well, the first known troubadour, William IX, duke of Aquitaine (1071–1126), had started to compose

his songs. Thus, it may be said that no later than 1100 the Carolingian-inspired pan-Gallo-Romance *scripta* had come to an end. The subsequent history of Gallo-Romance will become largely that of the expansion of *francien*, at the expense of the other literary and spoken dialects.

14. *La Vie de saint Alexis*, ed. Gaston Paris, Classiques Français du Moyen Âge, 4 (Paris: Champion, 1911); *La Chanson de Roland, publiée d'après le manuscrit d'Oxford et traduite*, ed. Joseph Bédier (Paris: Piazza, 1937).

15. Thus, although the king of France was, like the count of Champagne or the count of Flanders, a great feudal baron (whose fief was France, that is, *Île-de-France*), he was also superior to these barons, something more than merely first among equals. The Capetian ideal was that the king should be—as the pope would recognize eventually—"emperor" in his kingdom. The king's primacy extended to the language of his fief, *francien*, but only as this language was rendered literarily superior—as it became, like Latin, a genuine *scripta*.

16. Something analogous might have been on the mind of the poet whom we now identify as "Marie de France," when in the Prologue to one of the works attributed to her, she explains: "Marie ai num, si sui de France" (Marie is my name, I am from France). Marie de France lived and wrote in England.

17. Later generations, up to and including Dante (*De vulgari Eloquentia*, 1302), would identify the primacy of French with narrative, while Old Provençal would be viewed as the natural vehicle for lyric song.

18. This may well be something of a dig at the Norman-Angevin court of Henry II, where the quality of the French spoken—and the level of *courtoisie!*—left much to be desired.

19. In the midst of the meal Arthur astounds his guests by rising from the table in order to join the queen in her bedroom; he eventually falls asleep there.

20. Such "Cities" of men and of ladies exist in counterpoint to one another in the early romance, *Roman d'Énéas* (ca. 1155). Here the "City of Men" is addressed by the history of Énéas's transfer from Troy to Carthage to Italy and the prehistory of the founding of Rome. Meanwhile, Énéas's relationship to Woman—his mother, Venus, Dido, the *bellatrix* Camilla, and his second wife, Lavinia—forms another plot no less significant than the first. Chivalric arms and love are conjoined. Chrétien's debt to the *Énéas* is considerable.

Chapter 3

1. Wace's masterpiece, of course, does far more than merely translate Geoffrey's work; through the use of elaborate and fascinating descriptions, inventions like that of the Round Table, as well as by frequent narratorial interventions—the narrator, who calls himself Wace, appears to be speaking directly to his audience—Wace addresses the interests and the curiosity of his Anglo-Norman aristocratic public. His influence on subsequent narrative was

immense until well into the thirteenth century.

2.   Indeed, there are several precise textual references to Iseut in *Érec et Énide*. For example, when Chrétien alludes to the wedding night of the newly married couple, the narrator remarks that there was no need to substitute a Brangien for Énide, a clear allusion to Énide's chastity, since, on the wedding night of Mark and Iseut, the latter's serving-maid replaced the no longer virginal bride.

3.   Some of the confusion in these matters is probably due to the fact that, whereas *roman* was used in Old French to indicate "romance narrative," often specifically, and in contrast, say, to *chanson* (song), it also served to designate any substantial literary composition in the vernacular.

4.   In Chrétien's time Champagne was not a French province, but its counts were decidedly pro-French. Count Henry I had married Marie, daughter of Eleanor of Aquitaine and King Louis VII of France, in 1164. Moreoover, the archdiocese of Rheims had traditionally been affiliated with the interests of the Capetian Crown. It is in most ways accurate to refer to Chrétien de Troyes as a—self-consciously—*French* poet.

5.   These stories, presumably Celtic in origin, may well have been at the source of the early-thirteenth-century *Gereint*, a Welsh work of perhaps ultimately Irish origin loosely constituting part of the Welsh *Mabinogion*. *Gereint* is one of five Arthurian compositions traditionally associated with the more purely *Mabinogion* of non-Arthurian subject matter. *Gereint*, clearly influenced by twelfth- and thirteenth-century French style and manner, bears a close resemblance to Chrétien's *Érec et Énide*, although it is unlikely that Chrétien's poem influenced it directly.

6.   It may be argued, furthermore, that Érec's removal of himself and his wife from Arthur's court and their subsequent adventures in strange lands—adventures that prove very hazardous but that culminate in their final reconciliation—parallel Abelard's installation of Heloise at the Paraclete, their subsequent correspondence (which Heloise initiates, as Énide bravely breaks Érec's rule of silence), and the sublime reconciliation articulated by Abelard in the final pages of his last "personal letter" to his wife.

7.   I acknowledge my great debt to the pioneering study by Fanny Le Moine, whose revised Bryn Mawr dissertation was published as *Martianus Capella, A Literary Re-evaluation*, Münchener Beiträge zur Mediävisktik und Renaissance-Forschung, 10 (Munich: Bei der Arbeo-Gesellschaft, 1972). This indispensable study constitutes the first recent monograph-length attempt to describe and evaluate the *De Nuptiis* on its own terms.

8.   Their names are given in a manner reminiscent of Chrétien's long list of the knights attending Arthur at his court (*Érec et Énide*, vv. 1691–1750).

9.   Textual references to *De Nuptiis* are taken from Martianus Capella, *De Nuptiis Philologiæ et Mercurii*, ed. Adolf Dick, rev. by Jean Préaux, Bibliotheca Scriptorum Græcorum et Romanorum Teubneriana (Stuttgart: Teubner, 1978). English translations are taken from *The Marriage of Philology*

and Mercury, in *Martianus Capella and the Seven Liberal Arts*, vol. 2, trans. William Harris Stahl and Richard Johnson, with E. L. Burge (New York: Columbia University Press, 1977); hereafter cited in text as Martianus. Although Stahl's translations are not invariably as precise as one might wish and his obvious lack of sympathy for Martianus's procedure and thought is at times annoying, his (and his colleagues') scholarly notes are of great value, and it is a pleasure to record my gratitude for the work that went into this annotated translation and commentary.

10. See Otto von Simson, *The Gothic Cathedral*, Bollingen Series, 48 (Princeton, N.J.: Princeton University Press, 1974), especially chapters 1 and 2.

11. Guenevere's present to Énide might well constitute a reprise of Philology's abandonment of the earthly garments that her mother, Phronesia, had given her; one also recalls the welcome made to her by Juno Pronuba, her *vera genia* (tutelar deity).

12. She reiterates the same phrase as she blames herself for having caused Érec's death (or so she believes) during the Count of Limors episode (v. 4635).

13. After a night of love, Érec lies sleeping, while a melancholy Énide remains awake, weeping and thinking of her husband's tarnished reputation. What Jupiter had feared for Mercury has actually occurred with Érec, and Énide behaves exactly as Juno had predicted Philology would.

14. Macrobius, *Commentarii in Somnium Scipionis* (*Commentary on the Dream of Scipio*), ed. James Willis (Leipzig: Teubner, 1963) I, 2:7–9; cited by Fanny Le Moine, *Martianus Capella, A Literary Re-Evaluation*, Münchener Beiträge zur Mediävistik und Renaissance Forschung, 10 (Munich: Bei der Arbeo Gesellschaft, 1972), 34–35.

15. Yet, as Frappier and others have pointed out, unlike the *romanciers antiques* who at times almost mechanically dragged out their mastery of the conventional *descriptio*, Chrétien's narrator not infrequently interrupts the description with remarks like "To continue in this vein would be tedious," or "Why list the names of all the dishes served?" during Érec's coronation feast (vv. 6920–46). In this manner he subverts pure clerkly technique by speaking directly to his audience.

16. "Chrétien de Troyes: The Narrator and His Art," in Kelly 1985, 19. To Kelly's remark it might be added that for Chrétien, a Continental French vernacular writer, the celebration of King Arthur, a figure deemed to be an historical antecedent by the Plantagenet rulers of England, was hardly something to be desired. For Frenchmen, the great king-emperor of the past was Charlemagne.

17. Kelly ("Chrétien de Troyes: The Narrator and His Art," in Kelly 1985, 23) quotes Huon de Méry, author of the *Torneimenz Antecrit*, as declaring (concerning Chrétien) that "never did Christian mouth speak so well" (vv. 1336–37). See also Frappier 1968, 236–37.

18. This figure, as stated earlier, consists in repeating the root of a word,

or word family, and varying it by changing the desinence (such as *fin*, *fine*, *fine-ment*).

    19. The 15-year-old Cligés is described "formally" (vv. 2760–61) as "more handsome and charming than Narcissus who, beneath the elm tree, gazed upon his reflection in the fountain" (vv. 2766–68).

    20. The text is somewhat—probably deliberately—ambiguous: it is not perfectly clear whether both *chevalerie* and *clergie* removed to France, or, in fact, just *clergie*. The subject pronoun (*ele*) could grammatically refer either to both or exclusively to *clergie*. The fact of the matter is that none of the action of *Cligés* takes place in France, whereas, obviously, the "learned" composition of the romance does take place there. Chrétien is clearly distancing himself somewhat from the events of the story (which are, in many respects, quite preposterous). For a full discussion of this interesting issue, see Michelle A. Freeman, "Chrétien de Troyes' *Cligés*: A Close Reading of the Prologue," *Romanic Review* 67 (1976): 89–101.

    21. Chrétien explores here the role of the *losangier*, "gossiper, evil tongue," which is so prevalent in courtly lyric song; Fénice is genuinely worried about her public reputation. In this manner Chrétien seems to deal with Iseut's conflict between her loyalty to her beloved Tristan and her nostalgia for the public respect she understands is her due as queen at Mark's court.

    22. The following remarks owe a great deal to the pioneering studies of *Cligés* by Michelle A. Freeman. See her *The Poetics of "Translatio" and "Conjointure": Chrétien de Troyes's "Cligés,"* French Forum Monographs, 12 (Lexington, Ky.: French Forum, 1979); and *"Cligés"* in Kelly 1985, 89–131, 320–23. *"Cligés"* hereafter cited in text as Freeman 1985.

Chapter 4

    1. In the following pages I borrow heavily from the arguments and text of my *"Le Chevalier au Lion (Yvain),"* in Kelly 1985, 182–90.

    2. Whereas Gaston Paris argued vigorously on behalf of the anteriority of the *Charrette*, Wendelin Foerster called for caution on this issue, suggesting the possibility that the romances were composed more or less simultaneously. See Foerster's note to vv. 3707–08 in his edition of *Le Chevalier de la Charrette {Der Karrenritter}*, vol. 4 of the *Sämtliche erhaltene Werke*, 312.

    3. Anthime Fourrier, "Encore la chronologie des œuvres de Chrétien de Troyes," *Bulletin Bibliographique de la Société Internationale Arthurienne* 2 (1950): 69–88.

    4. See Frappier, *Étude sur "Yvain" ou le "Chevalier au Lion" de Chrétien de Troyes* (Paris: Société d'Édition d'Enseignement Supérieur, 1969), 16; hereafter cited as Frappier 1969. See also Mario Roques's Introduction to his edition, *Le Chevalier de la Charrete*, Classiques Français du Moyen Âge, 86 (Paris: H. Champion, 1958), vii.

    5. There is some question as to whether Laudine is named by Chrétien;

several manuscripts do not name her, and so a "Laudine" does not appear in Roques's C. F. M. A. edition of *Le Chevalier au Lion (Yvain)*, even though in his introduction he refers to her by this name! The available evidence suggests, however, that the scribes who do not mention a "Laudine" are in error. See Alfred Foulet and K. D. Uitti, "Chrétien's 'Laudine': *Yvain*, vv. 2148–55," *Romance Philology* 37, no. 3 (February 1984): 293–302.

6. Jean Misrahi, "More Light on the Chronology of Chrétien de Troyes?" *Bulletin Bibliographique de la Société Arthurienne* 11 (1959): 89–120.

7. "Note sur la date du *Chevalier de la Charrette*," *Romania* 92 (1971): 118–26; hereafter cited in text as Ménard.

8. Following Fourrier, David Shirt has suggested that *Yvain* vv. 4743–44, because of its seeming unawareness of the Noauz episode, had been completed either before or while Godefroi wrote his conclusion. See his "Godefroi de Lagny et la composition de la *Charrete*," *Romania* 96 (1975): 27–52.

9. The narrator explains that for a nobleman in the days of King Arthur, riding in a cart was equivalent to the dishonor of being pilloried.

10. *Gorre*—sometimes referred to, as in the Tristan story, as *Voire*, "glass"—appears to indicate a kind of Celtic version of Hades—a Land of the Dead.

11. An episode in the *Charrette* sometimes known as that of the "Importunate Lover"—in which Lancelot defends a maiden from the unwanted advances of another knight—contains a passage in which the narrator explains that a lady or damsel who travels alone must be not be molested by anyone, but that, if she is accompanied by a knight, he runs the risk of being challenged. If defeated, he must give up custody of the lady or damsel to the victor, who then may do as he will with her. That is precisely the case of Guenevere, who has been abandoned by Arthur to Méléagant; by vanquishing Méléagant, Lancelot, in principle, or "legally," has the right to dispose of Guenevere as he sees fit. Chrétien's narrator emphasizes the importance of this ancient custom. The Importunate Lover cannot contain his joy at discovering the object of his passion accompanied by another knight: "Since I find you in such a situation, I can carry you off with me without incurring any shame for it" (vv. 1589–91). If she had been traveling alone, he would have been obliged honorably to have respected her wishes. Seen in the global context of the romance, this episode serves to legitimize Lancelot's passion for Guenevere: their adultery does not count alongside the great benefit that accrues to Arthur's court when Lancelot restores to it its queen. We might add that the Importunate Lover quite closely resembles Méléagant, just as his father, a very prudent and courteous man, resembles King Bademagu, the father of Méléagant. Chrétien seems to underscore the fact that Lancelot is not taking Guenevere away from Arthur; he frees her from Méléagant.

12. The *Lanzelet* contains an episode (which could be entitled the Episode of the Badly Cut Mantle) that reflects somewhat on the moral purity of

Guenevere; the mantle does not fit her perfectly, as it should have had her virtue been entirely free of possible reproach.

13. Countess Marie is one of the central figures in the love courts depicted by Andreas Capellanus in his celebrated *De Arte honeste amandi* (usually dated between 1174 and 1186, that is, roughly at the time of composition of *Le Chevalier de la Charrette*).

14. Interestingly, *Amor(s)*, which could be either feminine or masculine when personified in Old French, is invariably feminine in the *Charrette*; in *Yvain*, meanwhile, it is sometimes one sometimes the other. Conversely, in *Cligés*, *Amors* is invariably masculine—Cupid instead of Venus.

15. See his "II. Le *Conte de la charrette*," *Romania* 10 (1881): 465–96; 12 (1883): 459–534; 16 (1887): 100–101. Present-day readers are less inclined to see in Chrétien so doctrinaire a theorist (or "follower" of Andreas Capellanus). For a more nuanced discussion of the lyric elements present in *Lancelot*, consult Emmanuèle Baumgartner, *Chrétien de Troyes: "Yvain," "Lancelot"—la charrette et le lion* (Paris: Presses Universitaires de France, 1992), 59–67 and *passim*.

16. Indeed, we recall, shortly after the start of *Yvain*, Arthur, to his guests' consternation, leaves the dinner table in order to join Guenevere in bed. However, as is the case with Mark and Iseut, the couple is never said to have had children.

17. In Old and Middle French narrative, the beautiful fairy with whom the knight errant falls in love is a well-recognized motif. Furthermore, her domain generally conflicts with the court to which, ostensibly, the knight belongs; he tarries there, sometimes to his greater fulfillment, at other times to his detriment. The fairy's place represents an almost private alternative to the far more socially focused court. Chrétien exploits this contrast in *Le Chevalier au Lion*.

18. A brief and highly useful summary of the scholarship devoted to the Celtic origins of *Yvain* is provided by Jean Frappier in Frappier 1969, 81–118.

19. See in particular *Recherches sur les sources latines des contes et romans courtois du moyen âge* (Paris: Champion, 1913); also useful is Foster E. Guyer, "The Influence of Ovid on Crestien de Troyes," *Romanic Review* 12 (1921): 97–134, 216–47.

20. For example, vv. 575–76 ("I went there thus, I returned from there thus; / While returning I held myself to be a fool") are almost an exact quotation from a passage of the *Roman de Rou* in which Wace describes a trip he made to the Fountain of Barenton in order to experience the "marvel" of the tempest. "I went there a fool, I returned a fool" (vv. 6393–98), Wace comments, after failing to provoke the storm.

21. Lunete's role resembles somewhat that of Godefroi de Leigni in the *Charrette*; it is this *clerc* who is entrusted by Chrétien to bring Lancelot and Guenevere back together again at court. Godefroi's "continuation" of Chrétien foreshadows the many rewritings of the *Lancelot* story that will take place in the thirteenth century.

Chapter 5

1. Unless otherwise noted, English versions of Chrétien's text—and their line references—given here correspond to the facing-page translation provided by William W. Kibler to the edition prepared by Rupert T. Pickens (New York and London: Garland, 1990).

2. Philippe d'Alsace, count of Flanders, is thus described as of greater worth than Alexander the Great, a figure of Greek antiquity who had become the symbol in the Middle Ages of largess and generosity.

3. The use of the indefinite article *un* (v. 3186) implies the *graal* was not an unknown object in Chrétien's day. Since this is the earliest significant use of the object (and word) in Old French literature, *graal* has inspired an entire bibliography of scholarly commentary. Suffice it to say at this juncture that it appears to be a slightly concave serving dish, not dissimilar in shape to a modern soup dish (or *assiette creuse*), which, we learn later, contains a single Host. (Jean Frappier quotes Hélinand de Froidmont, who described a grail in these terms: "*Graal* is what is said in French to mean a broad plate that is somewhat concave"; see his *Chrétien de Troyes et le mythe du graal. Étude sur "Perceval" ou "le Conte du Graal"* (Paris: Société d'Édition d'Enseignement Supérieur, 1972), 7–8, 174; hereafter cited as Frappier 1972. Later traditions will transform Chrétien's *graal* into the Holy Grail, identified first with the plate used by Christ at the Last Supper (Robert de Boron) and then with the chalice in which Joseph of Arimathea is said to have collected the blood of the crucified Christ.

4. The color configuration of red and white, which occurs with a certain frequency in *Le Conte du Graal* (as with the drops of blood falling from the shining, silvery lance), is usually associated in medieval color symbolism with love and/or with the beauty of the beloved (white skin/red lips, and so on).

5. Throughout the twelfth century weeping was taken to be a sign of genuine repentance; it is thus that Perceval's tears should be understood here. Although it would not be considered officially a sacrament until the Lateran Council of 1214, confession was increasingly practiced over the course of the twelfth century.

6. I make no pretense in the following pages to study the phenomenon, or the myth, of *courtoisie* in all its many historical and social contexts; I shall refer mainly to the traditions of Old French courtly romance and, to a lesser degree, the *chanson courtoise* of troubadours and *trouvères*. For a more exhaustive study, see Aldo Scaglione, *Courtliness, Chivalry, and Courtesy from Ottonian Germany to the Italian Renaissance* (Berkeley-London-Los Angeles: University of California Press, 1991).

7. The English translation is from *Eneas: A Twelfth-Century Romance*, translated, with an Introduction and Notes by John A. Yunck (New York and London: Columbia University Press, 1974).

8. Virgil's Camilla was a king's daughter; he had been unjustly deposed, and Camilla, who loved her father greatly, sought to avenge him.

9. Thus, "Ne sui si *nice* ne si *fole* / Que bien n'entande une parole" (vv. 1565–66) and "Une response *nice* et *fole*" (v. 6399).

10. The fifth occurrence of *nice* takes place during the Gauvain section when a lord refers to his daughter as "enfes" (childish) and "*nice* chose *fole*" (v. 5324; foolish simpleton), to which Gauvain replies, interestingly, "Certes, fait me[s]sire Ga[u]vains, / Dont seroie je tro[p] vilains, / Se sa volenté ne feisoie" (vv. 5325–27; "Indeed," said my lord Gawain, / "then I'd be very ill-mannered/ not to do what she wants").

11. Or, perhaps, even a bit earlier. Thus, when Gauvain meets Perceval alone on the snow-strewn field, he enquires of him what he has been doing there. Perceval explains how the three blood drops reminded him of "le vis m'amie," to which Gauvain replies: "Cist pansers n'estoit pas vilains, / Einz estoit mout *cortois* et dolz" (vv. 4424–25; "This was no vulgar thought, / but a most sweet and courtly one").

12. It is perhaps in order to contrast Perceval's taking Blancheflor to his bed with Dido's receiving Énéas in her bed that the tantalizingly chaste and passionate bundling episode in *Le Conte du Graal* remains inexplicit. Also, unlike Énéas's departure from Dido, Perceval's leaving Blancheflor is not sneaky. Furthermore, he promises her that he will return.

13. On the surface the situation appears to resemble the argument proposed by Gauvain to Yvain shortly after the latter's wedding; however, as the rest of the song demonstrates, this is not truly the case.

14. I am indebted to conversations with Rupert T. Pickens and Michelle A. Freeman for further support for what I have said here, namely, for noting the fact that the narrator of the *Conte du Graal*, a bit like that of *Yvain*, undergoes an important transformation. His authority in telling Perceval's story diminishes as Perceval himself grows in *courtoisie* and self-knowledge: the narrator comments less on what is going on and contents himself with reporting what, so to speak, he "sees."

15. To use Rupert T. Pickens's terminology here, Perceval is neither on "Arthurian" nor on "Grail Kingdom" territory during this obscure five-year period. He journeys in a kind of no man's land.

16. I believe that we are being reminded here of the period of Yvain's madness after his disavowal by Laudine and before the intervention of the Dame de Noroison.

17. In the first episode it is simply stated that Perceval "recited the whole creed" (v. 156); here the Credo, as spoken to Perceval by the knight, is reproduced virtually verbatim.

18. For a brief and judicious summary of this scholarship, see Frappier 1972, 182–89.

19. Pickens and Kibler remind us (465) that this counsel "recapitulates his mother's (492–580) and that of Gornemant (1619–68)." They also quite usefully summarize biblical antecedents for what the Hermit says.

20. This overriding Pauline presence in *Le Conte du Graal* may be what

explains Chrétien's erroneous attribution to him of a quotation deriving from Saint John in the prologue. For a more extensive discussion of the presence of Saint Paul in *Perceval*, see Rupert T. Pickens, "*Le Conte du Graal (Perceval)*," in Kelly 1985, especially 237–38.

21. Just as in the prologue to *Cligés*, Chrétien gives enlightened *chevalerie* its due, not sacrificing it to *clergie*, so *imperium* undergoes here a process of *translatio* as thoroughly as *studium*.

22. Chrétien's overriding interest in education has led some scholars (who base their suppositions on the importance of Philip of Flanders to the education of the son of the king of France) to consider Chrétien de Troyes as having been employed in the tutoring of young princes and noblemen. The closeness of the courts of Flanders, at Bruges, and Champagne, at Troyes, along with the intimacy they shared with the royal court of France, evidenced in Philip's proposing marriage to the widowed Countess Marie de Champagne (daughter of the king of France), has reinforced the plausibility of these hypotheses. The nature of Chrétien's relationship to Philip is unclear in many respects, to the point that it is not certain that he left Champagne for Flanders in order to be "officially" in Philip's service; they could have discussed *Le Conte du Graal* during one of the count's many sojourns at the court of Champagne.

23. Only a few fragments of Thomas's *Le Roman de Tristan et Iseut*—the so-called courtly version of the tale—survive. Gottfried's masterpiece, used with suitable caution, permits a plausible reconstruction of that of Thomas. It is widely believed that Chrétien was very familiar with the Thomas version of the *Tristan* story.

24. Indeed, Joseph Bédier, the great *Tristan* scholar, begins his delightful modern French translation of the entire tale (as provided by Béroul, Thomas, Gottfried, Marie de France, and others), with the formula: "Seigneurs, vous plaît-il d'entendre un beau conte d'amour et de mort?" ("My lords, would it please you to hear a beautiful story of love and death?"). See Joseph Bédier, ed. and trans., *Le Roman de Tristan et Iseut* (Paris: H. Piazza, 1929), 1.

25. Gottfried von Straßburg, *Tristan, with the Surviving Fragments of the Tristran of Thomas*, trans. Arthur Thomas Hatto (London: Penguin, 1960), 42–44.

26. See his *L'Amour et l'Occident* (Paris: Plon, 1939); English trans., *Love in the Western World* (New York: Harcourt Brace, 1940).

Appendix

1. As Jean Frappier has pointed out, "Philomena" was far more common in medieval usage than the more classically correct "Philomela" (nightingale). See Frappier 1968, 63.

2. The *Ovide moralisé* comprises some 72,000 rhyming octosyllabic lines. It is ostensibly a translation of Ovid's *Metamorphoses*, but interpolates earlier French versions of Ovid (like *Piramus et Tisbé* and, of course, Chrétien's

Philomena). Each fiction leads up to an interpretation that seeks to explain the hidden meaning of that fiction, either as a prefiguration of the New Testament or in terms of an allegory of some sort—moral, historical, geographical, or even scientific. The work is a kind of Ovidian encyclopedia. "De la Hupe" appears in Book 6. The standard edition of the text is that of Cornelis De Boer, et al., *Ovide moralisé, poème du commencement du XIVe siècle, publié d'après tous les manuscrits connus*, 5 vols., Verhandelingen der K. Akademie van Wetenschappen te Amsterdam, Afdeeling Letterkunde, Nieuwe Reeks, Deel 15, 21, 30, 37, 43 (Amsterdam: J. Müller/H.I. Paris, 1915–38).

3.   A mystery pervades, however, the naming of the author at the exact midpoint of the tale in the *Ovide moralisé*. At v. 634 his name is given as "Crestïens li Gois." No one has as yet come up with a fully satisfying explanation of "li Gois." The standard edition of the poem is *Philomena: conte raconté d'après Ovide*, ed. Cornelis De Boer (Paris: Geuthner, 1909).

4.   Frappier insists that when one compares the literary workmanship of *Philomena* with that of the romances of certain authorship, no serious objection can be raised against firmly placing the *Ovide moralisé* text within the Chrétien canon, and similarities of tone, style, and so on, appear to argue very strongly in favor of this attribution. See Frappier 1968, 64.

5.   This European bird possesses a distinctively patterned plumage, a fanlike crest, and a slender, but powerful, downward-curving bill.

6.   See her *Les Chansons courtoises de Chrétien de Troyes: édition critique avec introduction, notes et commentaire*, Publications Universitaires Européennes (Bern: Herbert Lang; Frankfurt/M.: Peter Lang, 1974), 101; hereafter cited in text as Zai. Zai distinguishes between two songs of "certain" attribution (R[aynaud].121, beginning "Amors, tençon et bataille," and R.1664, beginning "D'Amors, qui m'a tolu a moi") and two "doubtful" songs which, she believes, can reasonably be assigned to Chrétien (R.66: "De joli cuer chanterai," and R.1380: "Quant li dous estez decline"). Our textual references correspond to this edition, which offers, in addition to the texts, exhaustive discussions of the various manuscripts—or *chansonniers*—as well as detailed notes and commentary, at once textual, musical, and bibliographic.

7.   Scholars have traditionally pointed to *Lancelot* as the romance by Chrétien that most closely adheres to the troubadour "system" of *fin'amors*. See Frappier 1968, 68.

8.   Here is the text:

> Onques du buvrage ne bui
> Dont Tristan fu enpoisonnez;
> Mes plus me fet amer que lui
> Fins cuers et bone volentez.
> Bien en doit estre miens li grez,
> Qu'ainz de riens efforciez n'en fui,
> Fors que tant que mes euz en crui,

Par cui sui en la voie entrez
Donc ja n'istrai n'ainc n'en recrui.

(Zai, 78)

(Never did I drink of the brew that poisoned Tristan; but a refined heart
and good will make me love more deeply than he. I must consent willingly therefore to this love in that I was not forced by anything to love,
apart from believing what I was told by my eyes by whom I was led into
the road from which I shall never depart and which I have always wished
to follow.)

Selected Bibliography

Editions of Works by Chrétien de Troyes

Collected Editions

Christian von Troyes. *Sämtliche erhaltene Werke*. Edited by Wendelin Foerster. Halle: Max Niemeyer, 1884–99. Reprint. Amsterdam: Éditions RODOPI, 1965. Grosse Ausgabe. 4 vols. 1. *Cliges* (1884); 2. *Der Löwenritter (Yvain)* (1887); 3. *Erec und Enide* (1890); 4. *Der Karrenritter und das Wilhelmsleben* [*Le Chevalier de la Charrette* and *Guillaume d'Angleterre*] (1899). Kleine Ausgabe. 4 vols. 1. *Erec und Enide* (1896; rev. ed. 1909, 1934); 2. *Cliges* (1888; rev. ed. 1901, 1910, 1921 [abridged by Alfons Hilka], 1934 [edited by Hermann Breuer]); 3. *Yvain* (1891; rev. ed. 1902, 1906, 1912, 1913, 1926 [edited by Alfons Hilka], 1942 [edited by T. B. W. Reid. Manchester: Manchester University Press]); 4. *Wilhelm von England* (1911).

Foerster's editions (except some of those revised by other editors) do not provide glossaries. This lack is made up for by Wendelin Foerster, *Wörterbuch zu Kristian von Troyes sämtlichen Werke* (Halle: Niemeyer, 1914; rev. ed. [ed. Hermann Breuer], Tübingen: Max Niemeyer, 1964).

These editions, to which may be added *Der Percevalroman (Li Contes del Graal)*, edited by Alfons Hilka (Halle: Niemeyer, 1932; reprint. 1966), are of very high literary quality, but, because Foerster in effect rewrote the manuscripts he utilized in order to conform to a *champenois* literary language in which he deemed Chrétien to have written, they are of very little linguistic value. However, he furnishes a rich set of variant readings and numerous useful notes. The texts are somewhat dated in that they do not take into consideration the evidence provided by manuscripts unknown to the editor, such as MSS Annonay and Princeton University Library, Garrett 125, which would have helped him solve a number of cruxes in both the *Charrette* and *Yvain*. Nevertheless they must be consulted by any serious student of Chrétien de Troyes.

Les Romans de Chrétien de Troyes, édités d'après la copie de Guiot (Bibl. nat. fr. 794). Edited by Mario Roques et al. Classiques Français du Moyen Âge (C.F.M.A.). Paris: H. Champion, various dates: *Érec et Énide*. Edited by Mario Roques. C.F.M.A., 80 (1952); *Cligés*. Edited by Alexandre Micha.

C.F.M.A., 84 (1957); *Le Chevalier de la charrete*. Edited by Mario Roques. C.F.M.A., 86 (1958); *Le Chevalier au lion (Yvain)*. Edited by Mario Roques. C.F.M.A., 89 (1960); *Le Conte du graal*. 2 vols. Edited by Félix Lecoy. C.F.M.A., 100 (1973) and 103 (1975).

An extreme partisan of conservative editorial policy, Roques does little more than punctuate and correct the most glaring errors of his base manuscript, B.N. f. fr. 794, also known as the Guiot manuscript. For all intents and purposes, the C.F.M.A. Chrétien de Troyes is little more than a transformation into modern book form of the Guiot text. Yet, mainly because of the prestigious label of the Classiques Français du Moyen Âge, these editions held sway in Chrétien scholarship from their introduction in the late 1950s to the mid-1980s. They are now being replaced.

Editions of Single Romances

Érec et Énide. Edited and translated by Carleton W. Carroll. The Garland Library of Medieval Literature. Series A. New York and London: Garland, 1987.

Cligés. Edited by Stewart Gregory and Claude Luttrell. Arthurian Studies. Cambridge: D. S. Brewer, 1993.

Le Chevalier de la Charrette (Lancelot). Edited and translated into Modern French by Alfred Foulet and Karl D. Uitti. Classiques Garnier. Paris: Bordas, 1989 (contains a facing-page Modern French translation).

Lancelot, or The Knight of the Cart. Edited and translated by William W. Kibler. The Garland Library of Medieval Literature. Series A. New York and London: Garland, 1981.

Le Chevalier au Lion (Yvain). Edited by Karl D. Uitti (with Modern French translation by Philippe Walter). In *Œuvres complètes de Chrétien de Troyes*, edited by Daniel Poirion. Bibliothèque de la Pléiade. Paris: Gallimard, 1994. This volume also contains the texts and Modern French translation of the other four romances of certain attribution.

The Knight with the Lion, or, Le Chevalier au Lion (Yvain). Edited and translated by William W. Kibler. The Garland Library of Medieval Literature. Series A. New York and London: Garland, 1985.

Le Roman de Perceval ou le Conte du graal. Edited by William Roach. Textes Littéraires Français. Geneva-Lille: Librairie Droz, 1956. Reprint. Geneva-Paris: Librairie Droz, 1959.

The Story of the Grail (Li Contes del Graal), or Perceval. Edited by Rupert T. Pickens and translated by William W. Kibler. The Garland Library of Medieval Literature. Series A. New York and London: Garland, 1990.

"Le Roman de Perceval" ou "Le Conte du Graal," édition critique d'après tous les manuscrits. Edited by Keith Busby. Tübingen: Niemeyer, 1993.

Editions of Works of Doubtful Attribution

Guillaume d'Angleterre. Edited by Maurice Wilmotte. Classiques Français du Moyen Âge, 55. Paris: H. Champion, 1927.

Guillaume d'Angleterre. Edited by Anthony J. Holden. Textes Littéraires Français. Geneva: Librairie Droz, 1988. (This work has been at times attributed to Chrétien de Troyes; I do not believe he composed it, and therefore do not deal with it in the present monograph.)

Les Chansons courtoises de Chrétien de Troyes: édition critique, avec introduction, notes et commentaire. Edited by Marie-Claire Zai. Bern: Herbert Lang, 1974. Reprint. Frankfurt/M.: Peter Lang, 1974.

Philomena: conte raconté d'après Ovide. Edited by Cornelis De Boer. Paris: Geuthner, 1909.

Translations into English and Modern French

Arthurian Romances by Chrétien de Troyes (*Érec et Énide, Cligés, Yvain,* and *Lancelot*). Translated by W. Wistar Comfort. Everyman's Library, 698. London and Toronto: J. M. Dent; New York: E. P. Dutton, 1914.

Arthurian Romances by Chrétien de Troyes. Translated by D. D. R. Owen, with Introduction and Notes. London: J. M. Dent, 1987.

The following Modern French translations, based largely on the C.F.M.A. editions, have been published by H. Champion, in Paris: *Érec et Énide.* Translated by René Louis (1954). *Cligés.* Translated by Alexandre Micha (1969). *Le Chevalier de la Charrette (Lancelot).* Translated by Jean Frappier (1971). *Le Chevalier au Lion (Yvain).* Translated by Claude Buridant and Jean Trotin (1972). *Le Conte du Graal (Perceval).* Translated by Jacques Ribard (1979).

Érec and Énide. Translated by Dorothy Gilbert, with Introduction and Notes. Berkeley and Los Angeles: University of California Press, 1992.

Yvain, the Knight of the Lion. Translated by Burton Raffel. New Haven, Conn.: Yale University Press, 1987.

"Lancelot," or, "The Knight of the Cart." Translated by Ruth Harwood Cline. Athens: University of Georgia Press, 1990.

The Story of the Grail (Perceval). Translated by Robert White Linker. Chapel Hill: University of North Carolina Press, 1952.

Perceval le Gallois ou le Conte du Graal. Translated into the Modern French by Lucien Foulet. Paris: Stock, 1947. Reprint. Paris: A. G. Nizet, 1970.

Perceval, the Story of the Grail. Translated by Nigel Bryant. Cambridge: D. S. Brewer; Totowa, N.J.: Rowman and Littlefield, 1982.

Other Prima ry Texts

Bernard of Clairvaux. *On the "Song of Songs".* Vols. 2– 5 of *Works.* Spencer, Mass./Kalamazoo, Mich.: Cistercian Publications, 1971–80.

Abelard and Heloise. *The Personal Letters between Abelard and Heloise.* Edited by J. T. Muckle, C.S.B. *Mediæval Studies* 15 (1953)–17 (1955). Translated into English as *The Letters of Abelard and Heloise.* Introduction and English trans. by Betty Radice. New York: Penguin Books, 1974.

Andreas Capellanus. *De Amore et Amoris remedio.* Edited and translated by P. G. Walsh. London: Duckworth, 1982.

Énéas, roman du XIIe siècle. 2 vols. Edited by J.-J. Salverda de Grave. Classiques Français du Moyen Âge, 44, 62. Paris: Champion, 1925–31. An English translation is *Eneas: A Twelfth-Century Romance.* Translated, with an Introduction and Notes by John A. Yunck. New York and London: Columbia University Press, 1974.

John of Salisbury. *Metalogicon.* Edited by J. B. Hall (with K. S. B. Keats-Rohan). Turnholt: Brepols, 1991. An English translation is *The Metalogicon of John of Salisbury, a Twelfth-Century Defense of the Verbal and Logical Arts of the Trivium.* Edited and translated by Daniel D. McGarry. Berkeley and Los Angeles: University of California Press, 1955.

La Vie de saint Alexis: texte critique. Edited by Gaston Paris. Classiques Français du Moyen Âge, 4. Paris: Champion, 1911. An Old French text with facing page English translation is *The Life of Saint Alexis.* Edited by C. J. Odenkirchen. Leyden, The Netherlands and Brookline, Mass.: Brill, 1978.

Le Roman de Thèbes, édition critique d'après tous les manuscrits connus. 2 vols. Edited by Léopold Constans. Paris: Société des Anciens Textes Français, 1890.

Le Roman de Troie, par Benoît de Sainte-Maure, publié d'après tous les manuscrits connus. 6 vols. Edited by Léopold Constans. Paris: Société des Anciens Textes Français, 1904–12.

The Mabinogion. Translated by Gwyn Jones and Thomas Jones. London: J. M. Dent; Rutland, Vt.: C. E. Tuttle, 1991.

Macrobius. *Commentary on the Dream of Scipio.* Translated with Commentary by William H. Stahl. New York: Columbia University Press, 1952.

———. *Opera.* 2 vols. Edited by James Willis. Leipzig: Teubner, 1963.

Marie de France. *Les Lais.* Edited by Karl Warnke and translated into the Modern French by Laurence Harf-Lancner. Paris: Librairie Générale Française, 1990.

Martianus Capella. *De Nuptiis Philologiæ et Mercurii.* Edited by Adolf Dick and revised by Jean Préaux. Bibliotheca Scriptorum Græcorum et Romanorum Teubneriana. Stuttgart: Teubner, 1978.

————. *Martianus Capella and the Seven Liberal Arts*. 2 vols. Edited and translated with Commentary by William H. Stahl and Richard Johnson, with E. L. Burge. New York: Columbia University Press, 1971–77.

Narcisse: conte ovidien français du XIIe siècle. Edited by Martine Thiry-Stassin and Madeleine Tyssens. Bibliothèque de la Faculté de Philosophie et Lettres de l'Université de Liège. Paris: Société d'Éditions "Les Belles Lettres," 1976.

Peter Abelard. *Historia calamitatum: Texte critique avec une introduction*. Edited by Jacques Monfrin. Paris: Vrin, 1978.

Peter of Riga. *Evangelium Ægidi: Aurora Petri Rigæ: A Verse Commentary on the Bible*. Edited by Paul E. Beichner. Part 2, Publications in Medieval Studies, 19. Notre Dame, Ind.: Notre Dame University Press, 1965.

Peter the Venerable. *Letters*. 2 vols. Edited by Giles Constable. Cambridge, Mass.: Harvard University Press, 1967.

Piramus et Tisbé: Introduzione-Testo critico-Traduzione e Note. Edited by F. Branciforti. Florence, Italy: Olschki, 1959.

Tristan et Yseut. Edited and translated by J. C. Payen. Classiques Garnier. Paris: Éditions Garnier, 1974. Gives the Old French text and Modernized French translation of Béroul, Thomas, the two *Folies Tristan* of Berne and Oxford, and Marie de France's *Chèvrefeuille*.

Wace. *Le Roman de Rou*. 2 vols. Edited by Anthony J. Holden. Paris: Société des Anciens Textes Français, 1970–73.

————. *Le Roman de Brut*. 2 vols. Edited by Ivor Arnold. Paris: Société des Anciens Textes Français, 1938–40.

Secondary Works

Studies of Chrétien de Troyes—Books

Frappier, Jean. *Chrétien de Troyes: l'homme et l'œuvre*. Connaissance des Lettres, 50. Paris: Hatier, 1957. Reprint. 1968. Translated into the English by Raymond J. Cormier under the title *Chrétien de Troyes, the Man and His Work*. Athens: Ohio University Press, 1982.

Kelly, Douglas, ed. *The Romances of Chrétien de Troyes: A Symposium*. The Edward C. Monographs on Medieval Literature, 3. Lexington, Ky.: French Forum, 1985. This work contains the following essays: "Chrétien de Troyes: The Narrator and His Art" (Douglas Kelly); *"Érec et Énide"* (Edward J. Buckbee); *"Cligés"* (Michelle A. Freeman); *"Le Chevalier de la Charrette (Lancelot)"* (Matilda Tomaryn Bruckner); *"Le Chevalier au Lion (Yvain)"* (Karl D. Uitti); *"Le Conte du Graal (Perceval)"* (Rupert T. Pickens); "On Editing Chrétien's *Lancelot*, Chrétien's Indebtedness to the *Alexandre décasyllabique*" (Alfred Foulet); Selected Bibliography (Sandra Ihle).

Loomis, Roger Sherman. *Arthurian Tradition and Chrétien de Troyes*. New York: Columbia University Press, 1949.

Micha, Alexandre. *La Tradition manuscrite des romans de Chrétien de Troyes*. Paris: Librairie Droz, 1939. Reprint. Geneva: Librairie Droz, 1966.

Topsfield, Leslie T. *Chrétien de Troyes: A Study of the Arthurian Romances*. Cambridge: Cambridge University Press, 1981.

Uitti, Karl D. *Story, Myth, and Celebration in Old French Narrative Poetry 1050–1200*. Princeton, N.J.: Princeton University Press, 1973, especially 128–231.

Studies of Chrétien de Troyes–Articles

Foulet, Alfred. "On Grid-Editing Chrétien de Troyes," *L'Esprit Créateur*, Special Issue entitled "The Poetics of Textual Criticism: The Old French Example," 27, no. 1 (Spring 1987): 15–23.

Fourrier, Anthime. "Encore la chronologie des œuvres de Chrétien de Troyes," *Bulletin Bibliographique de la Société Internationale Arthurienne* 2 (1950): 69–88.

Hunt, Tony. "Tradition and Originality in the Prologues of Chrestien de Troyes," *Forum for Modern Language Studies* 8 (1972): 320–44.

Ménard, Philippe. "Note sur la date du *Chevalier de la Charrette*," *Romania* 92 (1971): 118–26.

Misrahi, Jean. "More Light on the Chronology of Chrétien de Troyes?," *Bulletin Bibliographique de la Société Internationale Arthurienne* 11 (1959): 89–120.

Ollier, Marie-Louise. "The Author in the Text: The Prologues of Chrétien de Troyes," *Yale French Studies* 51 (1974): 26–41.

Paris, Gaston. "Études sur les romans de la Table Ronde. Lancelot du Lac, I. Le *Lanzelet* d'Ulrich de Zatzikhoven; Lancelot du Lac, II. Le *Conte de la Charrette*," *Romania* 10 (1881) 465–96; 12 (1883) 459–534; 16 (1887) 100–101.

Reid, T. B. W. "Chrestien de Troyes and the Scribe Guiot," *Medium Ævum* 45 (1976): 1–19.

Roques, Mario. "Le Manuscrit fr. 794 de la Bibliothèque Nationale et le scribe Guiot," *Romania* 73 (1952): 177–99.

Uitti, Karl D. "Autant en emporte *li funs*: Remarques sur le Prologue du *Chevalier de la Charrette* de Chrétien de Troyes," *Romania* 105, nos. 2–3 (1984): 270–91.

Studies of Individual Romances–Books

Baumgartner, Emmanuèle. *Chrétien de Troyes: "Yvain," "Lancelot"—la charrette et le lion*. Études Littéraires. Paris: Presses Universitaires de France, 1992.

Frappier, Jean. *Étude sur "Yvain," ou le "Chevalier au Lion" de Chrétien de Troyes*. Paris: Société d'Édition d'Enseignement Supérieur, 1969.

———. *Chrétien de Troyes et le mythe du graal: étude sur "Perceval," ou le "Conte du Graal."* Paris: Société d'Édition d'Enseignement Supérieur, 1972.

Freeman, Michelle A. *The Poetics of "Translatio studii" and "Conjointure": Chrétien de Troyes's "Cligés."* French Forum Monographs, 12. Lexington, Ky.: French Forum, 1979.

Kelly, Douglas. *"Sens" et "Conjointure" in the "Chevalier de la Charrette."* The Hague and Paris: Mouton, 1966.

Maddox, Donald. *Structure and Sacring: The Systematic Kingdom in Chrétien's "Érec et Énide."* French Forum Monographs, 8. Lexington, Ky.: French Forum, 1978.

Pickens, Rupert T. *The Welsh Knight: Paradoxicality in Chrétien's "Conte del Graal."* French Forum Monographs, 6. Lexington, Ky.: French Forum, 1977.

Studies of Individual Romances–Articles

Uitti, Karl D. "Vernacularization and Old French Mythopoesis, with Emphasis on Chrétien's *Érec et Énide*," in Rupert T. Pickens, ed., *The Sower and His Seed: Essays on Chrétien de Troyes*. French Forum Monographs, 44. Lexington, Ky.: French Forum, Publishers, 81–115.

General Studies–Books

Curtius, Ernst Robert. *European Literature and the Latin Middle Ages*. Translated by Willard R. Trask. Bollingen Series. Princeton, N.J.: Princeton University Press, 1953.

De Ghellinck, J., S. J. *L'Essor de la littérature latine au XIIe siècle*. 2 vols. Museum Lessianum Brussels: L'Édition Universelle; Paris: Desclée de Brouwer, 1946.

Dronke, Peter. *Fabula: Exploration into the Uses of Myth in Medieval Platonism*. Mittellateinische Studien und Texte, 9. Leyden, The Netherlands and Cologne: Brill, 1974.

Faral, Edmond. *Les Arts poétiques du XIIe et du XIIIe siècle: Recherches et documents sur la technique littéraire du moyen âge*. Bibliothèque de l'Ecole des Hautes Études. Sciences historiques et philologiques, 238. Paris: Champion, 1923. Reprint. Slatkine, 1982.

—————. *Recherches sur les sources latines des contes et romans courtois du moyen âge*. Paris: Champion, 1913. Reprint. 1983.

Köhler, E. *Ideal und Wirklichkeit in der höfischen Epik: Studien zur Form der frühen Artus- und Graldichtung*. Beihefte zur Zeitschrift für romanischen Philologie, 97. Tübingen: Niemeyer, 1956. 2d ed. 1970).

—————. *L'Aventure chevaleresque: Idéal et réalité dans le roman courtois: études sur la forme des plus anciens poèmes d'Arthur et du Graal*. Translated by Éliane Kaufholz. Paris: Gallimard, 1974.

Le Moine, Fanny. *Martianus Capella, A Literary Re-Evaluation*. Münchener Beiträge zur Mediävistik und Renaissance-Forschung, 10. Munich: Arbeo-Gesellschaft, 1972.

Manitius, Max. *Geschichte der lateinischen Literatur des Mittelalters*, 3, *Vom Ausbruch des Kirchenstreites bis zum Ende des zwölften Jahrhunderts*. Revised by Paul Lehmann. Munich: Beck Verlagsbuchhandlung, 1931.

Raby, F. J. E. *A History of Secular Latin Poetry in the Middle Ages*. 2 vols. Oxford: Clarendon Press, 1934.

Scaglione, Aldo. *Knights at Court: Courtliness, Chivalry, and Courtesy from Ottonian Germany to the Italian Renaissance*. Berkeley-Los Angeles-Oxford: University of California Press, 1991.

Setton, Kenneth, ed. *A History of the Crusades*, vol. 2. Philadelphia: University of Pennsylvania Press, 1962.

Simson, Otto von. *The Gothic Cathedral: Origins of Gothic Architecture and the Medieval Concept of Order*. Bollingen Series, 48. Princeton, N.J.: Princeton University Press, 1974.

Southern, R. W. *The Making of the Middle Ages*. New Haven, Conn. and London: Yale University Press, 1953.

Stock, Brian. *Myth and Science in the Twelfth Century: A Study of Bernard Silvester*. Princeton, N.J.: Princeton University Press, 1972.

Vinaver, Eugene. *The Rise of Romance*. New York: Oxford University Press, 1971.

Wetherbee, Winthrop. *Platonism and Poetry in the Twelfth Century: the Literary Influence of the School of Chartres*. Princeton, N.J.: Princeton University Press, 1972.

General Studies–Articles

Freeman, Michelle A. "*Fergus*: Parody and the Arthurian Tradition," *French Forum* 8, no. 3 (1983): 197–215.

Guiette, Robert. "Li conte de Bretaigne sont si vain et plaisant," *Romania* 88 (1967): 1–12.

Bibliographies

Kelly, Douglas. *Chrétien de Troyes: An Analytic Bibliography*. Research Bibliographies and Checklists. London: Grant and Cutler, Ltd., 1976. An update of this 1976 listing, compiled by Sandra Ihle, may be found in Douglas Kelly, ed., *The Romances of Chrétien de Troyes: A Symposium*. The Edward C. Armstrong Monographs on Medieval Literature, 3. Lexington, Ky.: French Forum, 1985, 343–53.

Yearly *Bibliography* of the Modern Language Association of America (also on-line).

Bulletin Bibliographique de la Société Internationale Arthurienne— Bibliographical Bulletin of the International Arthurian Society, published yearly in Paris since 1949.

Index

The Author

Karl D. Uitti is the John N. Woodhull Professor of Modern
Languages and former chairman of the Department of Romance
Languages and Literatures at Princeton University. He received his
Ph.D. from the University of California–Berkeley. His chief work has
been in medieval Romance studies, with an emphasis on French; some of
his studies include *Story, Myth, and Celebration in Old French Narrative
Poetry—1050—1200* (1973); a critical edition with modern French
translation (in collaboration with Alfred Foulet) of Chrétien de Troyes's
Le Chevalier de la Charrette (Lancelot) (1989), and a critical edition (for the
Bibliothèque de la Pléiade) of Chrétien's *Le Chevalier au Lion (Yvain)*. At
present he is engaged on a long-term project involving the computeriza-
tion of the *Lancelot* manuscript tradition, and is general editor of *The
Edward C. Armstrong Monographs on Medieval Literature*. Professor Uitti
has been decorated *Officier dans l'Ordre des Palmes académiques* and has
been a Guggenheim Fellow and a Senior Fellow of the National
Endowment for the Humanities.